Tort Law in Serbia

Marija Karanikić Mirić

This book was originally published as a monograph in the International Encyclopaedia of Laws/Tort Law.

Founding Editor: Roger Blanpain
General Editor: Frank Hendrickx
Volume Editor: Britt Weyts

Wolters Kluwer

Published by:
Kluwer Law International B.V.
PO Box 316
2400 AH Alphen aan den Rijn
The Netherlands
E-mail: lrs-sales@wolterskluwer.com
Website: www.wolterskluwer.com/en/solutions/kluwerlawinternational

Sold and distributed by:
Wolters Kluwer Legal & Regulatory U.S.
920 Links Avenue
Landisville, PA 17538
United States of America
E-mail: customer.service@wolterskluwer.com

ISBN 978-94-035-2897-7

e-Book: ISBN 978-94-035-2907-3
web-PDF: ISBN 978-94-035-2917-2

This title is available on www.kluwerlawonline.com

The Author

Marija Karanikić Mirić is a professor of Civil Law at the Faculty of Law of the University of Belgrade (Serbia) and holds visiting appointment at the Faculty of Legal Sciences of the University of Donja Gorica (Montenegro). She has published in the fields of contracts, torts and consumer law. She received an LLB (1999) and PhD (2008) from the Faculty of Law of the University of Belgrade, and an LLM (2002) from the Duke University School of Law as a Ron Brown Scholar. She has authored three monographs, respectively on fault (2009), strict liability (2013), and charge of debtor (2017). She has spent nine months at Trinity College at Oxford University under Chevening Scholarship and has also researched at the Max Planck Institute for Comparative and International Private Law in Hamburg, the Institute for European Tort Law in Vienna, and the Paris Institute of Political Studies (*SciencesPo*).

The Author

Table of Contents

List of Abbreviations

APFB	Anali Pravnog fakulteta u Beogradu (1953 –) – Law Journal (1953 –)
Arhiv	Arhiv za pravne i društvene nauke (1946 –) – Law Journal (1946 –)
CCP	Zakonik o krivičnom postupku iz 2011 – Code of Criminal Procedure of 2011, last changes in 2021
CCS	Krivični zakonik iz 2005 – Criminal Code of 2005, last changes in 2019
Comm CPA Poz	Komentar Zakona o parničnom postupku (Borivoje Poznić), Beograd 2009 – Commentary CPA of 1976
Comm LO BK	Komentar Zakona o obligacionim odnosima (eds. Borislav Blagojević, Vrleta Krulj), Beograd 1983 – Commentary LO
Comm LO Per	Komentar Zakona o obligacionim odnosima (ed. Slobodan Perović), Beograd 1995 – Commentary LO
Comm LO PS	Komentar Zakona o obligacionim odnosima, (eds. Slobodan Perović, Dragoljub Stojanović), Kragujevac / Gornji Milanovac 1980 – Commentary LO
COTIF	Convention Concerning International Carriage by Rail
CPA	Zakon o parničnom postupku iz 2011 – Civil Procedure Act of 2011, last changes in 2020
CRS	Ustav Republike Srbije iz 2006 – Constitution of the Republic of Serbia of 2006, amended in 2021
DCC	Draft Civil Code of Serbia (May 2019)
FRY	Federal Republic of Yugoslavia
GDP	Gross Domestic Product
Glasnik	Glasnik Advokatske komore Vojvodine (1952 –) – Law Journal (1952 –)
GUSG	Opšte uzanse za promet robom iz 1954 – General Usages of Sale of Goods of 1954
HCC	Visoki savet sudstva – High Court Council

List of Abbreviations

HIA	Zakon o zdravstvenom osiguranju iz 2019 – Health Insurance Act of 2019
HIF	Fond za zdravstveno osiguranje – Health Insurance Fund
HPA	Zakon o zdravstvenoj zaštiti iz 2019 – Health Protection Act of 2019
Ingpro	Ingpro – a commercial searchable electronic database of court decisions and other legal documents
LA	Zakon o radu iz 2005 – Labour Act of 2005, last changes in 2018
LCP	Zakon o zaštiti potrošača iz 2021. – Law on Consumer Protection of 2021
LCRR	Zakon o autorskim i srodnim pravima iz 2009 – Law on Copyright and Related Rights of 2009 (last changes in 2019)
LCTI	Zakon o obaveznom osiguranju u saobraćaju iz 2009 – Law on Compulsory Traffic Insurance of 2009 (last changes in 2013)
LCTR	Zakon o ugovorima o prevozu u drumskom saobraćaju iz 1995 – Law on Contracts for Transport by Rail of 1995
LEP	Zakon o zaštiti životne sredine iz 2004 – Law on Environmental Protection of 2004, last changes in 2018
LGE	Zakon o rodnoj ravnopravnosti iz 2021 – Law on Gender Equality of 2021
LJ	Zakon o sudijama iz 2008 – Law on Judges of 2008, last changes in 2021
LO	Zakon o obligacionim odnosima iz 1978 – Law on Obligations of 1978, last changes in 2020
LOC	Zakon o uređenju sudova iz 2008 – Law on Organization of Courts of 2008, last changes in 2018
LPR	Zakon o javnim putevima iz 2005 (nije na snazi) - Law on Public Roads of 2005 (not in force)
LR	Zakon o putevima iz 2018 – Law on Roads of 2018
LRNSS	Zakon o radijacionoj i nuklearnoj sigurnosti i bezbednosti iz 2018 – Law on Radiation and Nuclear Safety and Security of 2018 (last changes in 2019)
LRVC	Zakon o ratifikaciji Bečke konvencije o građanskoj odgovornosti za nuklearne štete iz 1977 – Law on Ratification of Vienna Convention on Civil Liability of 1977
NATO	North Atlantic Treaty Organization
NBS	National Bank of Serbia

NPAA	National Programme for the Adoption of the EU Acquis of 2014
NZ	Naša zakonitost (1947 –) – Legal Journal (1947 –)
OG RS	Službeni glasnik Republike Srbije – Official Gazette of the Republic of Serbia
PDIA	Zakon o penzijskom i invalidskom osiguranju iz 2003 – Pension and Disability Insurance Act of 2003 (last changes in 2022)
PDIF	Pension and Disability Insurance Fund
PLex	Paragraf Lex, a commercial searchable electronic database of court decisions and other legal documents
PZ	Pravni život (1951 –) – Legal Journal (1951 –)
RSK	Republic of Srpska Krajina
SCC	Srpski građanski zakonik iz 1844 – Serbian Civil Code of 1844
SCS	Supreme Court of Serbia / Supreme Court of Cassation of Serbia (as of 2010)
SFRY	Socialist Federal Republic of Yugoslavia
Skica	Skica za zakonik o obligacijama i ugovorima iz 1969 – Draft Code on Obligations and Contracts of 1969
SPZ	Strani pravni život (1956 –) – Law Journal (1956 –)
WWI	World War I
WWII	World War II

List of Abbreviations

General Introduction

§1. The General Background of the Country

I. Geography

1. Serbia is a small, landlocked country, located in Southeast Europe, with a total land area of 88,499 km^2, covering the southern parts of the Pannonian Plain and the central part of the Balkan Peninsula.[1] It borders Bosnia and Herzegovina (371 km), Croatia (262 km) and Montenegro (250 km) to the west; Hungary (175 km) to the north; Bulgaria (361 km) and Romania (548 km) to the east; and to the south, it adjoins Macedonia (283 km) and Albania (114 km, through the disputed territory of Kosovo, administrative border to Kosovo being 366-km long). The Capital of Serbia is Belgrade, one of the largest cities in southeastern Europe, situated at the confluence of the Sava and Danube rivers. Belgrade is the country's administrative, economic and cultural centre, with a population of over 1.6 million.

2. Serbia's terrain is extremely diverse. It ranges from the rich, fertile plains of the north, to the limestone ranges and basins in the east, and the ancient mountains and hills in the southeast. The plains of the northern region lie at heights between 60 and 100 metres above sea level. The central body of the country is characterized by hills and high mountains. The country's western parts include sections of the Dinaric Alps, and its eastern borderlands are part of the Carpathian and Rhodope mountain systems. Differences in elevation, proximity to the sea, and exposure to wind lead to significant climatic differences within Serbia. In general, however, the climate is continental, with cold, relatively dry winters and warm, humid summers. The difference between average temperatures in January and July in Belgrade is 22°C.[2] A major part of Serbia has a continental precipitation regimen, with a peak in the earlier summer period, except for the southwest, which receives the highest precipitation in autumn. Annual sums of solar radiation are in the interval from 1,500 to 2,200 hours annually. Serbia's drainage is primarily to the Danubian system and flows into the Black Sea. The Danube, the second largest European river, passes through Serbia across 588 km (21% of its overall length), it is completely

1. Unless otherwise indicated, the statistical data has been taken from the Statistical Yearbook of the Republic of Serbia for 2022. The latest census in Serbia was held in late 2022, but the results have not yet been processed and published.
2. http://www.britannica.com/EBchecked/topic/654691/Serbia.

navigable and represents the country's largest source of fresh water. Other than reservoirs behind hydroelectric dams, Serbia has no significant lakes. Its largest natural body of water is Lake Palić in Vojvodina, with a surface area of less than 5 km^2. With 29.1% of its territory covered by forest, Serbia is considered to be a middle-forested country. Forest coverage is somewhat lower than the European average of 35%.[3] Serbia is a country with a rich ecosystem and diverse species – covering only 1.9% of the whole European territory, Serbia is home to 39% of European vascular flora, 51% of European fish fauna, 40% of European reptile and amphibian fauna, 74% of European bird fauna, and 67% European mammal fauna.[4] There are 1,783 strictly protected wild species in Serbia, and 860 protected wild species of plants, animals and fungi. Serbia has five national parks and many national nature reserves, encompassing 7.66% of the state territory.

3. In terms of administrative and territorial division, Serbia is divided into provinces, regions, administrative areas, the City of Belgrade, cities and municipalities. The territorial organization of Serbia includes five regions (Belgrade, Vojvodina, Šumadija and Western Serbia, Eastern and Southern Serbia, Kosovo and Metohija). It encompasses 29 administrative areas, 23 cities, 28 urban municipalities, 150 municipalities, 6,158 villages and 195 urban settlements. The City of Belgrade has the constitutional status of a separate territorial unit. Serbia has two territorial autonomies: *Vojvodina* and *Kosovo and Metohija*.[5] The main communication and development line extends from Belgrade to the southeast, which is one of the major land routes from Western Europe to Turkey. Most major cities are placed on, or around that route, as well as the main railroad and highway.

4. According to the 2011 census, Serbia had a population of 7,186,862 (excluding Kosovo[6]). In 2021, the population of Serbia was estimated to be 6,834,326. The rate of population growth in relation to the previous year is negative. Serbia has a comparatively old overall population. The average life expectancy of the male and female population has been extended in the period 2011–2019, from 71.9 years to 73.1 years for men and from 77.0 to 78.3 years for women. However, in the period 2020–2021, due to illnesses that can be related to COVID-19, a shorter life expectancy was recorded compared to 2019 for both sexes: 70.0 years for men and 75.6 years for women. The average density of the population is 92.6 inhabitants per 1 km^2, with an uneven distribution: the population is five times denser than average in the areas around the capital. The average number of persons per household was 2.9 in 2011. Less than half of the population is economically active (41.3%), whereby the share of the male labour force (57.2%) prevails over the female (42.8%). The unemployment rate, i.e., the share of unemployed persons in the total economically active population is 22.4%. In the period from 2011 to 2021, the population decreased by 402,193 and the average annual growth rate was minus 5.2

3. http://srbijasume.rs/gazdovanje-sumama/sumski-fond/podaci-o-sumskom-fondu.
4. Institute for Nature Conservation of Serbia, https://www.zzps.rs/wp/osnovne-informacije/?lang=en.
5. More on the general background of the country at, http://www.srbija.gov.rs.
6. Kosovo held its own census in 2011 that numbered total population at 1,739,825 (estimated 1.78 million in 2021), ask.rks-gov.net.

per 1,000 inhabitants. In the same period, the proportion of the population aged under 15 and over 65 in the total population ranged as follows: the percentage of young people (0–14) remained at almost the same level, 14.4% in 2011 and 14.3% in 2021, while the percentage of the population aged 65 and over increased from 17.3% (2011) to 21.3% (2021). The population aged 15–64 decreased from 68.3% (2011) to 64.4% (2021). The average age of the population increased from 42.1 years (2011) to 43.5 years (2021). The registered number of employees in legal entities and unincorporated enterprises, with indefinite or fixed-term employment contracts and in temporary or occasional employment, as well as persons individually founding or running business amounted to 2,212,631 in 2021, presenting an increase of 3.0% relative to 2020. The average salary per employee in 2021, compared with 2020, registered a nominal increase of 9.4% and a real increase of 5.2%. The greatest salary increase in this period was recorded in the sections: Information and communication (a nominal increase of 19.4% and a real increase of 14.8%), Human health and social work activities (a nominal increase of 12.3% and a real increase of 8.0%), Professional, scientific and technical activities (a nominal increase of 11.7%, and a real increase of 7.4%). In this period, salaries decreased only in the section of electricity, gas, steam and air conditioning supply (a nominal decrease of 0.4% and a real decrease of 4.2%). In 2020, there were 90,111 active enterprises in Serbia, involving a total of 1,248,987 persons employed (of whom 1,181,664 were paid employees). In 2020, the value of total turnover generated by enterprises amounted to RSD 11,271 billion, while the value added at factor costs was RSD 2,567 billion. The value added per enterprise was RSD 28.5 million on average. The average number of persons per enterprise was 13.9 in 2020. Sections with the highest share in the total number of enterprises were Wholesale and retail trade (33.3%), Manufacturing (17.3%) and Professional, scientific and technical activities (14.0%). Furthermore, 33.1% of employees were engaged in Manufacturing, followed by 21.9% in Wholesale and retail trade, and 8.4% in Transportation and storage.

5. Serbia used to have the largest refugee population in Europe in the 1990s: the total number of refugees and war-affected persons in 1998 exceeded 650,000 – approximately 10% of the entire population of Serbia did not live in Serbia prior to 1992.[7] In July 2018, there were 26,502 people in Serbia with refugee status, and the number of internally displaced persons from Kosovo and Metohija was 199,584.[8]

6. The ethnic composition of persons with Serbian citizenship shows an 83.3% majority of Serbs and a number of minorities (Hungarians 3.5%, Roma 2.1%, Bosniaks 2% and others 5.7%). More than 84% of the total population are Orthodox Christians, 5% of the total population are Catholics, while 3% are followers of Islam. Almost 90% of the population considers Serbian as their mother tongue, the second language is Hungarian (3.4%), then Bosniak (1.9%), and the Roma language (1.4%). Less than 2% of the population is illiterate (aged 10 and over). Illiteracy is higher in women, and when age is concerned, illiteracy is highest in the

7. https://www.unhcr.org/.
8. The Commissariat for Refugees and Migration of Serbia, https://kirs.gov.rs/eng .

age group of 65 and over. Computer literacy is at 49%, and complete computer literacy is at 34.2%. Almost 50% of the population over 15 years of age have completed secondary education, 20.7% have elementary education, one over six inhabitants have completed higher (third level) education. In the 2020/21 school year, a total of 1,214,733 persons participated in any of the education levels, whereof preschool education comprised 17.8%, primary and lower secondary education 41.9%, upper secondary 20.3% and tertiary 20%.

7. Natural resources of Serbia include oil, gas, coal, iron ore, copper, zinc, antimony, chromite, gold, silver, magnesium, pyrite, limestone, marble, salt, and arable land. In 2013, arable land participated with 64.6% of the total agricultural area, orchards with 4.7%, vineyards with 1.0%, permanent grassland with 12.8% and pastures with 16.2%. In 2013, the share of crop production in the total value of agricultural production equalled 67.4% and that of livestock production was 38.1%. When compared to 2012, the net index of the physical volume of agricultural production increased by 21.7%. The irrigated area in 2013 was 53,086 ha, and the most frequent type of irrigation, as in the previous year, was sprinkling irrigation. The industrial and mining sectors include ore and stone mining, the processing industry and the production and distribution of electricity, gas and water. In 2013, compared with 2012, industrial production increased by 5.5%. The largest influence on industrial production growth in 2013 compared to 2012 had the divisions of manufacture of motor vehicles and trailers, manufacture of refined petroleum products, generation of electricity, manufacture of chemicals and chemical products and manufacture of electrical equipment. The Electric Power Industry of Serbia (EPS) encompasses coalmines, electric power sources (hydroelectric power plants, thermal power plants, heating plants) and grid distribution systems. The largest share in energy commodities' production in 2012 related to the production of coal, 45.76%. Crude oil and petroleum products participated in imports with 50.23% in 2012, and electricity participated with 54.46% in export. When it comes to final consumption in 2012, 40.41% of coal was consumed in industry; 60.55% of petroleum products were consumed in transport; 53.44% of electricity was consumed in households; and 64.7% of natural gas was consumed in industry. In 2021, compared with 2020, industrial production in the Republic of Serbia increased by 6.3%. Observed by sections, in 2021, compared with 2020, the following trends were recorded: section of Mining and quarrying – an increase of 27.6%, section Manufacturing – an increase of 5.6% and section of Electricity, gas, steam and air conditioning supply – an increase of 0.7%. Data on industrial production in 2021 compared with the previous year expressed growth in the production of intermediate goods, energy excluded (by 13.2%), capital goods (by 11.0%), non-durable consumer goods (by 3.4%), and energy (by 1.6%), while fall was recorded in the production of durable consumer goods (by 3.0%). The largest influence on industrial production growth in 2021, compared to 2020, had the divisions of mining of metal ores, manufacture of coke and refined petroleum products, manufacture of other transport equipment, manufacture of electrical equipment and manufacture of machinery and equipment. In 2021, the share of crop production in the total value of agricultural production equalled 68.4%, and that of livestock production equalled 31.6%. When compared to 2020, the net index of the physical volume of agricultural production decreased by 5.6%. In relation to the previous year, crop production in 2021 decreased by 10.1%. The value of livestock production in relation to the previous year decreased by 1.4%. In 2021, arable land and kitchen gardens participated with 75% of the total utilized agricultural area, fruit plantations/orchards with 5.2%, vineyards with 0.6%, permanent grassland with 9.5% and pastures with 9.5%. In the structure of sown arable land areas and kitchen gardens, cereals participated with 67.7%, industrial crops with 18.5%, vegetables with 1.8%, and fodder crops with 8.7%. Compared to the previous year, noted was decreased number of livestock units (by 2.4%) and cow's milk production (by 1.4%), while meat production increased (by 1.2%).

8. Environmental issues[9] include air pollution in urban agglomerations, where the polluting substances exceed daily limit values, air emissions indicators show a fluctuating trend for sulphur dioxide and nitrogen oxides, due to a decline in industrial production. The most significant part of the total emission of these gases comes from the energy sector and agriculture. The majority of local soil pollution sources originate from public municipal waste dumps (43.5%) and oil excavation and production sites (22.5%). Other important soil pollution sources are industrial waste dumps and industrial facilities. Surface and ground water quality monitoring shows that in most cases water remains within excellent or good ecological status (I and II class of water quality). The worst quality has been detected in surface waters in the province of Vojvodina. Natural hazards include earthquakes – the last damaging earthquake (VIII category) was in 1998, and the last three powerful earthquakes (VII category) were in 1999, 2002 and 2010. In 2021, the quantity of drinking water abstracted from the water supply industry increased by 1.4% relative to 2020 and the quantity distributed to households increased by 0.8% compared to 2020. The number of households to which water was distributed increased in 2021 by 0.4% relative to 2020. In 2021, treated wastewater increased by 3.8% relative to 2020. From a total quantity of 101 million m^3 of wastewater in industry, in 2021, 29 million m^3 of water was purified, of which 61.2% was by primary treatment, 19.0% by secondary treatment and 19.7% by tertiary treatment. In 2021, there was a 15 thousand ha flooded area by surface and ground water, of which 52.9% referred to utilized agricultural land. The area of eroded land in 2021 amounted to 3,912 km^2. The irrigated area in 2021 was 52,236 ha, and the most frequent type of irrigation was, as in the previous year, sprinkling irrigation. Quantities of generated waste, observed by sections and in relation to the previous year, noted the following trends in 2020: Agriculture, forestry and fishing – decrease of 5.3%, Mining and quarrying – decrease of 15.0%; Manufacturing – decrease of 31.5; Electricity, gas, steam and air conditioning supply – increase of 5.3%, Water supply; sewerage, waste management and remediation activities – decrease of 17.1%, Construction – increase of 20.3% and Service activities – increase of 37.2%.

9. The European Environmental Agency data is available at, https://www.eea.europa.eu/countries-and-regions/serbia. *See also* the Serbian Environmental Agency Report for 2018, available at, http://www.sepa.gov.rs/download/Izvestaj2018.pdf.

II. History

9. The history of Serbia was marked by invasions – the Celts conquered most of Serbia in the third century BC, displacing the Illyrians; the Roman Empire took control over the region in the span of the next three centuries; the South Slavs settled in the Balkans in the sixth century and became firmly established throughout the Balkans by the late seventh century; the Turkish conquest started in the fourteenth century and resulted in a five-century long Ottoman rule; constant Turkish conflicts with the Austrians followed on; the Austro-Hungarian invasions took place mostly in the nineteenth century; while the German occupation ensued in World War II (WWII).

10. In the great division of the Roman Empire by Emperor Theodosius I in 395 AD, Serbia fell within the Byzantine authority. In the late ninth century, the Byzantine emperor Michael III appointed two brothers from Thessalonica, Cyril and Methodius, to evangelize the Slavs. In order to preach in the vernacular, Cyril and Methodius created a script, initially known as Glagolitic. The script was later revised to resemble characters of Greek. It became known as the Cyrillic alphabet and still represents one of the most visible features of Serbian culture.[10]

11. The first early South Slav State to which Serbs ascribe their political identity was created by Vlastimir around 850, in what is now eastern Montenegro and southern Serbia known as Raška. It evolved into a Grand Principality by the eleventh century. Stefan Nemanja assumed the throne of Raška in 1168, and a stable and continuous state and national church (Serbian Orthodox Church) were established under the Nemanjić dynasty. Stefan Nemanja abdicated in favour of his son Stefan Prvovenčani, who in 1217 received the title of 'king of Serbia, Dalmatia, and Bosnia' from Pope Honorius III. The autocephalous Serbian Eastern Orthodox church was declared in 1219, with Sava, the youngest son of Stefan Nemanja as archbishop, not reporting to any higher-ranking ordained or consecrated member of the clergy. He was canonized as St. Sava. The seat of the Church was later moved southward, to the city of Peć. The Serbian archiepiscopacy was promoted to an orthodox patriarchate in 1375. The Nemanjić period was the time when a number of churches and monasteries were endowed, that are to this day considered monuments of the greatest historical and symbolic importance for Serbs. The Nemanjić state reached its greatest extent under the reign of Stefan Uroš IV Dušan (1331–55): Serbian Empire was established in Skopje in 1346, where Dušan had himself crowned 'Emperor of the Serbs and Greeks', claiming succession of the Byzantine Empire. The Empire incorporated a significant part of the Balkans. Emperor Dušan promulgated the famous *Zakonik* (code of laws) in 1349, opened new trade routes and strengthened the state's economy (agriculture and mining).[11]

---

10. The main source: Encyclopaedia Britannica, http://www.britannica.com.
11. *Ibid.*

12. Turks got a strong position on the European mainland in the mid-fourteenth century, and the Ottoman sultanate started gradually spreading westward. Following Dušan's death, the Serbian Empire began to disintegrate under rival leaders, torn by domestic disputes and Ottoman conquest. The Turks defeated the temporarily united Serbian forces in 1371 at the Battle of the Maritsa River. The second important defeat of Serbs and their allies, commanded by Prince Lazar Hrebeljanović, ensued in 1389 at Kosovo Polje. Serb despots were forced to accept the position of vassals to the Turks. Their resistance ended in 1459, with the fall of Smederevo, and Serbia was ruled by the Ottoman Empire for almost five centuries. During that time, the majority of the population lived in local rural communities, literacy was generally confined to the clergy, towns were small, and the culture was shaped by non-Serb groups, such as the Turks and, in commerce, the Greeks, Ragusans, Vlachs, or Jews. The Ottoman authorities ruled through local headmen (*kneževi*). The institution of the *knez* became one of the most important symbolic focuses and practical resources around which Christian resistance could grow.[12]

13. The resistance increased from the seventeenth century, with the end of the territorial expansion of the Ottoman Empire. Early revolts were suppressed, but two uprisings against the Ottoman rule (in 1804 commanded by Đorđe Petrović Karađorđe, and in 1815 by Miloš Obrenović) resulted in the effective independence of Serbia in 1817. Still, Turkish troops continued to occupy Belgrade until 1867. In 1830, the Ottoman Government granted the Serbian principality full autonomy. The Principality of Serbia was finally recognized by the Great Powers in the Berlin Congress of 1878. The Proclamation of the Kingdom of Serbia came in 1882. The territory of today's Vojvodina was under Ottoman occupation for more than one century but was conceded to the Habsburg Empire by the end of the seventeenth century. As the Great Migrations depopulated most of southern Serbia, many Serbs moved across the Danube to Vojvodina, and to the Military Frontier province of the Habsburg Monarchy, where they were granted special rights by the Austrian crown. For some time in the eighteenth century, the Austrian Empire ruled most of Central Serbia (1718–1739). Southwestern Serbia remained under de facto Austro-Hungarian occupation from 1878 to 1913 when it was temporarily returned to the Ottomans.[13] The Ottoman domination in the Balkans was brought to an end with the Balkan wars of 1912–1913. National Balkan states were created in the territories from which the Ottoman Empire withdrew. Serbia expanded to the territories of Vardar Macedonia, Kosovo and Raška. Its area and population vastly enlarged.

14. The assassination of Archduke Franz Ferdinand, heir presumptive to the Austro-Hungarian throne, and his wife in Sarajevo in 1914, by those wishing to unite all of the territories with a majority South Slavic population, initiated a diplomatic crisis, an ultimatum from Austria-Hungary to the Kingdom of Serbia, and a conflict which in a short time expanded to become World War I (WWI). In the winter of 1914–1915, an epidemic of typhus struck Serbia, devastating both the civilian population and the army, forcing them to withdraw from the national territory

12. *Ibid.*
13. http://www.arhiva.serbia.gov.rs/enc/history.html.

marching across the Albanian mountain ranges to the Adriatic Sea. Having recuperated on Corfu, the Serbian Army returned to combat on the Thessaloniki front together with other Entente forces. Serbia had 1,264,000 casualties in WWI (28% of the total population, 58% of the male population).[14]

15. After the end of WWI and the downfall of Austria-Hungary and Ottoman Empires, the Kingdom of Serbs, Croats and Slovenians was proclaimed in December of 1918, under the Karađorđević dynasty. In 1929, following a severe political crisis driven by separatist tendencies and nationalist passions, King Alexander I declared a royal dictatorship, dissolved the parliament, banned all political parties, and changed the name of the state to Yugoslavia. During a state visit to France in 1934, King Alexander I was assassinated, and subsequently the regency was established, headed by Prince Paul, the uncle of Peter II, the heir to the throne. When the regents signed the Tripartite Pact with Hitler on 25 March 1941, mass demonstrations of protest arose, especially in Belgrade. In a coup of 27 March, the regency was replaced by senior officers, who repudiated the pact. Belgrade was bombed on 6 April and the country was invaded by Germany and its allies. On 14 April the king and government fled to Athens. By August 1941, a client regime had been established in Belgrade under Milan Nedić.[15]

16. The Communist Party of Yugoslavia instigated a Partisan uprising against the occupation in September 1941. A self-declared 'temporary government' was formed in 1942.[16] The Red Army and the Partisans liberated Serbia by the end of 1944, and the rest of the Yugoslav territories by May 1945. A new constitution was promulgated in January 1946. The monarchy was replaced by a federation of six republics, with borders drawn along ethnic and historical lines: Slovenia, Croatia, Bosnia and Herzegovina, Serbia, Montenegro and Macedonia. In addition, two autonomous provinces were established within Serbia: Vojvodina and Kosovo.

17. After distancing from Stalin in 1948, Yugoslavia remained a neutral nation, not formally aligned with or against any major power bloc. For the next four and a half decades, Yugoslavia maintained its own course between the Warsaw Pact and the West. This course included a specific model of state organization, the system known as workers' self-management – later refurbished in a direction of 'market socialism' as the middle ground between planned and liberal economy. The country underwent a period of relative political stability and economic growth, industrialization and urbanization until the 1980s, and developed into a society profoundly different from the economically backward rural economy of the pre-war years. Josip Broz Tito, president for life, died in 1980. In the period that ensued, the weak and destabilized system of the federal government was unable to cope with escalating economic and political difficulties.

14. *Ibid.*
15. http://www.britannica.com.
16. *Ibid.*

18. After a period of political crisis in the 1980s, the federated states of Yugoslavia broke off. The breakup of the multi-ethnic federation along the ethnic and historical lines resulted in a series of ethnic conflicts and wars, primarily in Bosnia and Herzegovina and Croatia. A new state emerged in April 1992, consisting only of the federated states of Serbia and Montenegro. The capital and assembly of the new Federal Republic of Yugoslavia (FRY) were in Belgrade. In early 2003, FRY was reconstituted as a loose political union officially known as the State Union of Serbia and Montenegro. The Union converted into two independent nations by 2006: Montenegro held a referendum in the spring of that year, resulting in a formal declaration of independence and separation from Serbia on 3 June.

19. After the conflicts between Serbs and Albanians and The North Atlantic Treaty Organization (NATO) bombing of Serbia in 1999, the southern Serbian province of Kosovo and Metohija was left under international protection, with more than 200,000 Serbs being relocated from the province. At present, some 100,000 Serbs live there, predominantly concentrated in the northern part of Kosovo.

20. During the Thessaloniki European Council Summit in 2003, Serbia was identified as a potential candidate for EU membership. European partnership for Serbia was adopted in 2008, setting out priorities for the country's membership application, and in 2009 Serbia officially applied for European Union membership. In March 2012, European Council granted Serbia official candidate status for EU membership. In September 2013, a Stabilization and Association Agreement between the EU and Serbia (SAA) entered into force. In December 2013, the Council of the EU approved opening negotiations on Serbia's accession, and the first Intergovernmental Conference was held on 21 January 2014 in Brussels.

III. Political System

21. The fundamentals of the Serbian political system are governed by the Constitution of 2006, as amended in 2021. The Republic of Serbia is a state of Serbian people and of all citizens who live in it, based on the rule of law and on the principles of social justice, civil democracy, human and minority rights and freedoms, and commitment to European values and principles.[17] The constitutional order of Serbia is founded on the republican and democratic principles, the rule of law and inalienability of human rights, the principle of division of powers, secularity, gender equality and protection of national minorities. Serbia has an effective multiparty system of parliamentary democracy, as normally no single party has a majority of its own accord.

17. Article 1 of CRS. The amendments to the CRS came into force in February 2022, on the day of their promulgation in the National Assembly. In order to give practical effect to the constitutional amendments, the relevant implementing legislation still needs to be adopted. According to the Constitutional law for the enforcement of the said amendments, this legislation should be adopted within one year for judicial laws, and within two years for the alignment of all other relevant legislation.

22. The unicameral National Assembly (*Narodna skupština*) is the supreme representative body in the country, holding constitutional and legislative powers. Its members are elected to serve four-year terms, by secret vote in direct elections, using the proportional electoral system (by voting for the electoral list; 250 parliamentary seats are distributed in proportion to the number of votes the electoral lists received). Universal, equal and secret suffrage exists as of 18 years of age.

23. The Constitution defines the position of the National Assembly in light of the principle of separation of powers.[18] The National Assembly holds constitutional and legislative powers, and performs representative, overseeing and electoral functions. It adopts and amends the Constitution; decides on changes concerning borders and may call for a referendum; ratifies international agreements; decides on war and peace and declares the state of war and emergency; supervises the work of intelligence services; enacts laws and other general acts within the competence of the Republic;[19] gives preliminary approval to the autonomous province statutes; adopts the defence strategy, development plan, land using plan and the state budget; grants amnesty for criminal offences, etc. In addition, the National Assembly elects the Government, supervises its work and decides on the expiry of the term of its office; elects four members of the High Court Council (HCC), four members of the High Prosecutorial Council, elects the Supreme Public Prosecutor and decides on the termination of his office; elects and supervises the work of, and removes the Governor of the National Bank and the Ombudsman, etc. The right to propose laws belongs to every MP, the Government and assemblies of autonomous provinces or at least 30,000 voters. The Ombudsman and the National Bank of Serbia (NBS) are entitled to propose laws within their competences.[20]

24. The President of the Republic signifies the unity of the Republic of Serbia and represents the country at home and abroad. The president is elected by universal suffrage, for a term of five years (eligible for a second term).[21]

25. The national government is the holder of executive power in the Republic of Serbia. It executes or enforces the laws and has the authority for daily administration of the Republic. The national government is headed by the prime minister and is responsible to the parliament. The ministries of the state act as a cabinet. While the role of the president of the Republic is largely ceremonial, the government is the head of the executive branch and is responsible to the legislature.

26. The Constitution provides that the Government shall determine and carry out policies; execute or enforce the law as enacted by the legislature; pass regulations and other general acts for the purposes of law enforcement; propose to the National Assembly laws and other general acts, and give an opinion on the laws and general

18. Articles 98 and 99 of CRS.
19. 'General act' should be understood as an act of a general character, addressed to an indeterminate number of individuals.
20. Article 107 of CRS.
21. Articles 111–112 of CRS.

acts proposed by other initiators; direct, coordinate and supervise the work of public administration bodies, etc.[22] The Government accounts to the legislature with regard to the policy of the Republic of Serbia, the enforcement of laws and other general acts of the National Assembly, and the work of the public administration bodies. The public administration is autonomous, bound by the Constitution and law, and accountable for its work to the Government.[23]

27. The role of political parties in the democratic shaping of the political will of the citizens is guaranteed under Article 5 of the Constitution of the Republic of Serbia (CRS). Political parties may be established freely. Activities of political parties aiming at forced overthrow of constitutional system, violation of guaranteed human or minority rights, or inciting racial, national or religious hatred, are prohibited. Political parties may not exercise power directly or submit state power to their control.

28. The last elections for the National Assembly and the President of the Republic were held on 3 April 2022. The final voter turnout was reported to be at around 59%. Serbian Progressive Party (SNS) won 120 out of 250 parliamentary seats, while the coalition around the Socialist Party of Serbia (SPS) won 31. The coalition 'United for Victory' came second with 38 seats and now shares the opposition benches with four other coalitions. National minority parties of Hungarians, Bosnians, Croats, and Albanians also entered the parliament.[24]

29. Local government is organized on the principle of local self-government through municipal or town assemblies, councils and administrative bodies. Local self-government is exercised via local self-government units – municipalities, cities and the City of Belgrade. Local self-government means the right of citizens to manage the affairs of direct, collective and general interest for the local population, directly and through freely elected representatives in the units of local self-government, and the right and capacity of the units of local self-government, within the law, to regulate and manage public affairs under their jurisdiction and of interest to local residents.[25]

30. Independence is granted to the NBS.[26] NBS is responsible for the monetary policy of the state and is accountable to the National Assembly of the Republic of Serbia. The Governor of NBS is elected by the National Assembly.[27]

31. The independence of the judiciary is guaranteed under the Constitution.[28] The judiciary power is independent, unified in the territory of the Republic, and

22. Articles 122–124 of CRS.
23. Article 136 of CRS.
24. http://www.parlament.gov.rs.
25. Articles 2–3 of the Law on Local Self-Government of 2007 (last changes in 2021).
26. Though there are no further practical constitutional guarantees for its independence such as a fixed-term of office of the Governor.
27. Article 95 of CRS.
28. Article 4 of CRS.

belongs to courts. Judicial decisions are made in the name of the people. A court decision may be reviewed only by the competent court in a procedure prescribed by law, as well as by the Constitutional Court in a procedure on a constitutional appeal. The hearings before the courts are public, and the public can be excluded only in accordance with the Constitution. A judge is independent and adjudicates on the basis of the Constitution, ratified international treaties, laws, generally accepted rules of international law and other general acts, adopted in accordance with the law. Any undue influence on a judge in the exercise of judicial office is prohibited by the Constitution.[29] Under the Law on Organization of Courts of 2008 (LOC), courts are autonomous and independent state bodies protecting the freedoms and rights of citizens, and the rights and interests of legal subjects stipulated by law, ensuring constitutionality and legality. They adjudicate in accordance with the Constitution, laws and other general acts, generally accepted rules of international law and ratified international agreements. Judicial authority is vested in courts and independent of the legislative and the executive branches of government. Judicial decisions are obligatory to all and may not be subject to extrajudicial control, they may be reviewed only by the court of competent jurisdiction in due proceedings established by law.[30]

32. There is a single judicial authority on the territory of the Republic of Serbia. Judicial power in the Republic of Serbia is vested in courts of general and special jurisdiction. Courts of general jurisdiction are basic courts, high courts, appellate courts and the Supreme Court of Cassation (SCS). The SCS consists of more than thirty judges, who are organized into Criminal department and Civil department, the Department for protection of the right to a trial within reasonable time, and Court practice department.[31] Courts of special jurisdiction are commercial courts, the Commercial Appellate Court, misdemeanour courts, the Misdemeanour Appellate Court, and the Administrative Court.[32] The constitutional reform of 2021 reintroduces the old name (the Supreme Court) for the highest court in the Republic (from 2010 until the reform, the name of this court used to be the Supreme Court of Cassation). However, the change in the name of this institution is yet to be effectuated by laws, which should be enacted in 2023.

33. The Public Prosecutor's Office is an independent state body that prosecutes the perpetrators of criminal offences and other punishable actions, and performs other competencies for the protection of public interest, as determined by law. The highest public prosecutor's office in the Republic is the Supreme Public Prosecutor's Office, which is headed by the Supreme Public Prosecutor. The function of the Public Prosecutor's Office is performed by the Supreme Public Prosecutor, Chief Public Prosecutors and Public Prosecutors. No one outside the Public Prosecutor's office can influence the Public Prosecutor's office and the holders of the Public Prosecutor's function in conducting and deciding a particular case. The Supreme Public

29. Articles 142 and 144 of CRS.
30. Article 142 of CRS, Arts 1 and 3 of LOC (last changes in 2018).
31. www.vk.sud.rs.
32. Article 11 of LOC.

Prosecutor is responsible to the National Assembly for the work of the Public Prosecutor's Office and for his own work. The Supreme Public Prosecutor is not responsible to the National Assembly for his actions in a particular case. The Supreme Public Prosecutor is elected by the National Assembly, for a term of six years, at the proposal of the High Prosecutorial Council after a public competition, by the votes of three-fifths of all deputies. The High Prosecutorial Council shall consist of eleven members: five Public Prosecutors elected by the Chief Public Prosecutors and Public Prosecutors, four prominent lawyers elected by the National Assembly, the Supreme Public Prosecutor and the Minister in charge of justice. The function of the public prosecutor is permanent. The same person cannot be re-elected as the Supreme Public Prosecutor.[33]

34. The Constitutional Court is an autonomous and independent state body that shall protect constitutionality and legality, as well as human and minority rights and freedoms.[34] The fifteen justices of the Constitutional Court are elected or appointed to a tenure of nine years. Five of them are elected by the National Assembly, five are appointed by the President of the Republic, and another five by the general session of the Supreme Court. The Constitutional Court decisions are final, enforceable and generally binding. The Constitutional Court decides on compliance of laws and other general acts with the Constitution, generally accepted rules of the international law and ratified international treaties; compliance of ratified international treaties with the Constitution; compliance of other general acts with the law; compliance of the Statute and general acts of autonomous provinces and local self-government units with the Constitution and the law; compliance of general acts (of organizations entrusted with the public powers, political parties, trade unions, civic associations), and of collective agreements, with the Constitution and the law. In addition, the Constitutional Court decides on the conflicts of jurisdictions between the courts and other state bodies, between the republic bodies and the provincial bodies or the bodies of local self-government, or between the provincial bodies and the bodies of local self-government. It resolves electoral disputes for which the jurisdiction of courts is not specified by law, may ban a political party, trade union or civic organization, and also performs other duties stipulated by the Constitution. The Court also decides on constitutional appeals, which may be lodged against individual acts or actions of the state bodies, or organizations entrusted with public powers, where such act violates or denies any of the constitutionally guaranteed human or minority rights and freedoms, if there are no other legal remedies for their protection, or if such remedies are already exhausted.

35. Serbia was granted candidate status for membership in the European Union in 2012, and is a member of the United Nations (UN), Organization for Security and Co-operation in Europe (OSCE), Council of Europe, Black Sea Economic Cooperation, NATO Partnership for Peace, Central European Free Trade Agreement,

33. Articles 155–165a of CRS, and the Law on Public Prosecutor's Office of 2008 (last changes in 2016).
34. Articles 166–175 of CRS, and the Law on Constitutional Court of 2007 (last changes in 2015).

International Monetary Fund, World Bank, Southeast European Cooperation Process, Stability Pact for South-Eastern Europe, Southeast European Cooperative Initiative and Central European Initiative, and is also party to the Rome Statute of the International Criminal Court.

IV. Economic and Social Values

36. The efforts of economic recovery and social restructuring after WWII in Yugoslavia included various types of collectivization of property and centralization of the economy.[35] A number of laws on nationalization and expropriation of private companies, land and buildings were enacted immediately after the war. Collective farming was introduced as government policy all over the federal state. Since the peasantry comprised about 75% of the population at the time, the impact of these measures had been massive. The land was taken away from wealthy pre-war owners, caps were put on the possessions in private ownership, and large state-owned cooperatives were established.

37. The Soviet-inspired centrally planned collective ownership model was largely abolished by the 1950s, and the government embraced the principles of a new economic system of socialist or workers' self-management. As a way of transferring economic management from the state to the workers, work organizations of associated labour were divided into smaller units at the level of factory departments, which were than self-managed, and made financially and commercially independent. This system was further elaborated in the Yugoslav Constitution of 1974, and in the Law on Associated Labour of 1976. The industrial sector boomed in the 1950s, manufacturing exports doubled between 1954 and 1960, and the country showed the world's second-highest economic growth rate between 1957 and 1960.[36] However, the first problems in the functioning of this system appeared in the early 1960s, and by the dissolution of Yugoslavia in the early 1990s, the idea and the practice of workers' self-management were abolished.[37]

38. Yugoslavia had made some initial efforts to deregulate and open the economy, and to encourage foreign investment. However, these attempts to reform collapsed by 1991, and what ensued were high inflation and unemployment, a decrease in production, and 'fracturing of the economy along republic and ethnic lines'.[38] The disintegration of the multi-ethnic federation (SFR Yugoslavia) along the ethnic and historical lines resulted in a series of ethnic conflicts and wars. Prolonged economic and political isolation of the country played a role in massive pauperization of the people and stratification of the society. The extended period of

35. In detail, J.K. Cox, *The History of Serbia* 111 (2002) and further.
36. From: www.nationsencyclopedia.com, where there is much more on socialist self-management in Yugoslavia.
37. On the reasons of failure of workers self-management in Yugoslavia: P.H. Liotta, *Paradigm Lost: Yugoslav Self-Management and the Economics of Disaster* (2001), http://balkanologie.revues.org/681.
38. *Ibid.*

international economic sanctions against what was left of Yugoslavia in the 1990s, along with the destruction of Serbian infrastructure and industry during the NATO airstrikes in 1999, and general mismanagement of the economy, resulted in negative long-term economic effects.

39. After the democratic changes in 2000, Serbia implemented measures of economic stabilization and entered into a market reform programme. The country has engaged in processes of trade liberalization, enterprise restructuring and privatization (though many large companies are still owned by the state).[39] The economy of Serbia is a service-based upper middle-income economy in Central Europe, with the tertiary sector accounting for two-thirds of the total Gross Domestic Product (GDP). The GDP in Serbia was worth USD 63.07 billion in 2021, according to official data from the World Bank. The GDP value of Serbia represents 0.05% of the world economy. The economy functions on the principles of the free market. Nominal GDP in 2023 is projected to reach USD 75.287 billion, which is USD 10,648 per capita, while GDP based on purchasing power parity (PPP) stood at USD 164.835 billion, which is USD 25,709 per capita. The strongest sectors of Serbia's economy are energy, the automotive industry, machinery, mining, and agriculture. The country's primary industrial exports are automobiles, base metals, furniture, food processing, machinery, chemicals, sugar, tires, clothes, and pharmaceuticals. Trade plays a major role in Serbian economic output. The main trading partners are Germany, Italy, Russia, China, and neighbouring Balkan countries. In 2020, the national debt of Serbia amounted to around USD 28.52 billion. The unemployment rate in Serbia increased by 2.8 percentage points in 2021. In total, the unemployment rate amounted to 11.81% in 2021. This increase was preceded by a declining unemployment rate. Serbia joined the International Monetary Fund in 1992 (succeeding to membership of the former Socialist Federal Republic of Yugoslavia (SFRY)), and later the World Bank and the European Bank for Reconstruction and Development. The country was granted candidate status for membership in the European Union in 2012. Serbia is not a member of the World Trade Organization as yet.[40]

40. The Constitution of 2006 states that the economic system of the country shall be based on the market economy, open and free market, freedom of entrepreneurship, independence of business entities and equality of private and other types of assets.[41] According to the National Programme for the Adoption of the EU Acquis (NPAA) of 2014,[42] there is a broad political consensus on the foundations of economic policy in Serbia. As NPAA asserts, the agreement was achieved among the state, the industries and businesses, and the trade unions, with respect to 'the development-oriented economic policy'.

39. Corporate governance and enterprise restructuring of former state-owned enterprises remained a challenge in Serbia, where weak governance and output price controls resulted in large enterprise losses at significant fiscal cost. Z. Murgasova et al., *The Western Balkans: 15 Years of Economic Transition* 22 (2015), www.imf.org.
40. www.imf.org; data.worldbank.org.
41. Article 82 of CRS.
42. *National Programme for the Adoption of the EU Acquis (NPAA)*, European Integration Office, July 2014, 71. The new NPAA for the period 2022–2025 has been adopted in July 2022.

41. Serbian economic situation reflects that of a transitional economy. For the most part, it is dominated by market forces, but the state sector still prevails in some areas and many institutional reforms are needed. A recent study indicated ten reform priorities for Serbia: wastefulness of government spending, transparency of policy-making, protection of minority shareholders, quality of air transport infrastructure, prevalence of trade barriers, intensity of local competition, prevalence of foreign ownership, agricultural policy costs, burden of government regulations and business impact of the rules on foreign direct investment.[43]

42. When it comes to the transformation of the welfare system in Serbia after the disintegration of Yugoslavia, the pension and healthcare systems, and the social and (un)employment protection policies have remained relatively inclusive, although the benefits provided are very modest, and certainly insufficient to help the beneficiaries break the cycle of poverty.[44] Under Article 69 of the Constitution, social protection is not granted generally, but only to citizens and families.

§2. Legal System

I. Primacy of Legislation and Codification

43. *Hierarchy of formal sources of law* is written into the Constitution of Serbia of 2006. Sources of law in a formal sense are various instruments through which rules of human conduct are expressed in a given legal order. The main formal sources of law in Serbia are the Constitution; ratified international treaties and 'generally accepted rules of international law'; laws and other general acts of the Republic (i.e., acts of general application, passed by the Republic and addressed to an indeterminate number of individuals); general acts of different organizations entrusted with public powers; general acts of political parties, trade unions and civic associations; collective bargaining agreements; and statutes, decisions and other general acts of autonomous provinces and of the units of local self-government.

44. For the most part, formal sources of law are written. In addition to the written sources, there are also *customary practices* (standards of community, established patterns of behaviour that are considered to be law by the relevant actors); *general principles of law* (basic rules whose content is abstract and very general; they may be codified eventually; they bear high interpretative importance; cannot be applied directly; and remain uncompromised even if they do not prevail over some other conflicting principle); *public order* (*ordre public*); and *good morals* (*boni mores*). However, the prevalent view is that the source of law is not the legal principle or the custom itself, but the law which refers to it.

43. Z. Murgasova et al., *The Western Balkans: 15 Years of Economic Transition* 31 (2015), www.imf.org.
44. M. Stambolieva & S. Dehnert (eds), *Welfare States in Transition: 20 Years after the Yugoslav Welfare Model* 12 (2011).

45. Where two sources of law are in conflict, some of them shall be applied in preference to others, meaning that there is a hierarchy of formal sources of law. Under Articles 194 and 195 of the Constitution of 2006, the legal order of the Republic of Serbia is undivided, and the Constitution is the highest source of law, i.e., the supreme legal instrument in the Republic. All other sources of law in a formal sense (laws and other general acts, that is, acts of general application, addressed to an indeterminate number of individuals) must be in keeping with the Constitution.

46. Furthermore, the ratified international treaties and generally accepted rules of international law are incorporated into the national law, they form a part of the legal order of the Republic. Laws and other general acts must be in conformity with ratified international treaties and generally accepted rules of international law, while ratified international treaties must be in compliance with the Constitution. Therefore, within the hierarchy of sources of law which is established by the Constitution, international sources of law are ranked *below* the Constitution and *above* other national sources of law.[45]

47. Moreover, all bylaws of general application, i.e., subsidiary legal acts of the Republic that are addressed to an indeterminate number of individuals, along with general acts of organizations entrusted with the public powers, political parties, trade unions and civic associations, as well as collective bargaining agreements, must be in keeping with the law. Statutes, decisions and other general acts of autonomous provinces and of the units of local self-government must also be in keeping with the law. In the end, all general acts of autonomous provinces and of the units of local self-government must be compliant with their respective statutes.

48. In addition, under Article 198 of the Constitution, all *individual acts and actions* (i.e., acts and actions addressed to specified individuals) of state authorities, holders of public authority (organizations entrusted with the public powers), and local authorities (autonomous provinces and the units of local self-government), must be based on law. Where an individual act decides on someone's rights, duties or legally protected interests, its legality may be challenged in administrative proceedings before the courts unless some other kind of judicial protection is stipulated by the law for a given type of issue.

49. The Constitutional Court is responsible for solving any inconsistency within the afore-elaborated hierarchy. To that end, the Constitutional Court decides on: compliance of laws and other general acts with the Constitution, generally accepted rules of the international law and ratified international treaties; compliance of ratified international treaties with the Constitution; compliance of other general acts with the law; compliance of the Statute and general acts of autonomous provinces

45. As per the Venice Commission: 'This does, however, not mean that the Constitution is interpreted without having regard to international law. On the contrary, this means that the national authorities, including the Constitutional Court, interpret the Constitution in a manner designed to avoid conflicts between national and international rules.' Opinion No. 405/2006, Strasbourg, 19 Mar. 2007.

and local self-government units with the Constitution and the law; compliance of general acts (of organizations entrusted with the public powers, political parties, trade unions, civic associations), and of collective agreements, with the Constitution and the law. The Court also decides on constitutional appeals, which may be lodged against individual acts or actions of the state bodies, or organizations entrusted with public powers, where such act violates or denies any of the constitutionally guaranteed human or minority rights and freedoms, if there are no other legal remedies for their protection, or if such remedies are already exhausted. Where there is a conflict between legal sources of the same position within the hierarchy, or between provisions of the same legal instrument, it should be resolved by applying the rules of statutory interpretation.

50. A judge shall be independent and adjudicate on the basis of the Constitution, ratified international treaties, laws, generally accepted rules of international law and other general acts, adopted in accordance with the law.[46] Court decisions are not considered to be sources of law. The courts are generally supposed to apply, and not to create the law. The wording of the laws is sometimes plain and straightforward, yet some amount of interpretation is often necessary. In many cases, there is ambiguity or vagueness to the words used by the legislator. In order to find the meaning of such words, courts have to utilize various tools and methods of interpretation. Moreover, courts cannot refuse to adjudicate in situations where, *wrongly*, there is no applicable law to a given legal case, i.e., where the existing legal rules do not provide for a conclusive answer to the case at hand. Where the law *should* regulate the case in question, but has erroneously failed to do so, the courts have to fill up the lacuna. To that end, they must employ the means of statutory interpretation, so as to identify the existence of a legal gap. After that, they need to create a rule in order to decide the case.

51. The nature of statutory rules of Serbian tort law is abstract, very general and not fact-specific. The legislator often employs broad legal standards, such as a reasonable person, foreseeable damage, etc. This leaves a great deal of freedom to civil courts in deciding on the merits. For example, the criterion against which the existence of the injurer's fault is determined is left to the courts, as well as the content of the notion of reasonableness. Also, where the defendant has proved that the injured party has contributed to the occurrence of damage, but the extent of such contribution is not possible to establish, the court shall determine the amount of damages taking into account all circumstances at hand.[47] Procedural rules follow the same line. For instance, if it is determined that a party is entitled to damages, but the amount of damages cannot be established, or could be established only with disproportionate difficulties, the court shall establish the amount of due compensation at its own discretion, that is, as per the principle of free evaluation of the evidence.[48]

46. Article 144, para. 1 of CRS.
47. Article 192, para. 2 of LO.
48. Article 232 of CPA.

52. The same matter that has been adjudicated by a competent court cannot be raised again. The same parties cannot pursue the same issue anew. They can do it neither in the same nor in a different court.

53. Relevance of a court decision is restricted to the parties in a given dispute. The decisions issued in individual cases cannot have a general effect, and can never extend to other cases, or to other persons. Even the decisions of the SCS are not binding on the lower courts, since they are not a formal source of law. However, lower courts are de facto inclined to keep to the holdings of higher courts, and above all to the holdings of the highest court, whenever they need to decide on similar situations of facts.

54. Before the breakup of Yugoslavia, the highest courts in the country occasionally held joint sessions, and in these sessions, they were adopting common opinions on important matters of law. Since the disintegration of the federal state and the abolition of military courts, common opinions may be held solely by different chambers or divisions of the highest court instance. Under Article 31 of LOC, the SCS shall determine general legal views in order to ensure uniform application of the law by courts. These general legal views have considerable impact on the development of the law, and certainly on the ways in which the lower courts reason.

55. From a historical perspective, one of the most important examples of such influence in the field of tort law would be as follows. Immediately after LO was enacted (1978) the question arose about the degree of fault which should be rebuttably presumed under Article 154, paragraph 1 of LO. Whether the statutory presumption of fault concerns intention, gross negligence, or plain negligence? In 1980, the highest courts of Yugoslavia (Federal Court, state Supreme Courts and the Supreme Military Court) jointly held that only ordinary (plain) negligence may be presumed under this rule.[49] If the injured party claims that damage has been caused by intention or gross negligence, he or she has to prove this. This clarification is considered to be part of Serbian tort law to this day.

II. Position of the Judiciary

56. Independence of the judiciary and of the judges is guaranteed under the Constitution. Judiciary is independent and every judge is independent and accountable only to the Constitution and the law.[50] Serbia underwent constitutional reform in 2021–2022, with a focus on the position of the judiciary. The amendments to the CRS came into force in February 2022. In order to give practical effect to the constitutional amendments, the relevant implementing legislation still needs to be

49. Conclusion of XIV Joint session of the Federal Court, state Supreme Courts and the Supreme Military Court of 25 and 26 Mar. 1980, *Zbirka sudskih odluka*, V, 1, 18.
50. Articles 4 and 142 of CRS.

adopted. According to the Constitutional law for the enforcement of the said amendments, this legislation should be adopted within one year for judicial laws, and within two years for the alignment of all other relevant legislation.

57. Under the LOC of 2008, courts are autonomous and independent state bodies that are ensuring constitutionality and legality and protecting freedoms and rights of the citizens and rights and interests of legal entities as stipulated by law. They adjudicate on the basis of the Constitution, ratified international agreements, generally accepted rules of international law, laws and other legal sources with general application. As explained before, judicial authority is vested in courts and independent of the legislative and executive branches of government. Judicial decisions are obligatory to all and may not be subject to extra-judicial control, they may be reviewed only by the court of competent jurisdiction in due proceedings established by law, as well as by the Constitutional Court in a procedure on a constitutional appeal.[51] Under Article 144 of CRS, every judge is independent and adjudicates on the basis of the Constitution, ratified international treaties, laws, generally accepted rules of international law, laws and other general acts, i.e., legal sources with general application.

58. There is a single judicial authority on the territory of the Republic of Serbia. The Constitution of 2006 establishes two courts: the Constitutional Court and the Supreme Court (of Cassation, for explanation *see* paragraph 32 here). All other courts are to be established and abolished by law. The establishment of provisional courts, courts-martial and extraordinary courts is explicitly forbidden.[52] State-level courts are Supreme Court (of Cassation), Administrative Court, Misdemeanour Appellate Court[53] and Commercial Appellate Court.[54] The court system of Serbia includes the courts of general jurisdiction and the specialized courts. The courts of general jurisdiction are the Supreme Court (of Cassation), courts of appeal, higher courts, and basic courts. The specialized courts include commercial courts, the Commercial Appellate Court, misdemeanour courts, the Misdemeanour Appellate Court, and the Administrative Court.[55]

59. The Constitutional Court is an autonomous and independent state body that protects constitutionality, legality, and human and minority rights and freedoms.[56] The fifteen justices of the Constitutional Court are elected or appointed to a tenure of nine years. Five of them are elected by the National Assembly, five are appointed by the President of the Republic, and another five by the general session of the Supreme Court. The National Assembly elects five judges of the Constitutional Court from among the ten candidates proposed by the President of the Republic, the President of the Republic appoints five judges of the Constitutional Court from

51. Article 142 of CRS, Arts 1 and 3 of LOC.
52. Article 143 of CRS, Art. 2 of LOC.
53. Known from 2010 to 2013 as the Higher Misdemeanour Court.
54. Article 13 of LOC.
55. Article 11 of LOC.
56. Articles 166–175 of CRS, and the Law on Constitutional Court of 2007 (last changes in 2015).

among the ten candidates proposed by the National Assembly, and the general session of the Supreme appoints five judges from among the ten candidates proposed by the HCC and the High Prosecutorial Council in a joint session. The Constitutional Court decisions are final, enforceable and generally binding. As stated before, the Constitutional Court decides on constitutionality and legality of legal sources, conflicts of jurisdictions, constitutional appeals and other matters as prescribed by law.

60. More precisely, the Constitutional Court decides on compliance of laws and other general acts with the Constitution, generally accepted rules of the international law and ratified international treaties; compliance of ratified international treaties with the Constitution; compliance of other general acts with the law; compliance of the Statute and general acts of autonomous provinces and local self-government units with the Constitution and the law; compliance of general acts (of organizations entrusted with the public powers, political parties, trade unions, civic associations), and of collective agreements, with the Constitution and the law. In addition, the Constitutional Court decides on the conflicts of jurisdictions between the courts and other state bodies, between the republic bodies and the provincial bodies or the bodies of local self-government, or between the provincial bodies and the bodies of local self-government. It resolves electoral disputes for which jurisdiction of courts is not specified by law, may ban a political party, trade union or civic organization, and also performs other duties stipulated by the Constitution. The Court also decides on constitutional appeals, which may be lodged against individual acts or actions of the state bodies, or organizations entrusted with public powers, where such act violates or denies any of the constitutionally guaranteed human or minority rights and freedoms, if there are no other legal remedies for their protection, or if such remedies are already exhausted.

61. According to Article 150 of the Constitution, the HCC is an independent state body that ensures and guarantees the independence of courts, judges, court presidents and lay judges. It has eleven members: six judges elected by judges, four prominent lawyers elected by the National Assembly, and the President of the Supreme Court. Presidents of the courts cannot be elected to the HCC. The election of members of the HCC from among judges is yet to be regulated by law. According to CRS, the National Assembly elects members of the HCC from among prominent lawyers with at least ten years of experience in the legal profession – from eight candidates proposed by the competent committee of the National Assembly. If the National Assembly does not elect all four members within the time limit set by law, the remaining members are elected by a commission consisting of the Speaker of the National Assembly, the President of the Constitutional Court, the President of the Supreme Court, the Supreme Public Prosecutor and the Protector of Citizens from among all candidates eligible. HCC elects judges and lay judges and decides on the termination of their offices; elects the President of the Supreme Court and presidents of other courts and decides on the termination of their offices; decides on the transfer and secondment of judges; determines the needed number of judges and lay judges; decides on other issues in relation to the status of judges, presidents of courts and lay judges; and performs other competencies determined by the Constitution and the law.

62. Under Article 143 of CRS, the highest court in Serbia is the SCS.[57] The constitutional reform of 2021 reintroduces the old name (the Supreme Court) for the highest court in the Republic (from 2010 until the constitutional reform, the name of the highest court used to be the Supreme Court of Cassation). However, the change in the name of this institution is yet to be effectuated by law, and these laws should be passed in 2023. The President of the Supreme Court shall be elected by the HCC, upon provided opinion of the general session of the Supreme Court, for a term of five years. The same person cannot be re-elected President of the Supreme Court. The presidents of other courts shall be elected by the HCC for a term of five years.[58] Under Articles 146–148 CRS, the judicial office is permanent and lasts from the election of a judge until the judge reaches working age. Also, a judge has the right to perform the judicial office in the court in which he has been elected and only with his consent can he be permanently transferred or temporarily moved to another court, except in the case provided by the Constitution. A judge may not be held liable for an opinion given in connection with the exercise of judicial office and for voting in a court decision unless he or she commits the criminal offence of 'violating the law by a judge or public prosecutor' (at this moment Article 360 of Criminal Code (CCS)). A judge may have his office terminated before the end of his working age: if he so requests, if he permanently loses his ability to perform the judicial office, if his citizenship of the Republic of Serbia ceases or if he is dismissed from office. A judge will be dismissed if he is sentenced to at least six months in prison or if, in a disciplinary procedure, he is found to have committed a serious disciplinary offence which, according to the HCC assessment, seriously damages the reputation of the judicial office or public confidence in the courts. The decision on the termination of the judicial office is made by the HCC. The judge has the right to appeal against the decision of the HCC on the termination of the judicial office to the Constitutional Court, which excludes the right to a constitutional appeal.

63. Jurisdiction in civil matters: Basic courts have primary jurisdiction over a wide range of civil cases, including enforcement and non-litigious proceedings, and also housing and labour disputes. Both higher courts and appellate courts hear appeals from decisions of the basic courts. Higher courts have first-instance jurisdiction in civil cases where review (as an extraordinary procedural remedy) is available, as well as in paternity and maternity cases, in a wide range of labour and intellectual property disputes, and in cases where the plaintiff seeks damages or other remedies against the publication of information. As courts of secondary jurisdiction, higher courts hear appeals against decisions of basic courts in civil disputes, against judgments of basic courts in cases of small value, and in non-litigious

57. Prior to enactment of the Constitution of 2006, the highest court in Serbia was the Supreme Court of Serbia, created by Serbia's Constitution of 1990.

58. Article 149 CRS.

proceedings. Appellate courts decide on appeals against decisions of high courts, and against judgments of basic courts in civil disputes unless they are under jurisdiction of high courts. Commercial courts and the Commercial Appellate Court adjudicate disputes between domestic and foreign companies, enterprises, cooperatives, entrepreneurs and their associations. They have jurisdiction over a wide range of commercial disputes, status of commercial entities, privatization, foreign investment, various intellectual property issues, etc.[59]

64. As mentioned before, judges are guaranteed independence in their judicial activities under Article 144 of CRS and Article 1 of Law on Judges (LJ). A judge is also *obliged* to preserve confidence in his independence and impartiality at all times.[60] There are constitutional guarantees of the permanence of judicial office and of the immunity, impartiality and immovability of judges.[61] A judge may not hold office in bodies enacting or enforcing legislation, public offices, and autonomous province and local units of local self-government. In addition, a judge may not be a member of a political party or act politically in some other manner, engage in any paid public or private work, or extend legal services or advice for compensation.[62] A judge is required to conduct proceedings impartially, in accordance with his/her own assessment of facts and interpretation of the law, ensuring fair trial and compliance with procedural rights of parties guaranteed by the Constitution, laws and international acts. Judges are obliged to adhere at all times to the Code of Ethics issued by the HCC.[63]

65. Under Article 145 of CRS, the conditions for the election of judges shall be regulated by law. The new laws to that effect are being currently drafted and are expected to be adopted in 2023. At this moment, under Article 43–46 of LJ, all judges must have formal university legal training. Basic court judges must have three years of experience in the legal profession following the bar examination, while judges of the higher instance courts are required to have between six and twelve years of experience to qualify for the appointment. They must have Serbian citizenship, meet the general requirements for employment in state bodies and be deserving of the position. Other requirements for their election are knowledge (theoretical and practical knowledge necessary for performing judicial function); skilfulness (abilities for efficient use of specific legal knowledge in dealing with cases); merit (ethical characteristics that a judge should possess, and conduct in accordance with those characteristics). Moral characteristics of a judge include honesty, thoroughness, diligence, fairness, dignity, perseverance, and esteem. Conduct in compliance with these characteristics involves upholding the dignity of a judge on and off duty; social responsibility; independence and impartiality; reliability and dignity

59. In detail on jurisdiction of the courts: Arts 22–33 of LOC.
60. Article 3 of LJ.
61. Articles 146–148 of CRS.
62. Article 30 of LJ.
63. Article 3 of LJ.

on and off duty, and acting responsibly with regard to internal organization and positive public image of the judiciary.[64] Discrimination on any grounds is prohibited in the election and nomination for the election of a judge. In electing and nominating for the election of a judge, special care shall be devoted to the national composition of the population, adequate representation of the members of national minorities, as well as knowledge of professional legal terminology in the national minority languages officially used in court proceedings.

66. Lay judges participate in trials of many cases as panel members, having the rights and duties of a judge. Under Article 145 of CRS, the conditions for the election and term of office of lay judges shall be regulated by law. Under the current rules, any citizen of the Republic of Serbia, of legal age but not older than 70 at the time of appointment, may be appointed as a lay judge, provided that he or she is deserving of the function. In appointing a lay judge, sex, age, profession and social status, knowledge, competence, and affinities for a specific type of matter shall be taken into account. Lay judges are appointed for a period of five years and may be re-appointed.[65] Civil Procedure Act (CPA) determines in which cases lay judges will sit on panels.

III. Distinction Between Public and Private Law

67. The distinction between public law and private law may have practical consequences in certain legal systems, with respect to the division of legislative jurisdictions (e.g., it may be provided that private law is among the exclusive competences of federal legislation, whereas public law is partly a matter of state legislation); the division of subject-matter jurisdiction of the courts; or the differentiation of private legal entities and public legal entities, and their respective legal regimes.

68. However, the Serbian legal system is not one of those in which the stated distinction bears much importance. A few legal sources do mention private or public rights or private or public legal entities, but these references are random, unsystematic and largely inconsequential in their results.[66] Vodinelić gives some examples of these haphazard mentionings. Article 514 of LO relates to the warranty for legal defects, and specifies that the seller is liable for *public-law limitations* to the transferred right, provided that they were unknown to the buyer if the seller was aware of those limitations, or knew that they can be expected, and if he failed to inform the buyer thereof. Article 189, paragraph 2 of the Law on Police of 2005 used to stipulate that individuals whose *private rights* are endangered may turn to the police for their protection if, in a particular case, there is no other legal protection, and if infringement of the private right in question is related to the safety of his person or property. As of 2016 (last changes in 2018), Article 35 of the new Law

64. Article 45, para. 5 of LJ.
65. Articles 81–82 of LJ.
66. V. Vodinelić, *Građansko pravo* (Beograd, 2012), 47–49.

on Police prescribes the same, but uses the term 'personal and property rights' instead of 'private rights'. Under Article 46, paragraph 1 of the Law on Enforcement and Security of 2015 (last changes in 2020), a foreign executive title indicating *a private claim*, and already recognized by the domestic court in accordance with the law, shall be enforced in the manner and in the procedure identical to the procedure of enforcement of domestic executive titles. The Law on Pledge of Movable Assets Recorded in the Pledge Registry of 2003 (last changes in 2019) mentions in Article 27 that certain provisions of that law equally apply to *public and private juridical persons*.[67]

69. Despite the fact that very little practical significance is attached to the distinction between public law and private law, legal theorists have continuously emphasized the epistemological importance of this differentiation.[68]

70. Numerous theories have emerged in relation to the distinction between public law and private law, the most prominent of them being the interest theory, the subject theory, the subjection theory, and the necessary subject theory. In a few words,[69] under the interest theory, public law is predominantly concerned with the public interest (or the interest of the state), while private law is predominantly concerned with private interests (or the interests of citizens). The subject theory states that public law regulates legal relationships in which the state or other public entity is involved, while legal relationships of private entities are a matter of concern of private law. Under the subjection theory, public law in concerned with legal relationships marked by one party being subordinate and inferior to another, whereas private law governs relationships that are symmetric and equal, and where the parties meet on a level playing field, i.e., where they are equal in status and play by the same set of rules. The necessary subject theory states that public law is only concerned with legal relationships in which at least one party is a public authority holding public powers and exercising a sovereign function (*imperium*). These theories are obviously neither exhaustive nor mutually exclusive.

71. The border between public law and private law is not always evident in particular cases. However, civil law (including the law of tort) undoubtedly fits into the private law bracket. The norms of civil law are *predominantly* concerned with private interests, they *mainly* regulate the relationships between the parties on a level playing field, and they *normally* do not require the participation of public authorities. Yet, some of the norms of civil law are concerned with the public interest (e.g., marital prohibitions, restrictions to property rights, forbidden contracts); some reinforce relationships of subrogation (e.g., of a child to his or her parent, of an

67. One may add the following: The Constitutional Court explained on several occasions that electoral rights are 'public subjective rights' of individuals entitled to vote for and stand as a candidate. Decision of the Constitutional Court of Serbia, IUp. 42/2008 of 14 Apr. 2011, Decision of the Constitutional Court of Serbia, IU. 197/2002 of 27 May 2003, Decision of the Constitutional Court of Serbia, IU. 23/2003 of 3 Jun. 2003, *PLex*.

68. The most comprehensive theoretical work in this field is dissertation of V. Vodinelić, *Public and Private Law*, defended at the Faculty of Law of the University of Belgrade in 1986.

69. V. Vodinelić, *Građansko pravo* (Beograd, 2012), 48.

employee to his or her employer); for some, the participation of public authorities is a necessity (e.g., guardianship authority, land registry).[70]

IV. Sources of Private Law in General and of Tort Law in Particular

72. The general legal framework for regulating private law matters is determined by the CRS of 2006, as amended in 2021. The Constitution guarantees, *inter alia*, the peaceful enjoyment of property and other patrimonial rights acquired in accordance with law (Article 58), the right to inheritance in accordance with law (Article 58), the right to marriage and the equality of spouses (Article 62), etc. A number of personal rights enjoy constitutional protection, such as life, physical and mental integrity, human dignity, privacy, personal freedom and security, inviolability of the home, etc.[71] Article 18 of CRS provides for the direct application of constitutional rights, their interpretation and the role of the legislature. The legislature may only prescribe a manner of exercising these rights if there is an explicit basis for such legislative enactment in the Constitution. Also, constitutional provisions on human and minority rights are to be interpreted in a way to promote values of a democratic society, and in line with the international standards in the field and the practice of international institutions supervising the implementation of those standards.

73. The main source of the law of obligations – including the law of tort – in Serbia is the Law on Obligations (*Zakon o obligacionim odnosima*) of 1978 (LO). It was enacted by the National Assembly of SFRY on 30 March 1978, as a landmark piece of federal legislation in the area of private law.[72] After the dissolution of SFRY in 1992, LO was received into the legal system of the newly formed FRY.[73] In early 2003, FRY was reconstituted as a loose political union officially known as the State Union of Serbia and Montenegro, and LO was received into the national laws of Serbia and Montenegro. The Union converted into two independent nations by 2006, and as of then, LO has remained the main formal source of law of obligations in the Republic of Serbia. One may say LO has outlived the country it was created for, as after the disintegration of Yugoslavia, LO was also received into the legal systems of Slovenia, Croatia, Bosnia and Herzegovina, Macedonia and Montenegro. Legislators of some of these countries have subsequently introduced some

70. *Ibid.*, 48–49.
71. Article 23 of CRS and further.
72. LO was published in the *Official Gazette (OG) of SFRY* No. 29/1978 and came into force six months later on 1 Oct. 1978. It was amended several times before the dissolution of SFRY, and those amendments were published in *OG SFRY* Nos 39/1985, 45/1989 and 57/1989.
73. The received LO was published with a few amendments in *OG FRY* No. 31/1993. On that occasion all references to the socialist (workers') self-management and the corresponding categories were eliminated from LO. The last changes in LO in Serbia were introduced in 2020 (*OG RS* No. 18/2020), in relation to the form of sales contract and the power of attorney for sale of real estate.

alterations to the received piece of legislation, and the changes made by the Croatian legislator were by far the most substantial.[74]

74. LO is modelled very closely after the Draft Code on Obligations and Contracts (*Skica za zakonik o obligacijama i ugovorima*) published in 1969 (*Skica*). Skica was written singlehandedly by Mihailo Konstantinović (1897–1982), a professor at the University of Belgrade, Faculty of Law and the country's most influential civil law scholar. Skica represents an original, well-structured and coherent system. Konstantinović conducted a thorough comparative research, especially taking into consideration the Swiss Code of Obligations (though Skica comprises some other obvious influences, coming from German, French and Austrian codifications) and consulted domestic legal traditions, the post-WWII practice of Yugoslav courts, the 1964 Hague Uniform Laws and other international models and sources. LO's departures from Skica may be largely explained by the political moment of the law's enactment. Yet, these departures are neither numerous nor substantial enough to disturb the structure, fundamental nature and mainstream provisions of the proposed codification. When it comes to obligations and contracts, the Commission which was appointed by the Government in 2006 to draft a new civil codification for Serbia, thoroughly revisited Skica and seriously considered, on numerous issues, to return to the initial proposals made by Konstantinović. However, the official work on the codification of civil law in Serbia has been terminated in 2019.[75]

75. LO comprises 1109 articles, including the chapters on fundamental principles of the LO, sources of obligations (contract, tort, unjust enrichment, *negotiorum gestio* (*gestion d'affaires*), unilateral promises), effects of obligations, extinction of obligations, various kinds of obligations, substitution of creditor or debtor, and different types of contracts. The general rules on tortious liability are contained in Articles 154–209 of LO. In addition to LO, other major sources of private law in Serbia are the Law on Property Relations of 1980 (last changes in 2005), the Law on Inheritance of 1995 (last changes in 2015), the Family Act of 2005 (last changes in 2015), the CPA of 2011 (last changes in 2020), the Law on Non-Contentious Proceedings of 1982 (last changes in 2022), and a number of other laws such as the Law on Pledge of Movable Assets Recorded in the Pledge Registry of 2003 (last changes in 2019), the Law on Consumer Protection (LCP) of 2021, the Notaries Act of 2011 (last changes in 2015), Law on Copyright and Related Rights (LCRR) of 2009 (last changes in 2019), Law on Business Companies of 2011 (last changes in 2021), etc.

76. In addition to the LO's general rules on tortious liability, there are some specific statutes relevant to the law of tort. For instance, the LCP of 2021 contains provisions implementing the Product Liability Directive. One should also mention the

74. On those changes in particular: T. Josipović & S. Nikšić, 'Novi Zakon o obveznim odnosima i hrvatsko obvezno pravo', *Evropski pravnik* 4/2008, 61–94.

75. Komisija za izradu Građanskog zakonika, *Prednacrt. Građanski zakonik Republike Srbije* (Beograd, 2019). The Commission for drafting the Civil Code of the Republic of Serbia was appointed by the Government of the Republic of Serbia in 2006. In 2019, the Government decided to dissolve the Commission (*OG RS*, No. 51/2019) and to archive the project.

Law on Environmental Protection (LEP) of 2004 (last changes in 2018), the Law on Game and Hunting of 2010 (last changes in 2018), the Law on Contracts for Transport by Rail (LCTR) of 2015 (last changes in 2021), the Law on Radiation and Nuclear Safety and Security (LRNSS) of 2018 (last changes in 2019), the Law on Ratification of Vienna Convention on Civil Liability (LRVC) for Nuclear Damage of 1977, the Law on Compulsory Traffic Insurance (LCTI) of 2009 (last changes in 2013), etc.

77. Prior to the enactment of LO, the LO was uncodified in Yugoslavia for some decades. Right after WWII, in October 1946, *the Law on Invalidity of Legal Regulations enacted prior to 6 April 1946 and During the Time of Enemy Occupation* (LILR) was enacted. This law has severed the continuity between the legal systems of the former Kingdom of Yugoslavia and the newly formed state. As a result, the regulations that were in force on the day of 6 of April 1941 (German bombing of Belgrade), as well as the regulations enacted during the German occupation, had lost their legal force and thus were no longer enforced (as per Article 2 of LILR). This meant that the 1844 Civil Code of the Kingdom of Serbia, one of the oldest European codifications of civil law, also went out of effect. Besides, the courts were no longer allowed to cite the pre-war and the wartime jurisprudence. However, under Articles 3–4 of LILR, the courts were left with the possibility of using the rules originating from the pre-WWII laws, if there was no applicable law for a given case, and if the old rule did not contradict the values of the new constitutional order. Still, even if there was a lacuna and if the old rule existed that was not in contradiction with the new constitutionally protected values, the courts were not obliged to resort to it, and were free to decide on other methods of filling the legal gap, and even to create the norm which is contrary to the pre-war law, as long as it is compliant to the new constitutional order. One of the consequences of LILR was a tremendous development of the practice of domestic courts in the period after WWII.

78. The possibility the courts have under LILR (not to cite the pre-WWII formal sources of law directly, but to make use of the rules stemming from those sources by indicating those rules as the 'pre-war law') has lost much of its importance in the field of commercial contracts once *the General Usages of Sale of Goods (GUSG)* was codified in 1954. Under Article 2 of GUSG, it used to be taken that the parties to the contract have agreed to its application unless they have contracted out of GUSG. This provision of GUSG was later abrogated by Article 1107 of LO. The possibility of resorting to the pre-war law has lost significance even further as LO was enacted in 1978.

79. To say a few words about the aforementioned Serbian Civil Code (SCC) of 1844: at the time of its enactment, Serbia was not a kingdom yet, so the exact title of the codification was the *Civil Code for the Dukedom of Serbia*. Such early adoption of the codex was of great historical importance for Serbian legal culture and society in general. Serbia became one of the few countries in the world at that time to have a civil codification. The Code prompted Europeanization of the country and its cultural emancipation from the centuries-long Ottoman influence and established the way the development of civil legislation in Serbia would continue.

80. It must be said though that the 1844 SCC was in fact an abbreviated and to some extent amended version of the Austrian Civil Code of 1811. Following the Austrian example, Serbian codification kept to a tripartite structure of civil law, developed by classical Roman Law. However, the Austrian model was reduced to not more than 950 paragraphs, with some of the Austrian provisions being left out of the Serbian Code without good reason. Thus, it is generally understood that the reception was poorly executed and that the structure and internal coherence of the Serbian Code were damaged from the beginning. The succeeding amendments have only exacerbated the issue.

§3. Function of the Law of Torts

81. The first and foremost function of Serbian tort law is to indemnify the injured person, that is, to secure compensation for her losses and to put her in the position she would have been in, was it not for the damaging event. One of the fundamental principles of tortious liability in Serbia is the principle of 'full or integral compensation:' While also taking into account the circumstances that have ensued following the occurrence of damage, the court shall award damages in the amount necessary for the recovery of the injured party's financial situation, i.e., the amount necessary in order to place the injured party into the financial position in which she would have been, was it not for the injuring action or omission.[76]

82. It is embedded in LO, clear for the courts, and undisputed by legal doctrine that the amount of damages awarded should put the victim in the position he or she would have been in, had the injuring action not been committed. The victim is entitled to full compensation, and nothing but the full compensation, for the legally recognized (recoverable) losses inflicted on him. The primary purpose of compensation is neither to punish the tortfeasor, to better the financial position of the victim, nor to deter the tortfeasor and others from engaging in certain conduct.

83. The extent of compensation the victim is entitled to does not depend on the gravity of the tortfeasor's fault. As it will be elaborated later, ordinary negligence of the injurer is sufficient for ascertaining his liability for the damage caused, and ordinary negligence is exactly the degree of fault that shall be rebuttably presumed, once the injured party has sufficiently proved the damage and the causal link. Irrespective of whether the tortfeasor has acted with ordinary or gross negligence, or with an intention to harm (*animus nocendi*), or even with *dolus coloratus*, the injured party shall be entitled to the same amount of damages: the amount needed for full or integral compensation. Regardless of the degree of the tortfeasor's fault, the victim shall be entitled to compensation for both actual patrimonial loss (*damnum emergens*) and lost profits (*lucrum cessans*). Also, in cases of strict liability, the principle of integral compensation will normally apply. Thus, in general, the injured party shall be entitled to full compensation (lost profits included), even if the liability in question is not based on fault.

76. Article 190 of LO.

84. There are, however, some mechanisms for keeping tortious liability within reasonable limits. As it will be later explained, they serve as tools for fine corrections of the effects of the principle of full compensation as, admittedly, the principle of full compensation fails to produce fair and reasonable results in some cases. For instance, depending on the conditions of the case, the courts may consider the fact that the tortfeasor is deprived of the financial means necessary for his own maintenance. Or, the fact that the tortfeasor has acted in the sole interest of the injured party may also be relevant. The purpose of these mechanisms is to ensure the fair balance of interests of the parties concerned and to make certain that, taking all circumstances into account, liability is not unjustifiably burdensome for the tortfeasor.

85. When non-patrimonial (moral) damage is concerned, the courts and legal doctrine understand the purpose of awarding equitable compensation for non-patrimonial damage to be *satisfaction*, i.e., reinstatement of the injured party's moral and psychological equilibrium. After finding that the circumstances of the case at hand, and particularly the duration and the intensity of the pain and fear sustained by the injured party justify such a decision, the court shall award equitable monetary compensation to the injured party, irrespective of compensation for patrimonial damage, and in the absence of any patrimonial harm. In deciding on the merits of the claim, and on the amount of equitable compensation for non-patrimonial damage in question, the court shall take into account the importance of the violated non-patrimonial interests, the purpose of the equitable compensation for non-patrimonial losses (i.e., *satisfaction*), but also that the awarded equitable compensation should not favour the goals which are otherwise incompatible with its nature and social purpose.[77]

86. To sum up: the first and most important function primarily attributed to the law of tort in Serbia is to indemnify the person suffering harm, that is, (1) to provide for integral compensation of the patrimonial losses the victim has suffered, irrespective of the gravity of the injurer's fault; and also, (2) to ensure the victim receives equitable compensation (*satisfaction*) for non-patrimonial losses, which should facilitate the recovery of her psychological equilibrium.

87. In addition to everything said, the law of tort may indirectly serve some other social purposes, but they remain in the background and never prevail over the compensatory function of tortious liability.

88. First, different institutions of tort law may contribute to preventing the negative consequences of human behaviour, as well as discouraging potential wrongdoers from engaging in injurious activities. Therefore, the secondary function of tort law may consist of prevention and deterrence (though this is reduced to a large extent by the possibility of taking out insurance against liability).

For instance, a clearly preventive function may be attributed to a preventive civil law claim which may be pursued by a member of the public, in the interest of public order (any person may demand from another to eliminate a source of danger of

77. Article 200 of LO.

considerable damage to him, or to an unspecified number of persons; each person may demand from another to refrain from an activity which causes a disturbance or generates a risk of damage if disturbance or damage cannot be prevented by appropriate measures).[78]

Besides, irrespective of the circumstance that no social stigma is generally attached to liability in tort (as opposed to criminal liability), normally the mere anticipation of tortious liability should serve a preventive purpose, all the more so if the potential tortfeasor has confidence in the legal system and in the chances of forced execution of the injured party's rights. Nevertheless, it remains undisputed that the central mechanisms of prevention and deterrence of socially unacceptable behaviours are the mechanisms of criminal law.

89. Second, certain institutions of Serbian tort law may have some retributive elements. It is extremely rare that a sanction is imposed on the tortfeasor that exceeds the mere compensation of the injury. One such solitary example is the 'triple compensation' in the field of copyright law, where, as it will be shown later, a victim of a violation of copyright or related right may claim the threefold amount of what would have been the normal adequate remuneration for lawful exploitation of the right in question.

More often, 'retributive' elements are limited to differential treatment of different tortfeasors, meaning that tortfeasors who have acted with higher degrees of fault shall not have certain options that are present for those who have acted with ordinary negligence. For example, where the financial status of the tortfeasor is so critical that paying the full amount of compensation would deprive him of financial means necessary for his own maintenance, the court may reduce compensation, taking into consideration the victim's financial status as well, but only if the tortfeasor acted neither with intent nor with gross negligence.[79] Also, in the work-related context, an employee shall be directly liable for damage caused during the course of his employment, only if there existed the highest degree of fault (intent) on his side, which must be proved by the injured party. And, after compensating the damage, the employer is entitled to reimbursement of the paid sum from the employee on the condition of proving the employee's intent or gross negligence. If the employee has acted with ordinary negligence, he shall escape direct liability, as well as the employer's claim for recovery of the sum paid to the victim.[80] To add one more example: where an item of property was destroyed by a criminal offence committed with premeditation, the court may determine the amount of indemnity against the value the item has had for the injured party.[81] Here, the compensatory nature of damages is not changed, but a special method of assessment of damages is allowed, in order to sanction an especially heinous injurious conduct.[82]

78. Article 156 of LO.
79. Article 191 of LO.
80. Articles 170 and 171 of LO.
81. Article 189 of LO.
82. In detail on purpose of fault-based liability: M. Karanikić Mirić, *Krivica kao osnov deliktne odgovornosti u građanskom pravu* (Beograd, 2009), 301–328. In detail on purpose of strict liability: M. Karanikić Mirić, *Objektivna odgovornost za štetu* (Beograd, 2013), 31–39.

§4. Relationship Between Torts and Criminal Law

90. The historical development of legal thought in Serbia includes Toma Živanović,[83] an influential legal philosopher, who expanded from Franz Liszt's idea of the generic term of *Unrecht*, and his conceptual unity of delict in civil law and delict in criminal law. Živanović heavily criticized the idea of a clear-cut distinction between civil and criminal wrongdoings and held that there existed the *unity of criminal and tortious liability*.[84] Yet, his line of thought was not received by other legal scholars, and in today's legal theory and legal dogmatics in Serbia, it is undisputed there is a clear difference between notions of delict in criminal law and delict in civil law.

91. Most recently, these differences have been elaborated by Miodrag Orlić.[85] Common characteristics of tortious and criminal liabilities (as opposed to, for instance, political and moral liabilities) are that both kinds of liability are determined before the courts and that for both kinds of liability, the courts impose sanctions of legal nature. In contrast, the differences between these two kinds of liability are numerous and will be outlined here briefly.

92. First of all, there is a difference in the ways in which delicts are formulated in criminal law and in civil law. Concerning criminal law, no crime can be committed and no punishment meted out, without a violation of law as it existed at the moment of the alleged offence (*nullum crimen nulla poena sine lege*).[86] Thus, a closed number (*numerus clausus*) of criminal offences exist in a given legal order.

In contrast, Serbian tort law is based on the idea of 'general civil delict'. The requirements of tortious liability are set out by statutes (laws made by legislative bodies) but in a flexible and very broad and general manner. They include legally recognized (recoverable) moral or patrimonial damage; causal link (normally established as per the theory of adequate causation); and fault, i.e., substandard behaviour of the injurer (normally measured against an abstract, depersonalized, objective yardstick). Any injurious conduct may lead to liability in tort, provided that general preconditions of civil liability are met. The norm is flexible in the sense that the new types of behaviour may fall under it, as long as they meet the general requirements. Along the same lines, the courts may qualify new things, or new human activities as excessively dangerous, which shall trigger strict tortious liability of their keepers, or performers.

93. Second, in criminal law, liability may only be based on fault, and established exclusively for the wrongdoer's own actions or omissions. There can be no criminal liability for the acts of another person. In contrast, tort law is marked by a

83. T. Živanović, *Sistem sintetičke filozofije prava* (Beograd, 1997 [1921, 1951, 1959]).
84. On the history of these ideas, and offering original stance: M. Orlić, 'Ogled o odnosu građanske i krivične odgovornosti', *PZ 10/2011*, 615–636.
85. *Ibid.* An older analysis: A. Lazarević, 'Razlike između građanske i krivične odgovornosti i njen značaj u teoriji i praksi', *APFB 5–6/1969*, 587–600.
86. Article 1 of CCS (*Criminal Code of Serbia* of 2005, last changes in 2019).

plurality of possible grounds of liability, and also by the existence of different categories of liability for acts of others. In addition, in criminal law cases, the fault of the wrongdoer must be proved by the prosecution. Instead, there is a rebuttable statutory presumption of fault in Serbian tort law: If the injured party proves before the court that he sustained either patrimonial or moral damage or both and that the damage he suffered was caused by the injurer's conduct, the court will assume that the injuring conduct was wrong from the standpoint of the legitimate social expectations, i.e., that the tortfeasor was at fault. Also, ordinary negligence is generally sufficient for establishing liability in tort. In contrast, criminal liability requires the existence of criminal intent, and only exceptionally a lesser degree of fault shall be sufficient. In addition, the standard of proof is higher in criminal proceedings.[87]

94. Third, the very notion of fault is understood differently in criminal law and in tort law. In the field of liability in tort fault is understood objectively; it is an attribute of the injurer's conduct, and not of the state of his mind, and in that sense, it includes the instances where the injurer has breached the legitimate expectations of the society by deviating from the legal standard of conduct. Even in the heavily regulated fields of social behaviour, such as road traffic, the unlawfulness of the injurer's conduct is not required as a separate, fourth, condition of his liability (in addition to damage, causation and fault). Unlawfulness of the injurious conduct is considered an indicator, or an element, of the injurer's fault. In contrast, in criminal law fault is comprehended as the wrongdoer's state of mind, his psychological stance toward his own actions and the consequences of those actions. And, as there can be no crime without a pre-existing statutory proscription, the unlawfulness of the wrongdoer's conduct represents an indispensable condition of his criminal liability.

95. Fourth, there is a significant difference between the criminal law sanctions and the remedies of tort law. The purposes of criminal punishment are general and special prevention and deterrence, expression of social condemnation for criminal offences, endorsement of social morality, and reinforcement of obligation to abide by the law.[88] Retribution is not explicitly identified as one of the goals of criminal punishment, though, even in modern systems of criminal justice, retributive elements can never be totally excluded from the notion of punishment.[89] In contrast, the first and foremost function of Serbian tort law is to indemnify the injured person, that is, to secure compensation for her losses, and to put her in the position she would have been in, was it not for the damaging event. Furthermore, tort law remedies affect the injurer's estate, and not his personality. They consist in paying damages for loss or injury inflicted upon the injured party, even if the loss in question

87. Clear and convincing evidence or preponderance of evidence in civil proceedings; conviction with certainty (beyond reasonable doubt) in criminal proceedings. Cf. Art. 8 of CPA (*Civil Procedure Act* of 2011, last changes in 2020), Art. 2, para. 1 (20) and Art. 16 of CCP (*Code of Criminal Procedure* of 2011, last changes in 2021).
88. Article 42 of CCS.
89. Z. Stojanović, *Komentar Krivičnog zakonika* (Beograd, 2006), 175.

is non-patrimonial (moral, non-pecuniary) by its nature.[90] In contrast, the main sanctions of criminal law, such as imprisonment, directly affect the wrongdoer's personality.

96. Criminal law sanctions 'public wrongs', it provides for the punishment of those acts that are harmful not only to some individual or individuals but also to society. Criminal proceedings are initiated in the public interest and by public prosecution. Their main purpose is general and special prevention of wrongdoings of certain seriousness and deterrence of potential wrongdoers. The fact the wrongdoer has promptly and fully compensated the victim for the losses caused by criminal offence, shall not cancel criminal proceedings, and may only have a limited impact on sentencing.[91]

97. The civil court is bound by non-appealable condemnatory judgment of the criminal court, concerning the issues of existence of a criminal offence and criminal liability of the wrongdoer.[92]

98. Where damage has been caused by a criminal offence, the injured party may claim damages in the course of criminal proceedings. Under Article 252 of Code of Criminal Procedure (CCP), the injured party may claim compensation from a defendant in the adjudication process of the criminal law, for the damage caused by the defendant committing the criminal offence at issue, provided that resolution of the civil claim would not cause significant delays in criminal proceedings.[93]

99. Also, if damage has been caused by a criminal offence, and if there is a longer statute of limitation for criminal prosecution than for damages, the claim for damages against the liable party shall become unenforceable only when the longer prescription period for criminal prosecution expires. Interruption and suspension of the prescription period for criminal prosecution shall affect the claim for damages as well.[94]

100. The question of whether a criminal offence was performed by the wrongdoer or not, may be resolved before civil courts as a preliminary issue, except for the case where criminal court has decided on the merits, i.e., handed down either a condemnatory or a verdict of acquittal. Otherwise, the civil court can temporarily halt the proceedings until the criminal court decides on the merits. In deciding on

90. These could be mental suffering or physical pain or fear, each of sufficient intensity and duration.
91. Article 54 of CCS (the wrongdoer's comportment after the crime, and particularly his attitude towards the victim, may be taken into account in sentencing).
92. Article 13 of CPA.
93. The Code of Criminal Procedure contains elaborate rules on civil claims filed in criminal proceedings. Articles 252–260 of CCP.
94. Article 377 of LO. The extended prescription period runs against both the tortfeasor and the vicariously liable person, even if criminal proceedings against the tortfeasor were discontinued, or the tortfeasor died before the criminal proceedings were initiated, or there was an amnesty or a pardon granted to the tortfeasor. Opinion of the Constitutional Court of Serbia, Su. I-400/1/3-11 of 14 Jul. 2011, *PLex*.

whether to pause civil proceedings or to decide on a preliminary issue, the court shall consider the principle of opportunity or the principle of expediency.[95]

§5. Relationship Between Contractual and Delictual or Tortious Liability

101. There is a clear and important distinction in Serbian law between tortious liability (i.e., liability in delict, extra-contractual liability)[96] and liability for the violation or failure of a pre-existing duty to the other party to the obligation.[97] The latter kind of liability is usually called contractual liability, though the infringed pre-existent duty in question does not have to be a *contractual* duty. Besides, it is well-established in Serbian law and legal doctrine that pre-contractual liability (*culpa in contrahendo*) represents a type of fault-based tortious (extra-contractual) liability.

102. Parties to the obligation must exercise due care in performing their commitments to one another (Article 18 of LO). In general, they have to observe the standard of a careful man, a careful businessperson, or a careful professional, depending on the context. This principle applies only if the parties are already legally bound one to another. When it comes to contracts, Article 18 of LO may not be invoked prior to entering into a contract. In the pre-contractual stage, while the parties are still in the process of negotiation, they may plead Article 12 of LO (the good faith principle), but not the statutory duty of care under Article 18 of LO.

Insofar as tortious liability is concerned, it is considered there are no pre-existing obligations between the parties, and the obligation (to compensate for the damage) arises from the very fact that damage to one was caused by the conduct of another. However, the codified principle of *neminem laedere* applies (Article 16 of LO). This is a general standard of behaviour that runs to all others, irrespective of any prior legally recognized relationship, and breaching this standard may trigger fault-based liability in tort.

103. A party to the obligation may claim compensation for patrimonial damage caused by non-performance or delayed performance. However, the debtor shall be excused from this type of liability if he proves that his inability to perform or to timely perform resulted from the circumstances which have occurred after the formation of the contract, and which he was not able to foresee, avoid or eliminate.[98]

104. Under the rules of contractual liability, the promisor is generally only liable for patrimonial damage (including loss of profits), foreseen or which could have been reasonably foreseen (by him) at the time when the agreement was made. In case of intentional, grossly negligent or fraudulent breach of contractual (or any

95. Comm CPA Poz, 58, B. Poznić & V. Rakić-Vodinelić, *Građansko procesno pravo* (Beograd, 1999), 209, A. Jakšić, *Građansko procesno pravo* (Beograd, 2012), 75–76.
96. Articles 154–209 of LO.
97. Articles 262–269 of LO.
98. Articles 262 and 263 of LO.

other pre-existent) duty, the injured party may claim compensation for both foreseeable and unforeseeable patrimonial damage.[99] In contrast, under the rules on tortious liability, the injured party may generally claim full compensation for both patrimonial and non-patrimonial damage, irrespective of their foreseeability at the time of the damaging event.

105. Pre-contractual liability. Under Article 30, paragraph 1 of LO, parties to the negotiations are not bound by the mere fact that they have entered the negotiations, and each of them may terminate the process of negotiating whenever they want.[100] In other words, the fact that the two are negotiating about the prospective contract does not create an obligation for either of them to negotiate successfully, i.e., to actually enter into the contract. Still, the meaning of this provision is not that the parties may act as they wish in the pre-contractual stage, or that they do not have a remedy against the reckless behaviour of another before the contract is concluded. In contrast, they may be held liable in tort for their conduct in pre-contractual negotiations.

106. It is undisputed in Serbian law and legal doctrine that parties to the negotiations have a duty to bargain in good faith. Thus, a party who negotiates or breaks off negotiations in bad faith shall be liable for the losses caused to the other party. Under Article 30, paragraphs 2 and 3 of LO, the party who was negotiating without intention to enter into a contract shall be liable for damage caused to another party by negotiating. Also, the one who had commenced the negotiations with the intention to enter into a contract but later broke off the negotiations for no justified reason shall be liable for damage caused to the other party by unjustified termination of the process of negotiating. The general rules of fault-based tortious liability shall apply, except for the rebuttable statutory presumption of fault, as it may not be generally taken that people enter negotiations without intention to contract, or that they leave negotiations for no justified reason.

107. Therefore, the conditions of liability for damage caused by substandard behaviour prior to contract formation are the existence of recoverable damage (patrimonial or non-patrimonial[101]); causal link between negotiation or termination of negotiation, on the one hand, and the damage, on the other hand; fault of the liable party, which may consist in negotiating with no intention to conclude a contract, or in ending the negotiation without justified reason. The burden of proof rests with the injured party.

---

99. Article 266, paras 1 and 2 of LO.

100. Under Art. 30, para. 4 of LO, unless the parties agree otherwise, each party to the negotiations shall bear their own expenses of negotiating, while joint expenses shall be shared equally between the parties. (It is obviously redundant to say 'unless the parties agree otherwise', as the principle of freedom of contract generally applies.).

101. For example, the author's psychological pain due to infringement of his moral (personal) rights by the loss of his manuscript through the publisher's fault, in the course of negotiation regarding publishing contract. Decision of the Federal Court of Yugoslavia, Gzs. 51/1977 of 11 Jul. 1977. Detailed analysis of this decision and its relevance for the understanding of pre-contractual liability even before the enactment of LO: M. Orlić, *Zaključenje ugovora* (Beograd, 1993), 54–68.

108. However, these are not the sole two ways in which fault may manifest itself in the pre-contractual stage. The idea is more general: the rules on *culpa in contrahendo* may apply whenever there is no contract, and one of the parties to the negotiations has suffered damage from the fact that the other party was negotiating in bad faith. In any case, the injured party must prove the fault of another. For instance, a person making an invitation to treat does not intend to be bound as soon as the invitation is accepted by the person to whom the statement was addressed. She reserves the right to refuse the offer received upon such invitation. However, if she declines such offer for no justified reason, she will be liable for damage for the losses caused in that way to the other party (i.e., the invitation-recipient).[102]

109. The rule of non-cumul. Liability in tort and liability in contract seem to coincide in some situations of fact, so the injured party may have a choice either to sue under contract or under tort. For instance, actions for damages against medical professionals and their employers are regularly brought in tort in Serbia, though the patient could, at least in theory, bring an action for breach of contract against a medical or health institution (which would be easier to conceive with regard to private institutions and voluntary health insurance). However, there are no such cases as yet. Or, where the lessee destroys or damages the asset he has obtained the right to use under a lease agreement, the lessor may claim damages either under contract or under tort.

110. In contrast to the general principle of French law that the injured party has no option but to sue in the contract where the contract exists, even if the prescription period has run out for the contractual remedy, as the parties have freely agreed that their relationship is to be governed by the contract (i.e., they *opted for* a specific contractual regime, and thus *opted out of* the regime of tortious liability),[103] Serbian law generally allows concurrent liability in contract and tort.[104] The injured party is free to choose among the actions available to him. However, he cannot cumulate compensation for the same damage on different grounds, that is, he cannot collect damages for the same loss both in contract and in tort.

111. If one damaging event qualifies both as a breach of contract and as a civil delict, the injured party may choose to claim damages either in contract or in tort. Moreover, the plaintiff is not obliged to state the legal basis of his claim, and if she selects to do so, the court shall not be bound by the plaintiff's statement of what the legal basis of his claim should be. It is enough that the plaintiff recounts the facts of the case, and that he asks the court to impose the consequences which follow from these facts under the law. Under the rules of civil procedure, the court shall deny the claim only if there is no legal ground for it whatsoever. The court shall determine the facts of the case, and then examine whether there are *any grounds* for

102. Article 35, para. 2 of LO.
103. H.L. et J. Mazeaud & F. Chabas, *Leçons de Droit Civil* (Paris, 1998), 401–405.
104. J. Radišić, *Obligaciono pravo* (Beograd, 2004), 188.

the plaintiff's claim, not limited to the grounds of the claim as stated by the plaintiff. When there is more than one possible basis for the plaintiff's claim, the court shall accept the claim to the fullest extent possible under the law.[105]

§6. Protected Interests

112. The protected interests for which compensation is recoverable are not expressly enumerated or listed in any statute in Serbian law. The idea of the types of interests that enjoy protection under the rules of tortious liability may be inferred from a catalogue of recoverable damages, that is to say, from a directory of the losses legally recognized as damage under the rules of Serbian tort law.

113. Such catalogue may be construed from Article 155 and Articles 200–202 of LO, and from the Constitution. The right to peaceful enjoyment of property and other patrimonial rights is guaranteed under the Constitution.[106] Certain personal rights also enjoy constitutional protection.[107] Still, the violation in itself (of legally protected non-patrimonial interests, or objects of non-patrimonial or personal rights) does not constitute recoverable damage under Serbian tort law. Only if such violation has further resulted in some sort of legally recognized patrimonial or moral damage to the bearer of the violated personal right, he shall be entitled to damages under the rules on tortious liability.

114. There are some legitimate interests that *are* legally protected, but *not* under the rules of tortious liability. More precisely, certain interests do enjoy legal protection, but their infringement is not recognized as a type of recoverable loss under the rules of Serbian tort law. For example, Serbian courts are firmly holding to the view that juridical persons cannot claim compensation for moral damage.[108] Reputation of a juridical person represents a legally protected interest, it is considered an object of a non-patrimonial right. Therefore, in cases of violation of some non-patrimonial right of a juridical person, the court *may* order, at the expense of the injurer, a decision of the court to be published, or a published information to be corrected, or a statement of the injurer to be retracted, or another remedy by which the purpose of redress may be achieved.[109] On the other hand, injury to the reputation of a juridical person cannot produce legally relevant mental suffering, and as a result, juridical persons are not entitled to equitable compensation for moral damage.[110] This is a logical consequence of the purely subjective concept of moral damage, which is accepted in Serbian tort law.[111] Mere infringement of non-patrimonial rights, or

105. Comm CPA Poz, 411.
106. Article 58 of CRS.
107. Article 23 of CRS and further.
108. Legal position of the Civil Chamber of SCS of 5 Feb. 2001, *PLex*.
109. Article 199 of LO.
110. SCS, Rev. 611/2001 of 25 Dec. 2002, *PLex*.
111. The Commission appointed to draft the new Civil Code of Serbia considered several modes of either partial or complete objectivization of the concept of moral damage in the prospective codification. However, the Commission was dissolved in 2019 by the Government.

violation of personal goods as objects of these rights, does not constitute moral (non-patrimonial) damage, unless such infringement has caused physical or psychological pain, or fear, to the plaintiff, and therefore disturbed his or her mental equilibrium.

115. Catalogue of recoverable losses: Recoverable damage may be either patrimonial (pecuniary, material) or non-patrimonial (non-pecuniary, moral).[112]

116. Patrimonial (pecuniary, economic) interests of both natural and juridical persons enjoy protection under the rules on tortious liability insofar as their infringement qualifies as recoverable patrimonial damage. Two kinds of recoverable *patrimonial damage* exist direct loss (actual or positive damage or *damnum emergens*), and loss of the expected gains or profits (*lucrum cessans*).

117. There are three kinds of recoverable (legally recognized) *non-patrimonial (moral) damage*:[113] physical pain, psychological pain and fear, each of sufficient duration and intensity.[114]

More exactly, psychological pain (mental suffering) qualifies as recoverable moral damage only if it is caused by the injured party's impairment of life activities; severe disfigurement; violation of her reputation, honour, freedom or personal rights; or by death or severe disability of the injured party's close relative.[115] Also, victim of a criminal offence against sexual freedom has a special right to equitable compensation for psychological pain.[116]

118. As stated before, personal reputation, honour, freedom and personal rights, in general, enjoy protection under the rules on tortious liability (Article 200 of LO), provided that their violation has caused their bearer mental suffering of sufficient intensity and duration. Still, personal rights whose infringement may cause psychological pain which amounts to moral damage are not itemized in LO. Some of those rights are expressly guaranteed under the Constitution, such as life, physical and mental integrity, human dignity, privacy, personal freedom and security, inviolability of the home, etc.[117] However, contrary to having a limited *numerus clausus* of property rights, personal rights are not exhaustively enumerated: neither they are fully listed in the formal sources of law, nor is their content categorically and conclusively determined.[118]

---

112. Article 155 of LO.
113. Also affirmed in: Conclusion of the Joint session of the Federal Court, state Supreme Courts and the Supreme Military Court of 15 and 16 Oct. 1986, *Bilten sudske prakse Vrhovnog suda BiH* 1/1987. Future moral damage is recoverable under Art. 203 of LO.
114. Article 200 of LO.
115. This is an all-in list. Thus, psychological pain due to a loss of item of property, even if the item in question is a piece of artwork, does not represent recoverable moral damage. SCS, Rev. I 2749/2004 of 25 Nov. 2004, *PLex*.
116. Article 202 of LO.
117. Article 23 of CRS and further.
118. V. Vodinelić, *Građansko pravo* (Beograd, 2012), 253.

119. There are some circumstances under which damages are not available, despite the negative effects of another person's conduct. Under Article 156 of LO, damage caused by an activity which was performed in the public interest and authorized by the public authorities shall be recoverable only if it exceeds the normal scope of damage under the circumstances. The potentially injured party can, however, demand socially justified measures to be taken, in order to prevent or mitigate the impending damage.

Also, the owner of immovable property is obliged to control and prevent noise, smells, smoke, heat, garbage and other emissions from his premises which cause significant damage to others, or obstruct the use of other immovable properties, and he must keep those emissions within customary limits, considering the nature and the purpose of his premises and the local settings.[119] However, it is legitimate to expect the neighbours to withstand the accustomed, normal, usual levels of unpleasant emissions from one's premises.

120. Hence, there are circumstances in which the injured party shall have no remedy against the injurious conduct. These circumstances are 'special' so they should be construed narrowly. Where damage originates from an activity which is carried out in the public interest and approved by competent public authority, the injured party shall have no remedy against it, unless it exceeds normal extent. But, the courts have held that the injured party is entitled to full compensation once the damage exceeds the normal scope.[120]

119. As per Art. 5 of the Law on Property Relations of 1980.

120. District Court in Kraljevo, Gž. 417/1991 of 26 Mar. 1991, in: B. Čolić & M. Samardžić, *Zbornik sudske prakse iz oblasti imovinskog prava*, Glosarijum, Beograd 1995, 65.

Part I. Liability for One's Own Acts

Chapter 1. General Principles

§1. Unlawfulness and Fault

121. One of the precepts of Serbian Tort Law is the principle of *neminem laedere*. Under Article 16 of LO (*Prohibition of inflicting harm*) everyone is bound to refrain from actions that may cause damage to another. If taken literally, this provision would suggest the existence of legal duty to abstain from pretty much all human activity, as almost all human actions are, under certain conditions, apt to cause damage. However, this statutory provision is understood as a codified general principle of civil law. It bears high interpretative importance and is intended to facilitate our understanding of other, more concrete statutory provisions on tort liability. Statutory prohibition of causing harm to another is merely a standard which does not lay out conditions that make the application of this principle compulsory; it does not determine the outcome of a dispute; it inclines a decision of a court one way and remains uncompromised even if it does not prevail.

122. Under the general rules of Serbian Tort Law, unlawfulness of injurious conduct does not count among the conditions of tortious liability. According to Article 154, paragraph 1 of LO whoever causes damage to another shall be liable to redress it, unless he proves the absence of his own fault. One may not escape liability by proving that his actions were not unlawful, i.e., that his harmful conduct was not prohibited by law. Still, some authors claim that unlawfulness of the injurious conduct (as a condition of tort liability) may be inferred from Article 16 LO.[121] This line of thought implies that any action which results in damage to another should generally be deemed unlawful under Article 16 of LO.

123. This does not hold for several reasons. First, the said statutory provision should be understood as a codified principle, as noted above, and not as a rule which sets out the conditions for its own application and the consequences of its own breach. Second, Article 16 of LO does not order abstention from the behaviours of a certain type, i.e., refraining from the conduct that holds certain attributes. On the contrary, it proscribes certain results of human conduct (the results that legally qualify as *damage*), irrespective of the attributes or characteristics of the behaviour that led to these results. Thus, Article 16 of LO may not be taken as some sort of a

121. J. Radišić. *Protivpravnost kao uslov građanske odgovornosti*, APFB 1–4/2001, 551.

'general' protective norm; it refers to damage as a legally proscribed consequence of human action, and not to the action itself. In other words, the fact that damage was caused does not by itself signify that the injuring behaviour was unlawful. And third, in line with Article 154, paragraph 1 of LO, Serbian courts neither require the plaintiff to prove that the injuring action of the defendant was unlawful at the time it was assumed nor do they allow the defendant to discharge himself from liability by proving that his conduct was not unlawful though it did cause damage to another.

124. There are three statutory conditions of subjective liability for one's own acts. First, it is necessary that damage occurred, i.e., that the injured party has suffered legally acknowledged patrimonial (material), or non-patrimonial (moral, intangible) loss. Second, it is required that the victim's loss occurred as a consequence of the injurer's conduct, that is, that there was a sufficient causal link between the injuring conduct and the loss which was inflicted on the injured party. Third, the injurer must be at fault. His behaviour must be of such properties, or characteristics, that it departs from legitimate social expectations.

125. Fault is a broad concept which brings about liability the moment it is connected to the victim's loss by adequate causation. Furthermore, fault is understood objectively; it is an attribute of the injurer's conduct, and not of the state of his mind, and in that sense, it includes the instances where the injurer has breached the legitimate expectations of society by deviating from the legal standard of conduct. Even in the heavily regulated fields of social behaviour, such as road traffic, unlawfulness of the injurer's conduct is not required as a separate, fourth, condition of his liability (in addition to damage, causation and fault). Unlawfulness of the injurious conduct is considered an indicator, or an element, of the injurer's fault. By breaking the rule that purports to regulate his behaviour, the injurer has acted contrary to what was legitimately expected from a hypothetical reasonable and careful person in the same or significantly similar situation. In addition, the fact that someone is authorized by law to engage in certain conduct does not relieve him from the general obligation to act as a reasonable and careful person in the course of such engagement.

126. Unlawful behaviour of the tortfeasor, his action or omission that is contrary to his pre-existing legal duty to act in a certain manner, signifies that there is fault at his side – that his conduct was not as it should have been – in so far as this breach of the mandatory rule is not excused by specific considerations, such as consent of the injured party, self-help, self-defence, etc. However, the tortfeasor may be at fault even if he did not breach any pre-existing duty to act in a certain manner, as long as his action deviates from what is legitimately expected from a reasonable and careful person.

127. Neither unlawfulness of the injuring conduct nor fault is requested for ascertaining strict liability. Article 154, paragraph 2 of LO contains a general norm on strict liability for both patrimonial and non-patrimonial damage, caused by either an object, or a human activity, that generate abnormal (increased) risk of damage to others. An object or an activity may be categorized, either by the legislator or by the courts, as atypically, abnormally dangerous, that is, as being a generator of an increased, abnormal risk of damage. The sole conditions for this type of liability are damage and causation.

128. Finally, some legal scholars focus on the unlawfulness of the result of the injuring action. They emphasize the fact that there can be no liability for damage unless the loss suffered by the injured party is recoverable under the law, that is, if the sustained loss does not qualify as legally relevant damage. However, that is just another way of saying that *damage* in law is a normative concept. In any case, unlawfulness of the results of the injurer's behaviour may not be stated as the fourth condition of subjective liability – along with damage, causation and fault – because this type of unlawfulness has already been addressed or covered by 'damage' as the first among those conditions.

§2. Concept of Fault

129. There is no statutory definition of fault in Serbian civil law. LO neither defines nor describes behaviour which leads to tort liability. A definition of fault was included in Skica, that is, the already-mentioned Draft Code on Obligations and Contracts of 1969, but it was omitted from the LO. However, the definition found in Skica has exerted a profound influence both on the courts and legal scholarship in Serbia. The notion of fault, as proposed in Skica, was not a novelty to the courts at the time Skica was originally published. This definition was rather a proposal for the codification of an idea that has already emerged in the decisions of the courts. So, the well-known Article 127 of the Skica (*When the fault exists*) stated that, when determining whether there is fault on the side of the person who caused damage, that is, when establishing whether the injurer has acted as he should have acted, the court takes into account the normal course of things, as well as what could have been legitimately expected from a reasonable and careful man under the given circumstances.

130. The notion of fault in civil law has departed from the notion of guilt in criminal law. Under the rules of Serbian tort law, fault is not an internal, psychological relation toward one's own acts and their consequences, it is not an attribute of the tortfeasor's state of mind, i.e., of his consciousness and will, but an attribute of the tortfeasor's injurious conduct – a certain type of behaviour, which deviates from the legitimate social expectations under the given circumstances. One is at fault if he does not behave as a reasonable and careful man would under the same circumstances. This applies both to actions and omissions, as there are instances where the very failure to act defeats the legitimate social expectations concerning a hypothetical reasonable and careful man under the given circumstances.[122]

122. In detail: M. Karanikić Mirić, *Krivica kao osnov deliktne odgovornosti u građanskom pravu*, Beograd 2009, passim, M. Orlić, 'Esej o krivici – u građanskom pravu', *PZ* 1–2/2009, 179–198.

131. The general standard for evaluating fault is an objective one. Fault is measured by an objective yardstick, meaning that personal traits, conditions and capabilities of the tortfeasor generally do not alter the contents of legitimate social expectations vis-à-vis a hypothetical reasonable and careful man in a given situation. In other words, legitimate social expectations with regard to careful and reasonable behaviour under certain circumstances are generally the same for everyone, irrespective of particular individual characteristics of a person who actually did act and did cause damage under those circumstances. Personal traits of the tortfeasor do not change what can be sensibly expected from a reasonable man in his situation. If the tortfeasor has sufficient capacity of discernment, i.e., if he is able to understand the significance of his actions and the potential consequences of his conduct, he should take into consideration his own personal traits, conditions and capabilities, which may obstruct his adherence to the legitimate social expectations, and consequently, he should refrain from actions he cannot complete without causing damage to others.

132. There are, however, some personal traits of the tortfeasor that are always relevant. First of all, the tortfeasor's capacity of discernment serves as a positive precondition of his fault. It is legitimate to expect a person to act as a reasonable and careful man under the given circumstances and to abstain from action if, for some reason, an objective standard of a hypothetical reasonable and careful man is unattainable for him, only if that person has the capacity of discernment, that is, if he or she is able to judge well. Second, it is always relevant if the tortfeasor acts in a professional role or in his capacity as an expert, i.e., if he is supposed to have some special professional insights and knowledge that could not be legitimately expected from a hypothetical reasonable and careful man. In such cases, a special yardstick applies, and the tortfeasor's conduct is measured against the conduct of a reasonable and careful expert (professional) under the given circumstances. Finally, leaning towards an objective yardstick of the injurer's fault should be understood as the continuing inclination of Serbian courts, and not as their intransigent position.

133. Article 154, paragraph 1 of LO contains a rebuttable presumption (*praesumptio iuris tantum*) of the injurer's fault.[123] If the injured party proves before the court that he sustained either patrimonial or moral damage or both and that the damage he suffered was caused by the injurer's conduct, the court will assume that the injuring conduct was wrong from the standpoint of the legitimate social expectations, i.e., that the tortfeasor is at fault. Fault may take two broad forms under Serbian tort law: intention or negligence. The latter may be further sorted as either gross or plain (ordinary) negligence. The form of fault is generally irrelevant to the existence and the scope of the tortfeasor's liability. As a rule, the slightest form of fault is sufficient for establishing liability in tort. It is the other way around when it comes to guilt as the basis of criminal liability. Proof of general criminal intent is required for the conviction of most crimes.

123. In detail: M. Karanikić Mirić, 'Pretpostavka krivice u građanskom pravu', *PZ* 11/2009, 941–958.

134. Immediately after LO was enacted (1978), the question arose about the type (or the gravity) of fault which should be rebuttably presumed under the aforesaid statutory provision, namely, whether the statutory presumption concerns intention or plain negligence. In 1980, the highest courts of Yugoslavia jointly held that only ordinary negligence may be presumed under this rule.[124] If the injured party claims that damage has been caused by intention or gross negligence, he or she has to prove this. Still, there are only limited situations in which the injured party may have interest in proving the tortfeasor's intention or gross negligence,[125] as the rule on integral compensation applies (Article 190 LO), under which the extent of compensation to which the injured party is entitled does not depend on the degree of the injurer's fault. To sum up: ordinary negligence of the injurer is sufficient for ascertaining his liability for the damage he caused, and ordinary negligence is exactly the type of fault that shall be rebuttably presumed – once the injured party has sufficiently proved the damage and the causal link.

135. The fact that there can be no fault if there was no capacity of discernment of the tortfeasor at the time he behaved injuriously towards the victim does not imply that fault should be understood subjectively, that is, as a specific psychological relation of the tortfeasor towards his own action and the consequences of that action. The injurer's capacity of discernment only legitimizes or validates the social request that he aligns his conduct to what is otherwise legitimately expected from a hypothetical reasonable and careful man under the given circumstances.

§3. Duty of Care

136. The concept of duty of care has never been as important for Serbian tort law as it clearly is in the systems of tortious liability that belong to the Common Law tradition.

137. Under Article 18 of LO, parties to the obligation must exercise due care in performing their commitments. In general, parties to the obligation have to observe the standard of a careful man, a careful businessperson, or a careful professional – depending on the context. However, this principle applies only if the parties are already legally bound one to another, that is, once there is a legal obligation between them (for instance, a contractual one) which, from that point on, needs to be performed. And more specifically, when it comes to contracts, Article 18 of LO may not be invoked prior to entering into a contract. In the pre-contractual stage, while the parties are still in the process of negotiation, they may plead Article 12 of LO (the good faith principle), but not the statutory duty of care under Article 18 of LO.

124. Conclusion of XIV Joint session of the Federal Court, state Supreme Courts and the Supreme Military Court of 25 and 26 Mar. 1980, *Zbirka sudskih odluka*, V, 1, 18.

125. For instance, this happens in case of liability of an employer for the damage caused by his employee to a third party while at work, or in connection to the work (Art. 170 LO). The employee is directly liable to the injured party only if damage is caused *intentionally*. The employer has the right to reimbursement from the employee for the sums paid to the third party only if the employee has caused damage to the third party *intentionally* or by *gross negligence*.

138. Insofar as tortious liability under Serbian law is concerned, it is considered that there are no pre-existing obligations between the parties and that the obligation (to redress the damage) arises from the very fact that damage to one was caused by the fault of another. Thus, the existence of the tortfeasor's preceding duty of care towards the injured party is never examined.

139. However, the codified principle of *neminem laedere* applies. Namely, Article 16 of LO contains general prohibition of causing damage to another, that is, general duty to refrain from actions that may result in damage to others. A general rule of behaviour is drawn from this principle, inspired by a number of moral and social considerations. It states that everyone should be liable for the damage caused to another by insufficiently reasonable and careful behaviour. In other words, there is a general standard of behaviour that runs to all others, irrespective of any prior legally recognized relationship, and breaching this standard may trigger fault-based liability in tort. Adherence to the standard of reasonable and careful conduct under given circumstances should not be observed as a legal obligation of the tortfeasor towards the injured party but as a paradigm of socially acceptable behaviour.

§4. CAPACITY

140. Capacity of discernment is an indispensable precondition of fault under general rules of Serbian tort law. Fault-based liability of the tortfeasor for the injury he has caused may not be established if the tortfeasor was not able to understand, at the time he engaged in an injurious action, the significance of such action and of the consequences it was likely to produce. Only those with capacity to judge well may be charged with liability for not acting in accordance with legitimate social expectations, including the expectation to refrain from actions which they cannot complete without inflicting damage to another person.

141. Under Article 160 of LO, there is a conclusive presumption (*praesumptio iuris et de iure*) that minors up to the age of 7 have no capacity of discernment, and hence, it is not possible to establish their fault-based liability. Liability for damage caused by children of such a young age lies with their parents, or with the persons responsible for supervising them at the time of the injurious event. When it comes to minors between the ages of 7 and 14, the statutory presumption of their lack of capacity of discernment is rebuttable (*praesumptio iuris tantum*). It is allowed under the law to rebut such presumption, i.e., to prove that a specific minor of age between 7 and 14 in a given situation was, in fact, able to judge well, and thus, may be liable for his own fault. Finally, when it comes to persons older than 14 years of age, it is rebuttably presumed that they possess the capacity of discernment and that their liability in tort may, therefore, be based on their fault. The stated age brackets are based on the presumed phases in an average psychological and physical development of a typical person. It is obvious that there are some children of the age of 6 that are more mature than some seven-year-olds. However, it is in the nature of legal presumptions to put aside this kind of comparison and to bypass discussion on the capacity of discernment of every particular child, as that would be burdensome for the courts.

142. In addition to the age of the tortfeasor, his mental illness or intellectual disability (formerly known as mental retardation) may also be legally recognized as the root of his incapacity of discernment. It should be noted that the mere fact of mental illness, or that of intellectual disability, does not prove that a person may not be at fault in the legal sense. For such a conclusion it would be necessary to ascertain that the tortfeasor's mental illness, or his intellectual disability, has resulted in his incapacity to judge well. Under Article 159 of LO, if a person is incapable of discernment due to mental illness, intellectual disability, or for some other reason, he cannot be liable for damage caused to another. This provision, without a doubt, relates to liability based on fault. 'Other reasons' for incapacity of discernment may include organic mental disorders, stroke, heart attack, or some other medical condition or emergency due to which a person may not make sound judgments.

143. If a person, who is otherwise incapable of discernment for the reasons of mental illness or intellectual disability, causes damage in a lucid interval, i.e., in a period of relative mental clarity which occurred between periods of incapacity of discernment, he may be held liable, but it would be necessary to prove both his accidental capacity of discernment and his fault. The codification of this rule was proposed in Article 128, paragraph 2 of Skica in 1969, but it has never entered LO. However, the courts sometimes allow for fault-based liability of an injurer who caused damage while in a lucid interval.[126] In such cases, statutory presumption of fault does not apply.

144. Apart from the aforesaid causes of incapacity of discernment, the tortfeasor may be incapable to discern due to psychoactive substances intake. In case the tortfeasor's incapacity of discernment has been induced, i.e., caused by something he had consumed, the tortfeasor shall remain liable for the damage he inflicts on others while in an incapacitated state of mind. The legislator identifies this type of incapacity as 'temporary' (Article 159 of LO). The tortfeasor may excuse himself from liability by proving that he is not at fault for falling into this state. It would not be enough for the tortfeasor to prove that he did not cause his own incapacity, as it may be his fault for exposing himself to the risk to be brought into such state by someone else. Finally, if someone has brought the tortfeasor into the state of temporary incapacity of discernment, he or she will be liable for the damage caused by the incapacitated tortfeasor.

145. By way of exception, the persons who lack capacity of discernment due to their age, mental illness or intellectual disability may be held liable in tort on the grounds of equity. Namely, if the damage was caused by a person who cannot be liable for fault, as he or she lacks capacity of discernment because of young age, mental illness or mental disability, and if compensation cannot be obtained from the

126. For example, SCS, Rev. 4115/01 of 18 Apr. 2002, *Bilten sudske prakse VSS* 1/2003.

person who had a duty to supervise the incapacitated tortfeasor, the court may award either full compensation or a part thereof to be paid by the incapacitated tortfeasor, if the reasons of equity demand such decision, especially when the values of the property of the injurer and of the injured party are taken into consideration.[127]

146. Furthermore, if the damage was caused by a minor who is fully capable of discernment (which is rebuttably presumed for minors who are older than 14, and may be proved by the interested party for minors between 7 and 14 years of age), but who is unable to redress the damage which he inflicted upon the injured party, the court may award either full compensation or a part thereof to be paid by the minor's parents, if the reasons of equity demand such decision, and especially when the values of the property of the minor's parents and of the injured party are taken into consideration.[128]

127. Article 169, para. 1 of LO.
128. Article 169, para. 2 of LO.

Chapter 2. Specific Cases of Liability

§1. Liability of Professionals

I. In General: Higher Standard of Care for 'Experts'

147. In Serbian tort law, fault is generally measured against an objective, depersonalized, abstract standard of legitimate social expectations towards a hypothetical reasonable and careful man under the given circumstances. The codification of this rule was proposed in 1969, in Article 127 of Skica, but it has never been made part of LO. However, the courts adhere to this objective yardstick, and the Commission appointed by the Government to draft a new civil codex for Serbia is considering codifying the aforesaid rule.[129] The Commission is also considering codification of the general rule on professional fault,[130] which has been in use in Serbian courts for a long period of time.[131] Under this rule, there is a higher standard of legitimate social expectations that run against an expert, at the time he is acting in his professional capacity. This is not limited to the regulated professions.[132]

148. An expert who causes damage may not alleviate himself from fault, and from the resulting liability, by proving that he acted in a manner a hypothetical reasonable and careful ordinary man would act under the given circumstances. When it comes to the qualities of professional conduct, the measure of fault is how would a hypothetical reasonable and careful expert of the same professional specialization conduct himself under the given circumstances.

149. The measurement of professional fault is objective and abstract. This does not mean that, in establishing the existence of this type of fault, the courts would not take into account the circumstances under which the professional had operated, but that his personal traits and capabilities (apart from the fact that he is an expert in the given field), such as the individual lack of knowledge and personal weaknesses, fatigue, distress, insomnia, or bad eyesight, do not influence the contents of legitimate social expectations towards him.

---

129. Article 290, para. 1 of DCC, Komisija za izradu Građanskog zakonika, *Prednacrt. Građanski zakonik Republike Srbije* (Beograd, 2019).
130. Article 290, para. 2 of DCC:

> In judging whether there is fault on the side of a person acting in a professional capacity (for example, medical doctor, veterinarian, medical personnel, engineer, architect, lawyer, notary), the court takes into account the rules of skill and science, the life experience, and the legitimate expectations towards a reasonable and careful professional under the given circumstances.

131. M. Orlić, 'Evolucija shvatanja o krivici (u srpskom pravu) sa osvrtom na pojam profesionalne krivice', in *Private Law Reform in South East Europe: Liber Amicorum Christa Jessel-Holst* (eds M. Vasiljević et al., Beograd, 2010), 263–279.
132. Liability for damage caused by an unprofessional conduct of a mailman (by him acting contrary to the work practices), SCS, Rev. 455/1997 of 3 Jun. 1998, *PLex*.

150. Apart from the elevated standard of legitimately expected behaviour, when it comes to professional liability in fault, general rules on tortious liability for one's own acts apply.

This means, among other things, that the statutory presumption of fault applies. Ordinary (and yet professional, i.e., measured towards the enhanced legitimate expectations) negligence is rebuttably presumed, and exactly this type of fault is sufficient for establishing the liability of the professional.[133]

151. To sum up: the general norm of fault-based liability in Serbian tort law sets the standard of legitimately expected behaviour. Jurisprudence and legal scholarship have constructed this standard from the relevant provisions of LO, primarily from Article 16 and Article 154, paragraph 1 of LO. In doing so, the courts and legal doctrine have confirmed the general rule of behaviour, which was applied by the courts even before the enactment of LO. The aforesaid standard of legitimately expected behaviour shall be more precise and determined more firmly in cases where the potential tortfeasor acts in a professional capacity. Legitimate social expectations towards an expert are that he or she acts with professional care, i.e., as the hypothetical reasonable and careful expert of the given specialization under the given circumstances would behave.

152. With regard to contractual liability and, more generally, liability for damage caused by the breach of a pre-existing obligation towards the creditor, Article 18 of LO sets the tone. In general, parties to the obligation have to observe the standard of a careful man, a careful businessperson, or a careful professional – depending on the context. When performing under a contract in a professional capacity, one has to observe a higher objective standard of care, i.e., to behave as a hypothetical reasonable and careful professional of a given specialization.

II. Medical Practitioners

153. When it comes to liability for damages caused by medical professionals, the relatively new pieces of Serbian legislation in the field of healthcare, medical profession and patient rights turn to the general rules on tortious liability. In case of a health professional causing harm to the patient's body, or worsening the condition of the patient's health, by a professional error committed in the course of providing healthcare, Article 31 of Patient Rights Act of 2013 (last changes in 2019) resorts to the general rules of liability for damage, and additionally stipulates that patient's right to compensation cannot be excluded or limited in advance.

154. Under Article 185 of Health Protection Act of 2019 (HPA), health professional shall temporarily lose a professional licence in the disciplinary proceedings before his professional chamber, for committing a professional error and thus causing harm to a patient, or worsening the condition of the patient's health. In addition,

133. SCS, Rev. 1000/2006 of 14 Sep. 2006, *PLex*.

health professional shall temporarily lose a licence if he is convicted of imprisonment for a criminal offence against human health. Professional error in this sense means negligent rendition of healthcare, including neglecting and omitting to provide healthcare, by deviating from professional standards and expectations.

155. The following should be stressed though: 'Professional error', as set under HPA, should not be understood as the fourth condition of tortious liability of health professionals (on top of damage, causation and professional fault). The sole intention of the legislator in HPA was to regulate the basis of the disciplinary liability of health professionals – and not to covertly amend the general rules on tortious liability of professionals. However, some lower courts examine the existence of professional error on the side of health professionals as tortfeasors, in addition to the question of their fault, which has been causing inconsistency and contradictoriness in the practice of the courts so far.[134]

156. In cases of tortious liability of health professionals operating within medicine, surgery, obstetrics, dentistry, nursing, pharmacy and other health professions, Serbian courts conventionally apply general rules of extra-contractual fault-based liability. Actions for damages against medical professionals are regularly brought in tort, as in the state medical and health institutions patients do not enter into contract with the institution, or with the healthcare professional who treats them, and are commonly covered by the mandatory health insurance. The patient may, at least in theory, bring an action for breach of contract against a private institution. However, there are no such cases as yet. In contrast, when it comes to medical injuries, patients bring claims in tort against private health institutions as well.

157. The standard of legitimately expected reasonableness and care in a professional setup is elevated, and this also applies to the provision of preventive, curative, or rehabilitative healthcare. If damage was caused by a health professional in the course of, or in connection to, rendering healthcare to a patient, the tortfeasor is considered to be at fault if, under the given circumstances, he has failed to act as a hypothetical reasonable and very careful health professional of the corresponding specialization.

158. The statutory presumption of fault also applies, so when a health professional causes bodily harm to a patient, or in another way worsens the condition of his health, the court shall refutably presume the existence of the health professional's fault – of course, only after the patient proves damage and causation. However, it is exceptionally difficult to prove causation in cases of medical malpractice before Serbian courts. The courts heavily rely on medical expert witnesses in these matters.

---

134. In detail: M. Orlić, 'Zakon o zdravstvenoj zaštiti i odgovornost lekara za prouzrokovanu štetu', separate imprint, Udruženje pravnika Srbije, Beograd 2012, 1–25, M. Karanikić Mirić, 'Krivica kao osnov deliktne odgovornosti lekara u građanskom pravu', *PZ* 10/2013, 623–638.

159. Plain or ordinary negligence is sufficient for establishing tortious liability of a healthcare professional. It is not necessary that his conduct was reckless. Still, the existence of ordinary negligence in a professional context will be measured against the higher objective standard of conduct (of a hypothetical reasonable and very careful expert under the given circumstances). If the particular health professional in question suffers from certain individual shortcomings, weaknesses or lack of knowledge, which prevents him from reaching this heightened standard of legitimately expected conduct, this may not excuse him from liability. Quite the reverse, if the specific health professional incidentally has possession of some additional special skill, knowledge or insight, which renders him even more capable and knowledgeable than normally requested, the measure of what is legitimately expected from him further elevates, and he shall be obliged to employ all of his extra capacities for the benefit of his patient.[135]

160. The said type of fault on the side of the health professional counts among the conditions of tortious liability of the health institution he was working for at the time of the injuring event. In other words, if the health professional was employed at a health institution at the time of medical injury, the institution shall be vicariously liable for the damage inflicted by the professional on the patient.[136] A health institution may relieve itself from liability if it proves that there was no fault on the side of its employee, i.e., that the health professional behaved in a manner a hypothetical reasonable and very careful expert of the corresponding specialization would behave under the given circumstances. The institution may not be excused from liability by proving a lack of its own fault, e.g., by proving that it has carefully chosen, supervised and instructed the professional-employee. The way in which the health institution acted is not relevant, as the liability of the health institution for medical injury caused by its employee is based on the employee's professional fault, and not on the fault of the aforementioned institution. The injured party has a direct claim in tort against the health professional only if she can prove tortious intention of the health professional.

161. The courts have generally rejected the idea of strict liability of medical doctors and other health professionals for medical malpractice. Some authors advocate strict liability for damages caused to the medical research participants and to the blood donors.[137] Furthermore, there are some special rules of Serbian tort law on tortious liability in emergency cases, i.e., special liability in tort for omitting to render help to a person whose life or bodily integrity is in obvious peril, if that help can be rendered without danger to self or others (Article 182 of LO). These rules

135. J. Radišić, *Medicinsko pravo* (Beograd, 2004), 170–171.
136. SCS, Rev. 1900/2005 of 5 Oct. 2005, *PLex.* Also: A hospital is liable under the general rules of employers' vicarious liability (Art. 170 and Art. 171 of LO), for damage caused (to a patient) by professional negligence of the hospital's employee (a medical professional). The employee's professional fault is rebuttably presumed. Decision of the Appellate Court in Belgrade, Gž. 12342/2010 of 11 Apr. 2013, *PLex.*
137. J. Radišić, *Medicinsko pravo* (Beograd, 2004), 170.

apply to medical professionals as well, but towards them, the legitimate expectations of care and self-exposure to danger are higher than towards non-professionals. Health professional liability insurance is not mandatory in Serbia as of yet.

III. Legal Practitioners

162. When it comes to liability of the attorneys for damages caused in the line of their work, the general rules of extra-contractual liability for professional fault apply.[138] The injured party may elect to claim compensation under the contract, but the scope of damages recoverable under the contract (normally, patrimonial damage that was foreseeable to the debtor at the time of contract formation, *see* paragraph 104) makes this path less favourable. Attorney's professional fault is measured against an elevated objective standard of the legitimate social expectations towards a hypothetical reasonable and very careful professional lawyer under the given circumstances.

163. Article 37 of the Attorney Profession Act of 2011 (last changes in 2012) lays down the rules on compulsory professional liability insurance for attorneys, which may be purchased individually, or as a bar association collective scheme.

164. There are no special rules concerning the attorney's liability in third-party situations, i.e., their liability for damages caused to the non-clients. Therefore, the general rules of extra-contractual liability apply. Neither the courts nor legal theory have specifically probed into this question so far. However, one must assume that in these situations at least two principles would have to be weighed against each other: the general principle of *neminem laedere*, and the ethical framework of the attorneys' profession, which presupposes acting in accordance with the best interests of their clients.

IV. Builders and Architects

165. There are several regimes of liability for damages caused by a man-made 'building', i.e., by an immovable structure fixed to the ground, either above or beneath the surface, manufactured, created, or constructed by human beings.[139]

166. First of all, LO contains mandatory rules on contractual liability of the contractors for solidity (sturdiness, solidness) of the building, not only to the employer (client, developer) but also to every subsequent acquirer of the building, for the

138. M. Orlić, 'Građansko-pravna odgovornost advokata u srpskom pravu', in *Odgovornost i osiguranje odgovornosti advokata* (Beograd, 2006), 13–26.

139. Under Art. 631 of LO, the term 'building' includes houses, dams, bridges, tunnels, water supply installations, sewerage systems, roads, railroad tracks, wells and other structures (edifices) whose manufacture requires larger and more complicated works. This statutory definition is intended for the purposes of regulating the construction contracts.

period of ten years from delivery and acceptance.[140] The same applies to the architect, where the flaws of the building arise from flaws in the architectural designs and plans. The contractor is also liable for the deficiencies of the ground (soil, terrain), for the period of ten years from delivery and acceptance, unless he has timely acquired an expert opinion from a specialized organization, as to the suitability of the ground for construction, and on the condition that throughout the process of construction, no new circumstances have occurred that would raise doubt as to the reliability of the expert opinion. In case of joint and several liability of a contractor (a builder) and an architect, their respective portions of liability and payment may be sorted out in the recourse proceedings in proportion to the gravity of their faults.

167. Second, there are statutory rules on joint and several strict liability of a client (i.e., an employer, a developer, a person who has hired a contractor to construct a building) and a contractor, for damages caused to third parties by construction works.[141] Neither of them may escape liability towards the injured party by proving the absence of their own fault, or by proving fault of another. The existence and gravity of their respective faults are relevant only within their mutual relationship, i.e., in the recourse proceedings.

168. Third, if the construction of a building constitutes a breach of a pre-existing obligation to refrain from construction, creditor may demand demolition of the building. In addition, the creditor may demand compensation for the foreseeable patrimonial damage suffered in connection to the illicit construction, under the rules of liability for damages caused by violation of a pre-existent duty (Article 262 and Article 266 of LO). If the builder has acted with gross negligence, intention or fraudulently, the creditor of the said negative obligation (obligation not to build) may seek compensation for total patrimonial damage, irrespective of its foreseeability. Finally, the court shall balance the public interest against the legitimate interests of the creditor, and where the first one prevails as 'obviously more useful', the court shall award monetary compensation for damage caused to the creditor by the illicit construction – instead of the demolition of the building at issue.[142]

169. Finally, an erected building qualifies as a dangerous object, that is, as a source of aggravated risk of damage to the surroundings. Therefore, the owner shall be liable under the general rules of strict liability for damages inflicted on others by position, usage, or the very existence of his building. He may release himself from liability by proving that the damage at hand was caused by force majeure, or entirely by an action of the injured party. If a third party has caused damage in connection to the building or contributed to its occurrence, the owner remains liable but may seek reimbursement from the third party. If the injured party has partially contributed to the damage, he shall be entitled only to partial compensation. The compensation he may ask for shall be reduced in proportion to his own involvement in the damaging event.

140. Articles 644–647 of LO.
141. Article 207 of LO.
142. Article 292, paras 2 and 3 of LO.

V. Others

170. When it comes to other experts, such as notaries, tax advisers, accountants or banks, and their liability for damages caused in the course of, or in connection to, their professional work, i.e., in their professional setting, the general rules on tortious liability of professionals shall apply.

171. Under Article 58 of the Notaries Act of 2011 (NA, last changes in 2015), the notary public is liable for damage caused in line of his work in accordance with the general rules on tortious liability of professionals. Tortious liability of notaries is based on their objective fault, i.e., on substandard behaviour of the notary as a learned legal professional, which is measured against the external yardstick of a hypothetical reasonable and very careful legal expert exercising public powers under the given circumstances.[143] In addition, notary public is liable for damage caused by his trainees, associates and assistants, as well as for the administrative staff working in his office, regardless of whether these persons are directly liable for the damage they caused. The notary who has paid compensation for the damage caused to a third party by his trainee, associate, assistant or administrative staff, may seek reimbursement from the injurer within one year from the payment if the damage was caused intentionally or by gross negligence. The state is excused from liability for damage caused by the notaries. However, the state should be held liable for unlawful or otherwise wrongful, improper, irregular, or insufficiently reasonable and careful actions of the state authorities responsible for appointing, supervising or instructing notaries. Notaries are bound by statutory duty to take out insurance against professional liability (Article 59 of NA). Insurance may be purchased individually or as a part of the Public Notary Chamber's collective scheme. The mandatory insurance must include notary's liability for damage caused by others (his trainees, associates, assistants, and the administrative staff working in his office).

172. There is a special statutory strict liability regime for the manufacturers of defective products (Article 179 of LO and the new legislation in the field of consumer protection, as will be shown later).

§2. Liability of Public Authorities

173. Under Article 35 of CRS, everyone shall have the right to compensation for material and non-material damages inflicted on him by unlawful or irregular work of a state body, entities exercising public powers, bodies of the autonomous province, or units of the local self-government, and the law shall further stipulate conditions under which the injured party may demand compensation for damage directly from the person who has inflicted the damage in question.

143. M. Karanikić Mirić, 'Odgovornost javnih beležnika u srpskom građanskom pravu', *PZ 10/2014*, 559–584.

174. The rules of Serbian tort law on liability of juridical persons are very broad and general, set down regardless of the type of legal entity, or its organ. The same regime of liability applies to the state, for public authorities as separate legal entities (e.g., NBS, State Audit Institution, independent regulatory bodies, etc.), for public and private organizations and their one person and collegial organs, institutions, associations, etc.

175. Under Article 172 of LO, juridical persons are liable for damages caused by their organs in the course of, or in connection to, the performance of their function. This applies to the state as well. Thus, the state is liable for damage caused by unlawful or otherwise wrongful, improper, irregular, or insufficiently reasonable and careful actions of its organs and other entities exercising public powers (notaries excluded by Article 58 of NA, *see* paragraph 171).

176. Organs of juridical persons have no legal personality; they are not themselves legal persons in that they have no ability to exercise legal rights independently of the corporation or political body of which they are a part. Organs of a juridical person do not have detached accountability, they are not separate legal entities. Thus, they cannot be individually sued for damages. Juridical person may exercise their rights and carry out their activities solely through their organs and shall be liable for damages so caused. Liability of juridical persons for damages caused by their organs is sometimes categorized as a type of liability for others. However, that 'other' person (for whom the juridical person should presumably be accountable) lacks legal personality, so strictly speaking, juridical persons account for the consequences of their own unlawful or otherwise wrongful, improper, irregular, or insufficiently reasonable and careful acts (including omissions), which they, by definition, carry out *via* their organs.[144]

177. Once a juridical person pays compensation to the injured party for damages caused by its organ, it may seek reimbursement from the natural person responsible for the said organ. This right of reimbursement exists solely if the natural person acted with intention or gross negligence, and it expires six months after the payment.[145]

178. Under Article 124 of Civil Servants Act of 2005 (CSA, last changes in 2020), the state is liable for damage caused by unlawful or irregular work of a civil servant to a third party. The injured party has a direct claim against the civil servant if damage was caused intentionally. The state has the right of recourse against the civil servant who acted intentionally or with gross negligence. The right of the state to recover the paid sum from the civil servant expires six months from the date of payment.

---

144. The courts also mention actions of the organs of juridical persons that are contrary to the rules or protocols of a particular service, biased, malicious, hounding, contrary to the legitimate expectations, arbitrary, contrary to the practices of good service. In detail: M. Karanikić Mirić, 'Tip odgovornosti pravnog lica po čl. 172 ZOO', in Đorđe Ignjatović (ed.), *Kaznena reakcija u Srbiji, IV deo* (Beograd, 2014), 166–187.
145. Article 172, paras 2 and 3 of LO.

179. Under Article 148 of CRS, a judge may not be held liable for an expressed opinion or voting in the process of passing a court decision, unless he has actually committed a particular criminal offence ('violation of law by a judge'). Under Article 6 of LJ, the state bears liability for damage caused by unlawful or irregular conduct of a judge. The state may not escape liability by proving a lack of its own fault, i.e., by proving that the judge was properly appointed, trained and overseen. In contrast, the judge's fault operates as a condition of liability of the state and has to be proven by the injured party. It manifests itself as an unlawful, or otherwise wrongful, improper, irregular, or insufficiently reasonable and careful behaviour of the judge. The standard of legitimately expected behaviour of a judge is elevated: his work is objectively measured against the behaviour of a reasonable and very careful legal professional exercising public powers under the given circumstances. Individual lack of knowledge or experience, personal flaws or limitations of a particular judge do not influence the contents of legitimate social expectations towards him.

180. The state is entitled to demand remuneration from the judge for the amount paid to the injured party, on the condition that there was an intention on the side of the judge. This particular rule was introduced in 2013, on one of the occasions of LJ being amended, and it is heavily criticized as being at odds with the practice of the European Court of Human Rights, and that of the Court of Justice of the EU.[146] Prior to this legislative change, the right of recourse of the state against a judge was generally limited to cases in which damages were caused either intentionally or with gross negligence.

§3. Abuse of Rights

181. Several statutory provisions prohibit the abuse of rights. Under Article 13 of LO, it is forbidden to exercise rights (which arise out of unilateral promises, contracts, torts, unjust enrichment, *negotiorum gestio*, etc.) against the purpose for which they were established or recognized. Social and economic purposes of a specific right may be violated irrespective of the motives of the transgressor, and of the existence of his intention to harm another, which suggests the objective criteria for determining the abusive conduct.[147]

182. Under Articles 4 and 6 of the Law on Property Relations of 1980 (last changes in 2005), it is prohibited to exercise the right of ownership, as well as the rights of an easement, real encumbrance and pledge, contrary to the respective purposes for which each of these rights has been established or recognized. The courts have sanctioned the abuse of housing rights under the Law on Housing of 1950 (last

146. V. Rakić Vodinelić, 'Ograničena odgovornost sudije za štetu – neophodna privilegija koja obezbeđuje nezavisnost ili učvršćivanje sudijske neodgovornosti?', *Zbornik Pravnog fakulteta u Zagrebu*, 3–4/2013, 736–742: The new approach can secure neither real judicial independence, nor the rule of law. In addition, it discourages formation of reliable corpus of case law regarding civil immunity of judges.

147. J. Radišić, *Obligaciono pravo* (Beograd, 2004), 227–228.

changes in 2016).[148] CPA lays down the duty of the court to prevent the parties from abusing their procedural rights, and also to penalize the abuse of these rights (Article 9). Under Article 187 of CPA, on the request of the injured party, the court shall award compensation for damage caused by the other party's abuse of her procedural rights. Under Article 14 of the Criminal Procedure Code of 2011 (last changes in 2021) it is the duty of the court to prevent the abuse of procedural rights which is directed at the undue protraction of criminal proceedings.

183. Where an injury was caused in the exercise of legal rights, it is nevertheless allowed to examine whether there was fault on the injurer's side. The fact that the injuring conduct was not prohibited, or that the tortfeasor was authorized by law to behave in a particular way, still leaves the question of whether the tortfeasor behaved as a hypothetical reasonable and careful man would behave in the course of exercising his rights under the given circumstances.

184. Damage caused by an activity which was performed in public interest and authorized by the public authorities, shall be recoverable only if it exceeds the normal scope of damage under the circumstances. The potentially injured party can, however, demand socially justified measures to be taken, in order to prevent or mitigate the impending damage (Article 156 of LO). Some lower courts have taken the position that, once the damage exceeds the normal scope, the injured party is entitled to full compensation.[149]

§4. Injury to Reputation and Privacy

185. Strictly speaking, injuries to reputation and privacy do not constitute specific instances or types of liability under Serbian tort law. Rather, both reputation and privacy are considered to be legally protected non-patrimonial interests, or objects of non-patrimonial rights. Their violation or injury in itself does not constitute recoverable damage. However, injury to a person's reputation or privacy may further lead to the occurrence of patrimonial or non-patrimonial damage or both. Such damages shall be recoverable in general, that is, irrespective of the applicable regime of tortious liability, as the Serbian legal system is one of a few systems that compensate all kinds of non-pecuniary harm indiscriminately and irrespective of the basis of liability. Of course, these types of injuries (of reputation and privacy) never occur in certain settings, that is, in certain damaging events (e.g., in motor vehicle accidents, or in product liability cases) and therefore, recoverability of damage stemming from the injuries to reputation and privacy is never discussed in these situations.

---

148. SCS, Rev. 443/2003 of 15 May 2003, *PLex.*
149. District Court in Kraljevo, Gž. 417/1991 of 26 Mar. 1991, in B. Čolić & M. Samardžić, *Zbornik sudske prakse iz oblasti imovinskog prava* (Beograd, 1995), 65.

186. Moral (non-patrimonial, non-pecuniary) damage in Serbian tort law includes physical and psychological pain and suffering, as well as fear, each of sufficient duration and intensity (Articles 155 and 200 of LO). This is obviously a purely subjective notion of moral damage. The mere infringement of non-patrimonial rights, or violation of personal goods as objects of these rights, does not constitute moral damage, unless they have further caused physical or psychological pain, or fear, to the plaintiff, and thus disturbed his or her mental equilibrium.

187. Objectivization of moral damage is a change in this paradigm, towards the understanding of moral damage as an abstract infringement of a non-patrimonial right of the injured party, irrespective of any pain or fear caused by such infringement. Within an objectivized model, moral damage shall exist whenever someone's personal (non-patrimonial) right, personal good or legally protected personal interest is violated, even if the injured party did not suffer any pain or fear due to this violation.

188. As of 2005, Croatian legislator has abandoned the long-standing subjective concept of non-patrimonial damage and re-conceptualized it as an abstract violation of personal rights, including personal rights of legal entities. The same happened in Montenegro in 2017. These ideas are emerging among Serbian legal scholars as well. The Commission appointed to draft the new Civil Code of Serbia considers several modes of either partial or complete objectivization of the concept of moral damage in the prospective codification. One of the considered options is to return to the mixed conception of non-patrimonial damage (which was proposed in Article 124 of *Skica* of 1969 but omitted from LO of 1978), that is, to adhere to the existing concept of non-patrimonial damage but also to allow for a violation of non-patrimonial goods, or legally protected interests, to be recognized as a type of moral damage, regardless of any psychological suffering coming out of such infringement.

189. For the time being, reputation and privacy are among legally protected interests and may be understood as *objects of personal rights*. Serbian law keeps to the constitutional inviolability of human dignity and physical and mental integrity (Articles 23 and 25 of CRS).[150] Besides, Article 46, paragraph 2 of CRS indicates 'reputation' as one of the justifications for statutory restriction of the freedom of expression, so the Constitutional Court does not question constitutional grounds for protection of reputation.

However, injuries to reputation and privacy do not, per se, stand for, or amount to a legally recognized and thus recoverable non-patrimonial damage. Serbian tort law recognizes physical and psychological pain and fear as types of moral or non-patrimonial damage, so, in cases of injury to reputation and privacy, moral damage exists only if these injuries induced psychological pain of sufficient intensity and duration.[151]

150. Decision of the Constitutional Court, Už. 3238/2011 of 8 Mar. 2012, *PLex*.
151. SCS, Gž. 74/2006 of 6 Jul. 2008, *PLex*.

Logical consequence of this position is that only natural persons may be entitled to compensation in these kinds of cases, as only they are capable of feeling psychological pain and distress. Serbian courts are firmly holding to the view that juridical persons cannot claim compensation for moral damage.[152] Reputation of a juridical person enjoys legal protection, i.e., it represents a legally protected interest and may be considered an object of a non-patrimonial right, but injury to reputation of a juridical person may not result in psychological pain. Therefore, juridical persons may not be entitled to moral damages.[153]

190. If injury to reputation or privacy of either juridical or natural person has led to patrimonial damage on the side of the injured party – such as, for instance, pure economic loss – the injured party may claim compensation for it, under the general rules of tortious liability.

191. There are, however, a few special statutory provisions in Article 198 of LO. Everyone is entitled to compensation for *patrimonial damage* inflicted by an injury to his honour or reputation, or by false statements about his past, knowledge, abilities and competences, or anything else of the kind, under the condition that the injurer was aware, or should have been aware, that these statements were untrue. And, even if the injurer should have known that the injuring statement was false, he shall not be liable for the so-caused patrimonial damage, if either he or the recipient of his statement, had serious interest in conveying the given information.

§5. Interference with Contractual Relations

192. Generally, contractual relations are considered to be *res inter alios acta* for the persons outside the contract. The existing obligation is a thing done between the debtor and the creditor, and it is not of the third party's concern. However, this does not mean that the third party who is aware of the existing contract between the others may interfere and obstruct their performance under the contract. The contract between the two is opposable to others (*l'opposabilité du contrat aux tiers*), and the others must respect its existence as a juridical fact. For instance, if the owner concludes two consecutive contracts of sale of the same real property with two different buyers, the preceding buyer has the stronger legal title (irrespective of the fact that the property was delivered to, and accepted by the subsequent buyer, or even the fact that the subsequent buyer has registered as the new owner with the Real Estate Cadastre), if the subsequent buyer was not acting in good conscience, i.e., if he was aware, or should have been aware, of the earlier contract of sale between the same seller and the previous buyer.[154] In addition, the subsequent buyer may be held liable in fault for damages caused by interfering with the pre-existing contract he was or should have been, aware of.

152. Legal position of the Civil Chamber of SCS of 5 Feb. 2001, *PLex*.
153. SCS, Rev. 611/2001 of 25 Dec. 2002, *PLex*.
154. Conclusion No. 3 of the Joint Session of civil and commercial chambers of the Federal Court, state Supreme Courts and the Supreme Military Court of 28 and 29 May 1986, in: T. Ralčić, *Vodič kroz*

193. Another example would be the case of a lessor (the owner) who sells the previously leased asset, and who does so at the time after the conclusion of the lease agreement, but before the delivery and acceptance of the leased asset to the lessee. Under Article 593 of LO, if the buyer has known (at the time of entering the sales contract) of the pre-existent lease agreement, he shall take on legal position of the lessor and assume his contractual obligations towards the lessee. The buyer who did not know about the lease at the time of purchase, bears no obligations towards the lessee, and the lessee may only sue the lessor for damages.

§6. OTHERS

194. There are several special types of liabilities in Serbian tort law, which do not have anything in common, apart from the fact that they cannot easily fit within the standard categories of tortious liability. The legislator has gathered these tortious regimes under one title: *Special Cases of Liability* (Articles 180–184 of LO).

195. First, the state is strictly liable for both patrimonial and non-patrimonial damages resulting from death, bodily injury, or from impairment or destruction of property which belongs to a natural person, if such damage was caused by an act of public violence or terror, or during mass public demonstrations (irrespective of their political goals). If the identity of the direct tortfeasor is known, the state has not only the right but also the duty, to seek reimbursement from him for the sum paid to the victims. Organizers, participants, accomplices and instigators of acts of public violence and terror cannot claim compensation from the state on these grounds (Article 180 of LO).

196. Second, an organizer of a gathering of a large number of people, in either enclosed, or open-air spaces, bears strict liability for both patrimonial and non-patrimonial damage resulting from death, or bodily injury, inflicted on a person due to extraordinary circumstances which may occur in these situations, such as disorderly crowd behaviour, general turmoil, etc. (Article 181 of LO).

197. Third, there is a statutory provision on tortious liability in emergency cases (Article 182 of LO) – though it is almost never used. It is a type of fault-based liability of a person who causes foreseeable damage, by omitting to render help to another person whose life or bodily integrity was in an obvious peril. Liability for failure to rescue may be established solely if the help that was needed could have been rendered without risk to oneself or to others. Here, the general statutory presumption of fault (Article 154, paragraph 1 of LO) shall not apply: the plaintiff must prove fault on the side of the tortfeasor. The court may exonerate the tortfeasor from duty to compensate, or reduce the awarded compensation, on the grounds of equity

sudsku praksu u oblasti građanskog i upravnog prava (Beograd, 1989), 57. However, this practice has changed with the ongoing trend of affirmation and further strengthening of the principle of confidence in veracity of the land registry. It is mentioned here solely to illustrate the idea of opposability of the existing contract.

(e.g., he was able to help only some of the injured, as there were too many of them and not enough time, or he had a phobia, or he made an erroneous decision under time pressure, etc.)

198. In the fourth place, a person who is charged with statutory duty to conclude certain types of contracts shall be liable for damages for failure to conclude such contract without delay and at the request of the interested party (Article 183 of LO). The legislator sometimes prescribes the duty to contract in public interest, in order to keep provision of certain goods and rendering of certain services from inexcusable interruptions. This is a type of extra-contractual liability for a breach of statutory duty, and the excuses are very limited. The liable party must prove the absence of duty to conclude a contract under the given circumstances, e.g., that the other party failed to meet the prescribed criteria for contracting.

199. And finally, a juridical person providing services of general (economic) interest shall be liable for damage if they cease to perform, or irregularly perform their activity for no justified reason (Article 184 of LO). The courts understand the excuses for this type of liability in a very narrow and restrictive manner. This is a type of extra-contractual liability, strict in nature, as the courts accept only those excuses or justifications from the providers that amount to force majeure.[155]

200. When it comes to liability for unsafe conditions on public roads, the courts sometimes apply the above-explained provision of Article 184 of LO to the cases of tortious liability of both public and private utility companies for damages caused by interruptions or irregularities in the maintenance of public roads.[156]

201. On other occasions, the courts resort to the provisions of the Law on Public Roads of 2005 (LPR). Under Article 2 of LPR, a 'public road manager' is a public company, another juridical person, or an entrepreneur, registered for public road management activity. Under Article 15 of LPR, every public road manager shall ensure uninterrupted and outstanding maintenance and protection of public roads, and continuous and safe traffic flow, and shall be liable for damage inflicted upon public road users by failure to correctly perform routine maintenance operations, as prescribed by LPR, or by operating contrary to the prescribed technical specifications and methodology.[157] Substandard maintenance, or lack thereof, must be

155. For instance, electric company remains liable for suspended delivery of electricity even if it proves that the power lines were cut-off by a third party. The same goes for the water supply companies. Comm LO Per, 425.

156. Decision of the Appellate Court in Belgrade, Gž. 7182/2011 of 30 Jan. 2013, *PLex*: A company in charge of maintenance of public roads *cannot be excused* from liability for damage caused by lack of maintenance by proving that it has entrusted another company with this job. Cf. next footnote.

157. Decision of the Commercial Appellate Court in Belgrade, Pž. 2752/2012(1) of 18 Jun. 2012, *PLex*: A company in charge of maintenance of public roads *shall be* excused from liability for damage caused by lack of maintenance, by proving that it has entrusted another company with this job. No grounds for joint and several liability.

proved by the injured party, i.e., the user of the road.[158] LPR is no longer in force, but the relatively new piece of legislation contains the same rule vis-à-vis the duties of public road managers (Article 13 of the Law on Roads (LR) of 2018).

158. Decisions of the Commercial Appellate Court in Belgrade, Pž. 10385/2012 of 26 Jun. 2013 and Pž. 4456/2012 of 30 Jan. 2013, *PLex*.

Part II. Liability for Acts of Others

Chapter 1. Vicarious Liability

202. In a general tort case, the role of liable party and the role of tortfeasor coincide. The person that is liable for damage is the same person who has caused damage to another. If there are multiple tortfeasors, they may be jointly and severally liable. Liability of any of the multiple tortfeasors towards the injured party may exceed his respective contribution to the damage in question, but still, his liability is not secondary. Each of the multiple tortfeasors accounts for the consequences of his own injurious action, i.e., for what he has done, or participated in personally. In contrast, liability for acts of others presupposes that the liable party and the tortfeasor are not the same person. The injured party has a direct claim against the liable party, for damages caused by someone else. Of course, a direct claim against the liable party does not, in itself, exclude the injured party's claim against the perpetrator. If the victim has claims against both the labile party and the perpetrator, the two shall be jointly and severally liable towards the claimant.

203. Serbian tort law distinguishes several types or regimes of liability for acts of others. Their common characteristic, which differentiates these situations from a general tort case, is the separation of the two roles. The tortfeasor and the liable party are not the same person, rather, one person is held liable for damage caused by another. However, there must be a certain special relationship between the liable party and the tortfeasor (i.e., the perpetrator of damage), which gives rise to vicarious liability and justifies the idea that one person should be liable for acts of someone else. This may be employment, parenthood, guardianship, etc.

204. The fact that one person accounts for acts of another says nothing about the grounds of such liability. Vicarious liability may be strict, fault-based, or even based on equity (*see* paragraphs 146 and 230). When the liability for acts of others is *strict*, the quality of the liable party's conduct is legally irrelevant. Neither the victim needs to prove fault on the side of the liable party, nor the liable party can escape liability by proving that there was no fault on her side. The tortfeasor's fault, that is, the substandard injurious conduct of the perpetrator who has caused the damage in question, may stand, in certain regimes of liability for acts of others, among the conditions of the vicarious liability. In these cases, the vicarious liability remains *strict,* as it is considered that another man's fault may be a condition of someone's liability, but never its basis or ground.

205. In contrast, some regimes of vicarious liability are fault-based, meaning that a certain type of vicarious liability may not be established unless there is fault on the side of the liable party. In some cases, there is a rebuttable statutory presumption of fault of the liable party, and in other cases, the burden of proof of the liable party's fault lies with the victim. Serbian tort law recognizes some classical types of the liable party's fault. Not all of those types of fault shall be relevant in all the regimes of vicarious liability. The liable party's fault may present itself as substandard or erroneous supervision of the tortfeasor (*culpa in vigilando*), substandard or erroneous instructing or upbringing of the tortfeasor (*culpa in instruendo*), and finally, substandard or erroneous entrustment, that is, selection of an unsuitable person for a certain task or activity, which thereafter results in damage to another (*culpa in eligendo*).

§1. Employer/Employee

206. There are statutory rules in Serbian tort law which specifically provide for the liability of an employer for the injury an employee causes to another person during the course of his employment. Under Articles 170 and 171 of LO, an employer shall be vicariously liable for damage caused by his employee to a third party in the course of work, or in connection to the work, unless he proves that the employee acted as he should have acted under the given circumstances.[159]

207. An employer can be either a natural person (an entrepreneur) or a juridical person, which also includes the state institutions. An employee is always a natural person. The same rules on vicarious liability of an employer for damage caused by an employee to a third party apply to both full-time and part-time employment, both fixed-term employment and employment of indefinite duration, irrespective of whether there is any kind of contract between the employer and the injured party.

208. If the work in question presupposes the use of an atypically dangerous object, or if the work in itself represents an abnormally dangerous activity, statutory provisions on vicarious liability of the employer shall be without prejudice to the general rules on strict liability for dangerous objects or dangerous activities.[160] This actually means that the employee's fault will turn out to be irrelevant to the employer's liability if the damage in question (which was caused in the course of work, or in connection to the work) originates from a source of an increased, abnormal, atypical risk of damage to others. The employer will remain strictly liable even if the worker acted with the utmost reasonableness and care, that is, even if the level of the worker's cautiousness met or exceeded all legitimate expectations. Furthermore, under the general rules of strict liability, the liable party can be exempt from liability by proving that, although the damaging event did occur *in connection with*

159. There is no provision like the one of § 1313a ABGB, but there is some mention of contractual liability for associates in legal literature, inspired by legal writings in German. J. Radišić, *Obligaciono pravo* (Beograd 2004), 240, O. Antić, *Obligaciono pravo* (Beograd, 2008), 477.

160. Article 170, para. 3 and Art. 177, para. 5 of LO. *See*: SCS, Rev. 127/2006 of 5 Apr. 2006, *PLex.*

a dangerous object, or a dangerous activity, the damage in question was actually *caused* by a third party. However, a liable party's employee cannot be regarded as 'third party' for these purposes, since the employee will always be considered instrumental (implemental, subservient) in the employer's use of dangerous objects, or performance of dangerous activities (Article 177, paragraph 5 of LO).

209. Vicarious liability of the employer is strict under Serbian tort law, as the *employer's* fault is legally insignificant. Even if the employer has acted in full accordance with the legitimate social expectations, that is, even if he has selected, instructed and supervised the employee as a hypothetical reasonable and very careful employer would under the given circumstances, he will still be liable in damages for the damage caused by the employee in the scope of employment. Whereas the fault of the employer is legally irrelevant, the *employee's* fault serves as one of the conditions of the employer's liability and shall be rebuttably presumed. The employer may relieve himself from liability under the condition that he proves the absence of fault on the side of his employee. In the professional context, that is, when the work in question falls under the specific rules of profession and expertise, and requires some job-specific skills, knowledge and abilities, the employer may not escape liability by proving that his employee acted as a reasonable and careful person. What he needs to prove is that the employee's conduct, which eventually caused the damage in question, was that of a reasonable and very careful professional (expert) within the specific field and under the given circumstances.

210. In order to incite the statutory presumption of the employee's fault and, as a result, to substantiate the employer's tortious liability, the injured party needs to prove that he or she suffered actual damage, that damage was caused by a person who has been employed with the employer at the time of the damaging event, and that this event occurred in the course of their work, or in connection to their work. The employer cannot relieve himself from liability by presenting that it was the case of unreported or illegal employment, as no one can be heard to invoke his own turpitude. The damage will be considered to have been caused *during the course of the employment*, not only if the injuring conduct took place during working hours and at the working place, but also if it was merely carried out in connection to a working assignment or a work-function which was allocated by the employer to the employee. The employer remains liable for damages if he has granted access to the workplace, tools or other means of work to employees outside their normal work schedule. If the employee changed employers over time, the rules on vicarious liability shall apply to the person who was his employer at the time of the damaging event, i.e., when the employee carried out the injuring behaviour – and not necessarily when the damage presented itself. Where a company provides another with its employees, 'the employer' and vicariously liable should be the one who has the temporary benefit of the employee's services.

211. The victim may claim compensation for damage directly from an employee, under the condition of proving that the employee acted with tortious intent. In other words, an employee shall be directly liable for damage caused during the course of his employment, only if there was the highest degree of fault on his side, which must be proved by the injured party. In such cases, the employer and his employee shall be jointly and severally liable towards the victim, none of them can use the liability of another as a defence against the injured party.

212. The employer who has redressed the damage caused by his employee to the injured party shall be entitled, within six months from the payment, to reimbursement of the paid sum from the employee (i.e., the perpetrator of damage), on the condition of proving the employee's intent or gross negligence.[161] The statutory presumption of the employee's fault amounts to ordinary negligence, or, in a professional context, to his ordinary *professional* negligence.[162] This type of perpetrator's substandard injuring behaviour shall suffice for establishing the vicarious liability of his employer. On the contrary, the presumed ordinary (professional) negligence of the employee is sufficient neither for the victim's direct claim nor for the employer's recourse claim against the employee. The direct claim requires proof of the employer's intent, and the recourse claim requires proof of the employer's intent or gross (professional) negligence.

213. When it comes to tortious liability of an employee for the damage caused to his employer during the course of the employment, as well as to tortious liability of an employer for the damage suffered by his employee during the course of the employment, the statutory rules of labour law shall apply.[163] If an employee suffers damage at work, or in relation to work, special provisions of labour law refer back to the general regime of tortious liability. Thus, the employer shall be liable for damage sustained by his employee at work, or in relation to work, as per the general rules of liability in damages. As for an employee who causes damage to his employer at work, or in relation to work, he shall be liable in tort only if the employer proves he acted with intent or gross negligence. In case of multiple tortfeasors, that is, if a number of employees participate in a single damaging event, and all of them contribute to the damage suffered by the employer, their liability shall be several, i.e., proportionate to their respective shares in the damage. If it is not possible to discern their respective shares or contributions to the damage in question, the employees involved in the damaging event shall be liable in equal shares. However, if two or more employees in the scope of their employment commit a criminal offence with premeditation, their tortious liability for damage so caused shall be joint and several.

§2. Independent Contractors

214. There are no special statutory rules in Serbian tort law regarding the vicarious liability of independent contractors. An independent contractor is not

161. Article 171, para. 2 of LO. The same rule is repeated in Art. 163, para. 7 of LA.
162. A hospital is liable under the general rules of vicarious liability for damage caused by professional negligence of their employee – a medical professional. Decision of the Appellate Court in Belgrade, Gž. 12342/2010 of 11 Apr. 2013, *PLex*.
163. Article 163 and Art. 164 of LA.

necessarily a natural person. Unlike an employee, an independent contractor may be a juridical person. Furthermore, an independent contractor does not work for an employer on a regular basis and under the employment contract (*locatio conductio operarum*). In contrast, he works as and when required, and does so under the contract for services (*locatio conductio operis*), or under some other type of agreement with the liable party.

215. Actions of an independent contractor are to be attributed to the liable party, as it is generally considered that 'he who acts through another does the act himself' (*qui facit per alium facit* per se). The liable party may not invoke against the injured party, and as a defence to liability, the fact that he has outsourced the activity within his area of responsibility to an independent contractor.

216. In tort cases, the rules on vicarious liability of employers should apply by analogy in master-servant situations. Despite the fact there is no employment contract whatsoever between these two, a 'master' shall be vicariously liable for the damage caused by his 'servant' (a domestic worker, labourer, nanny, agency worker[164] and so forth), to a third party in the course of their engagement. Analogy requires that the master accounts for the consequences of the actions of his servant unless he proves there was no fault on the servant's side, i.e., that the servant acted in accordance with the legitimate social expectations. However, *he who acts through another does the act himself*. Therefore, the injurious conduct of the servant must be measured against the legitimate expectations towards a hypothetical reasonable and careful master – and not against the expectations towards a reasonable and careful servant.

217. When it comes to liability for breach of contract, a contractual party may not be released from liability by the mere fact of having hired another person to execute her obligations under the contract. This is only fair and logical, given that an independent contractor is not in a contractual relationship with the creditor. However, the independent contractor shall be liable under the general rules of tortious liability, for any damage caused to the creditor and to third parties. On the other hand, it seems that vicarious liability for an independent contractor may not be imposed where the parties have agreed to involve an independent contractor in the performance of their contract. Still, if the parties have solely agreed that one of them should decide on an independent contractor, the question of *culpa in eligendo* could be raised.

164. An agency worker is a person who has an agreement with an agency to work for another person. In such cases, 'the employer' and vicariously liable should be the 'master' – as he has the temporary benefit of the worker's services, and as he exercises direct control over the worker's performance. However, if it is the agency who is responsible for managing and delivering the service (under a so-called managed service contract), the agency should be vicariously liable for damages caused by its worker.

§3. Liability of Legal Entities for Acts of Their Organs

218. Under Article 172 of LO, juridical persons are liable for damages caused by their organs in the course of, or in connection to, the performance of their function. The courts have, however, added one condition to this statutory provision, so in their long-standing practice this type of liability can be established only if the injuring conduct of a legal entity (which may be, by definition, carried out solely via its organs) was substandard in a sense that it deviated from the legitimate social expectations. In other words, legal entities are liable for damage caused by unlawful or otherwise wrongful, improper, irregular, or insufficiently reasonable and careful actions (including omissions) of their organs. This needs to be proved by the victim: the general rule of Article 154, paragraph 1 of LO (the rebuttable statutory presumption of fault) does not apply.

219. The rule of Article 172 of LO is very broad and general, it applies no matter the type of legal entity or its organ. The same regime of liability concerns the state, public authorities as separate legal entities (e.g., the NBS, State Audit Institution, independent regulatory bodies, etc.), public and private organizations and their one person and collegial organs, institutions, associations, etc.

220. As previously explained, organs of juridical persons have no legal personality, they are not legal persons themselves, in that they have no ability to exercise legal rights independently of the corporation, or political body of which they are a part. Organs of juridical persons do not have detached accountability, they are not separate legal entities. Consequently, they cannot be individually sued for damages. Juridical person may exercise its rights, discharge its duties and carry out its activities solely through its organs, and thus, it shall be liable for damages caused via its organs. Liability of juridical persons for damages caused by their organs is sometimes categorized as a type of liability for others. However, the 'other' person (for whom the juridical person should presumably be accountable) lacks legal personality, so strictly speaking, juridical persons account for the consequences of their own unlawful or otherwise wrongful, improper, irregular, or insufficiently reasonable and careful acts (including omissions), which they, by definition, carry out *via* their organs.[165]

221. Legal entities cannot relieve themselves from liability by proving that the natural person (who was responsible within the organ) was properly appointed, trained and supervised. It would only be relevant if the legal entity acted (via its organ) in line with legitimate social expectations. The standard of legitimately expected behaviour of juridical persons (through their organs) is elevated. Their conduct is objectively measured against the behaviour of a reasonable and very

165. The courts also mention the actions of organs of juridical persons that are: contrary to the rules or protocols of a particular service, biased, malicious, hounding, contrary to the legitimate expectations, arbitrary, contrary to the practices of good service. In detail: M. Karanikić Mirić, 'Tip odgovornosti pravnog lica po čl. 172 ZOO', in Đorđe Ignjatović (ed.), *Kaznena reakcija u Srbiji, IV deo* (Beograd, 2014), 166–187.

careful professional under the given circumstances. Individual lack of knowledge or experience, personal flaws or limitations of the natural person responsible within the organ do not influence the contents of legitimate social expectations towards the legal entity.

222. A legal entity that has redressed the damage caused by its organ shall be entitled, within six months from the payment, to the reimbursement of the paid sum, from a natural person responsible within the said organ, on the condition of proving that this natural person acted with intention or gross negligence. It is the enduring understanding of Serbian courts that the injured party has no direct claim against the natural person who was responsible within the organ of the legal entity.[166] Legal scholars mostly agree.[167] The often cited reason for this position is that a natural person here does not appear in a private capacity but as an organ of a juridical person.

223. When it comes to persons to whom certain powers of the legal entities are delegated without formally being organs of the entity, i.e., persons entrusted with the power to act as legal entities short of being their organs: There are no special statutory rules on liability of legal entities for such persons. The aforementioned rules on vicarious liability for independent contractors could apply, provided that all the conditions for their application are met.

224. Still, some situations may be set apart. A director of a company or other legal entity may be a natural person who is not engaged under an employment contract with the legal entity in question, but under a contract for services (*locatio conductio operis*).[168] However, as this person acts as an organ of the legal entity in question, the above-stated general rules on liability of legal entities for acts of their organs shall apply.

225. Bankruptcy administrators are personally and directly liable for damage caused with intent, or gross negligence to the parties in the bankruptcy proceedings. They are obliged under the statute (Law on Bankruptcy) to take out professional liability insurance amounting to at least EUR 30,000. The creditors' committee may require the bankruptcy administrator to take out additional professional liability insurance. The costs of the supplementary insurance shall be considered an expense of the bankruptcy estate.[169]

---

166. For example, SCS, Rev. II–728/2003 of 18 Jun. 2003, Decision of District Court in Valjevo, Gž. 731/2008 of 21 Nov. 2008, Decision of Higher Commercial Court in Belgrade, Pž. 8297/2006(3) of 26 Sep. 2007, *PLex*.
167. V. Vodinelić, *Građansko pravo* (Beograd, 2012), 396, Comm LO PS, 522, B. Loza, *Obligaciono pravo* (Beograd, 2000), 237. *Contra*: J. Radišić, *Obligaciono pravo* (Beograd, 2004), 244; M. Karanikić Mirić, 'Tip odgovornosti pravnog lica po čl. 172 ZOO', in Đorđe Ignjatović (ed.), *Kaznena reakcija u Srbiji, IV deo* (Beograd, 2014), 183–186.
168. Article 48 of LA.
169. Articles 30 and 31 of Law on Bankruptcy of 2009 (last changes in 2018).

226. A company's representative, attorney-in-fact by virtue of employment, or procurator shall not be liable for damage to the company if they acted as permitted or approved by the company's organ in charge.[170]

227. When an agent exceeds its authority, the principal is not bound unless he subsequently approves the actions of the agent. However, if the principal refuses to give subsequent approval, the principal and the agent shall be jointly and severally liable in damages to the other contracting party, if that party did not know, or was not obliged to know of the fact that the authority was exceeded.[171]

170. Article 41 of Law on Companies of 2011 (last changes in 2021).
171. Article 87 of LO.

Chapter 2. Liability of Parents, Teachers and Instructors

228. Under Article 160 of LO there is a conclusive presumption (*praesumptio iuris et de iure*) that minors up to the age of 7 have no capacity of discernment, and hence, it is not possible to establish their fault-based liability. Liability for damage caused by children of such a young age lies with their parents, or with the persons responsible for supervising them at the time of the injurious event. When it comes to minors between the ages of 7 and 14, the statutory presumption of their lack of capacity of discernment is rebuttable (*praesumptio iuris tantum*). Namely, it is allowed under the law to rebut such presumption, i.e., to prove that a specific minor of age between 7 and 14 in a given situation was, in fact, able to judge well, and therefore, he may be liable for his own fault. Finally, when it comes to persons older than 14 years of age, it is rebuttably presumed that they possess the capacity of discernment, and consequently, that their liability in tort may be based on their own fault.

229. Under Article 159 of LO, if a person is incapable of discernment due to mental illness, intellectual disability, or for some other reason, he cannot be liable for damage caused to another. 'Other reasons' for incapacity of discernment may include organic mental disorders, stroke, heart attack, or some other medical condition or emergency due to which a person may not make sound judgments.

230. People who lack capacity of discernment due to their age, mental illness or intellectual disability may still be held liable in tort, by way of exception, on the grounds of equity. Under Article 169, paragraph 1 of LO, if damage was caused by a person who cannot be liable as he or she lacks capacity of discernment because of young age, mental illness or mental disability, and if compensation cannot be obtained from the person who had a duty to supervise the incapacitated tortfeasor, the court may award either full compensation or a part thereof to be paid by the tortfeasor, if the reasons of equity demand such decision, especially when the values of the property of the injurer and of the injured party are taken into consideration. And, as per Article 169, paragraph 1 of LO, if damage was caused by the minor who is fully capable of discernment, but unable to redress the damage he inflicted upon the injured party, the court may award either full compensation or a part thereof to be paid by the minor's parents, if the reasons of equity demand such decision, especially when the values of the property of the minor's parents and of the injured party are taken into consideration.

231. Parents (or adopters) are jointly liable for damage caused to another by their child, if the child in question was under the care and supervision of his parents at the time of the damaging event. If the child in question was under 7 years of age (at the time of assuming the injurious behaviour), the liability of the parents shall be strict. In such cases, the parents may not relieve themselves from liability by showing that they acted as they should have, i.e., that they took care of their child, supervised him and gave him instructions and guidance as a hypothetical reasonable and very careful parent would do. The quality of parental behaviour is legally irrelevant when it comes to their liability for children under the age of 7, parents are liable for a child that young regardless of any fault on their side. The general excuses from strict liability apply, so the parents can release themselves from liability by proving that, even though the damage came about in connection to their child, it was actually caused by the force majeure event, or entirely by unforeseeable or inexorable actions of either the injured party or a third party.[172]

232. The legal nature of parental tortious liability changes when a child turns 7. When the child-tortfeasor is older than 7 years of age (between the ages of 7 and 18), his parents are jointly liable for the damage the child causes to others while under supervision of either of them, unless they prove that there was no fault on their side. In other words, the liability of the parents is based on their rebuttably presumed fault (*culpa in vigilando*), and they can excuse themselves by proving that they acted in the way a hypothetical reasonable and very careful parent would act under the given circumstances.[173]

233. Parents are generally not liable for the damage their child causes while under the supervision of another person. Where another person is entrusted with the care and supervision of a child (irrespective of the child's age, that is, up to the tortfeasor's age of 18), liability will lie with the person entrusted to supervise the child and to take care of him in the absence of the parents. The liability of these 'overseers' is based on their rebuttably presumed fault (*culpa in vigilando*). Where a child, who is under supervision of a tutor, school or other institution, inflicts damage on another, the person in charge of taking care of, and supervising the child-tortfeasor will be exonerated from liability, under the condition of proving that he supervised the child in due manner (i.e., like a reasonable and very careful person or, if applicable, like a reasonable and very careful professional), or that the same damage would have occurred irrespective of the quality of the supervisor's conduct.[174]

234. There are no special statutory rules on the parents' liability for tortious consequences of the improper choice of a person to entrust the supervision of their child, but one may examine at least two possibilities. The first one would be to consider the child still under the care and supervision of his parents, in case the parents made poor choice of leaving the child with an unreliable person, and to apply the rules of parental liability for damages caused by a child under supervision of the parents. The second legal path would be to establish liability of the parents for *culpa in eligendo*, that is, for the tortious consequences of the unreasonable and incautious entrusting of a child to an unsuitable person.

235. There is one possibility to establish parents' liability for the damage their child causes to the injured party, while under the care and supervision of other persons (and again, irrespective of the child's age, that is, up to the tortfeasor's age of 18). Where the supervision of a child is not within the authority of the parents, but

172. Article 165, paras 1–3 of LO.
173. Article 165, para. 4 of LO.
174. Article 167, para. 1 of LO.

within the authority of another person, the injured party may claim compensation from the parents, under the condition of showing fault on the parents' side. This requires proving that the damage occurred because of the bad upbringing, poor examples, or corrupted habits the child was given by the parents (*culpa in instruendo*), or that the damage can otherwise be attributed to the parents' fault.[175] In this case, the person entrusted with the supervision of the child, who has already redressed the damage suffered by the injured party, may seek reimbursement of the paid sum from the parents of the child in question.

236. Where a child is also liable for damage, besides either his parent, or other person entrusted with the care and supervision of that child, the child and the liable person (either the parent or other vicariously liable person) shall be jointly and severally liable.[176] This can happen if it is proved that a child tortfeasor between 7 and 14 years of age had capacity of discernment at the time of the damaging event and that there was fault on his side. It also happens if a child tortfeasor is older than 14, but still younger than 18. Namely, there is the rebuttable statutory presumption of capacity of discernment,[177] as well as the rebuttable statutory presumption of fault,[178] for all tortfeasors over the age of 14. In these situations, the child tortfeasor and the person within whose authority was the care and supervision of that child will be jointly and severally liable.

237. Where damage is caused by a person who is deprived of capacity of discernment by reason of mental illness or intellectual disability, liability in damages shall lie with the person in charge of the care and supervision of the tortfeasor. The duty to take care of the tortfeasor and to watch over his conduct may be based on a statute or contract, or on a decision of the competent authority. This is a type of liability for acts of others based on the rebuttably presumed fault of the liable party in tending and supervising the incapacitated tortfeasor (*culpa in vigilando*). The liable party shall be exonerated from liability on the condition of proving that his conduct was that of a hypothetical reasonable and very careful man (or a hypothetical reasonable and very careful professional, if applicable) under the circumstances, or that the same damage would have occurred irrespective of the quality of the liable party's conduct.[179]

175. Article 168 of LO.
176. Articles 166 and 167, para. 2 of LO.
177. Article 160, para. 3 of LO.
178. Article 154, para. 1 of LO, under the condition of proving damage and causation.
179. Article 164 of LO.

Chapter 3. Liability for Things and Animals

238. Unlike the codifications of the Civil Law Tradition, Serbian LO does not contain specific provisions on the liability of owners of buildings and other constructions, and of keepers of animals. Provisions of this kind were proposed to the Yugoslav legislator in *Skica* – the Draft Code on Obligations and Contracts of 1969, but they were never included in the then-federal LO of 1978, which is still in force in Serbia.

However, LO contains a general norm on strict liability for damage caused by dangerous things and dangerous activities (Article 154, paragraphs 2 and 3 of LO). The courts comprehend both buildings and animals as dangerous objects and apply the general norm of strict tortious liability in these situations. Furthermore, there are some special rules on liability for wild animals in the Law on Game and Hunting of 2010 (LGH, last changes in 2018).

In any case, it is hard to categorize liability for either things, or animals as a type of liability for the acts of others, considering that both things and animals lack legal personality and, therefore, cannot be observed as 'others' (for whose acts someone else could be liable).

239. Most of the European jurisdictions took one of the two directions in developing the rules on strict liability. The first one is that of ad hoc legislation – in Zimmermann's terms – which means a casuistic approach of passing a series of special statutes for a number of singular sources of abnormal risk of damage, like road traffic, air transport, electricity, pharmaceuticals, and the like. The other approach was more general, like the development of the nineteenth-century French jurisprudence, where the courts have given a new and remarkably extensive interpretation of Article 1384 of Code Civil, and thus introduced the new tortious regime of strict liability for things under one's guard.[180]

240. In the period after WWII, the courts in Yugoslavia slowly developed a general norm on liability regardless of fault, for both patrimonial and non-patrimonial damage coming from a source of abnormal, atypical, elevated risk of damage to others.[181] A source of abnormal risk may present itself either as a dangerous thing (under the liable party's guard) or as a dangerous activity (conducted by the liable party).

Unlike the French court-made rule on strict liability for things under one's guard, here, strict liability was, from the very beginning, restricted to things that are dangerous, that is, the things that generate an abnormal risk of damage. In other words, liability regardless of fault has always been limited to the *dangerous* things (and activities) under one's guard.

---

180. R. Zimmermann, *The Law of Obligations. Roman Foundations of the Civilian Tradition* 1130–1142 (Oxford, 1996).
181. B. Bazala, 'Odgovornost za štetu prouzrokovanu uslijed povećane opasnosti', *NZ* 7/1952, 272, S. Mihajlović, 'Odgovornost za štetu pričinjenu izvorom povećane opasnosti', *Glasnik* 3/1975, 22. More on the pre-WWII and the post-WWII genesis of strict liability in the courts' reasoning and academic writings in former Yugoslavia, *see*: M. Karanikić Mirić, *Objektivna odgovornost za štetu* (Beograd, 2013), 24–31.

241. The general norm on strict liability for dangerous objects under one's guard, initially created by the post-WWII Yugoslav courts, was at one point proposed for codification to the Yugoslav legislator. The proposal was made by Professor Mihailo Konstantinović, the author of *Skica* of 1969. One version of the proposed legislative solution was integrated in Yugoslav LO of 1978 and is still in force in Serbia.

242. Where damage results from things or activities representing an increased source of danger for the surroundings, as well as in other cases prescribed by law, liability shall be imposed regardless of fault.[182] There is no statutory definition of either a dangerous thing or a dangerous activity. Both things and activities (or, to be more precise, *the types of* things and *the types of* activities) may be labelled as dangerous by the legislator (e.g., a motor vehicle in motion, or a defective product), or by the courts (e.g., a cement mixer, or a balance beam).

243. For the purposes of establishing strict liability, *dangerous thing* is a thing which generates an increased, atypical, abnormal, elevated risk of damage to the surroundings. The risk in question should be regarded as 'increased' or 'abnormal' or 'atypical' if it exceeds the normal, legitimately expected, typical chance of injury or loss in ordinary social interactions. Namely, people should reasonably expect some possibility of sustaining loss or injury by the mere fact of interacting with other people and engaging in the life of society. Where the chance of loss or injury significantly surpasses these reasonable expectations, then the thing involved or the activity assumed should be considered dangerous. Finally, the thing in question should be described as dangerous, if it generates atypical, abnormal, increased risk of damage to others *at its normal use*, that is, when it is used in a way a hypothetical reasonable and careful man would use it.[183]

244. In the absence of a statutory definition of a 'dangerous thing', the courts resort to the definition which was proposed in Skica but left out from LO. A thing is dangerous if its (normal) usage, position, or its very existence, generates an increased danger of damage to others. The author of Skica did not use the term dangerous activities. He believed that dangerous activity boils down to the utilization of a dangerous thing. If an activity does not include a dangerous object, it cannot be considered exceedingly dangerous. The reasoning is quite straightforward. Once a plain human movement (conducted without any dangerous objects) is understood as an abnormally dangerous social activity, we are left without any criterion or yardstick of normal, ordinary, reasonably expected risk of injury or loss in interacting with others.[184]

245. However, the legislator (Articles 173–177 of LO) differentiates dangerous things from dangerous activities and admits the possibility of human activity being

182. Article 154, paras 2 and 3 of LO.
183. In detail: M. Karanikić Mirić, *Objektivna odgovornost za štetu* (Beograd, 2013), 70–84.
184. M. Konstantinović, *Beleške s predavanja* (Beograd, 1969), 135.

abnormally dangerous when performed as a reasonable and careful man would perform it, even when it does not involve any dangerous object. The courts also affirm the distinction between dangerous things and dangerous activities (of which only some come down to the use of a dangerous thing) and have a long-standing understanding that an activity may be dangerous even when it is free from the use of dangerous objects. For instance, diving, skydiving, felling trees, gathering a large group of people in a limited space, extracting gravel from a riverbed, using a ladder sling, etc. However, the rules on strict liability for dangerous things and dangerous activities are the same, both situations fall under the same tortious regime, so the meticulous distinction between the use of a dangerous thing and the performance of a dangerous activity remains inconsequential. Along the same lines, the type of feature which makes a thing dangerous is also irrelevant or inconsequential. The courts hold a thing may be dangerous due to its very existence (like dangerous animals, or explosive materials), or due to the position it has been left in (e.g., a car parked downhill, or an elevator hanging high in the hoist way), or due to its use (like a motor vehicle in motion, or an electrical machine). However, once a thing is categorized as dangerous, due to any of these characteristics, the same rules on strict liability shall apply.

246. A 'dangerous activity' is a human activity which generates an abnormal, atypical, elevated risk of damage to others, when carried out in a legitimately expected manner, that is, in a way a hypothetical reasonable and careful man would perform it under the given circumstances. This may be, but does not have to be, a business activity, in a sense of an aggregate economic activity of the liable party. It may also be, but does not have to be, a regulated profession. For the purposes of establishing strict liability for dangerous activities, an 'activity' may be any human pursuit or engagement which is recognized in society as a coherent and rounded human effort. If the activity in question is such that a reasonable and careful man would not engage in it unless he is specially educated and trained for it, then the activity qualifies as 'dangerous' if it generates an abnormal, atypical, elevated risk of damage to others when performed in a way a hypothetical reasonable and careful professional (expert) would, under the given circumstances. In other words, this type of activity should be considered dangerous if it generates an abnormal risk of damage when carried out by a reasonable and careful expert. Finally, some activities are not dangerous in themselves, but they become dangerous if they need to be carried out under certain circumstances.[185] Some business activities increase the risk of occupational disease, and the courts tend to establish employers' liabilities in these cases as instances of strict liability for dangerous activities.[186]

185. M. Karanikić Mirić, *Objektivna odgovornost za štetu* (Beograd, 2013), 86.

186. SCS, Rev. 76/1998 (a business activity is dangerous if the process of work and working conditions increase the risk of proximate harm to human organism), SCS, Rev. 6875/1998 (vibration disease caused by machinery), SCS, Rev. 1215/1999 (employer's business activity is dangerous if it generates a proximate and longer detrimental effect on human body and wellbeing), *Sl. glasnik*.

247. The above-mentioned provisions of Article 154, paragraphs 2 and 3, and Articles 173–177 of LO represent, in fact, the 'general rules on strict liability'. There are, however, some special regimes of strict liability in Serbian tort law, such as liability for defective products.

Under the general regime of strict liability for dangerous things or dangerous objects, there are basically two conditions of liability. The first condition is the existence of recoverable damage, which must be proved by the injured party. This may relate to patrimonial damage, including direct loss (*damnum emergens*) and loss of expected gain or profits (*lucrum cessans, or lucrum interceptum*), as well as non-patrimonial damage (physical pain, psychological pain, fear – each of sufficient duration and intensity). The second condition is causation. In other words, the damage in question must be the consequence of the use, the position/location, or the very existence of a dangerous thing, or, it must be the consequence of a dangerous activity. Here, the statutory presumption of causation applies (Article 173 of LO).

248. Under the general rules on strict liability, the injured party must prove the existence of damage, and the fact that damage occurred 'in connection to' a source of an increased, abnormal, atypical risk of damage to surroundings.[187] In other words, the injured party must prove material, physical involvement of an abnormally dangerous thing, or an abnormally dangerous activity in the occurrence of damage. Once the link or the connection is established, the court shall rebuttably presume that it was *a causal* link or *a causal* connection, i.e., that the involvement of abnormally dangerous properties of the said thing, or activity, in the damaging event amounts to *causation*. That is to say, the court will take damage caused by a dangerous thing which participated in the occurrence of damage, or that damage which arose in connection to a dangerous activity was produced by this very activity. Thereafter, it will be up to the defendant to show that, irrespective of the fact the damage occurred in connection to his dangerous thing or activity, the true cause of damage was something else.

249. Who shall be liable under these rules? The legislator (and the courts) use the term 'proprietor' (Serb. *imalac*) to indicate the liable party.[188] This is a vague term, as it overlaps with the term 'owner' (Serb. *vlasnik, sopstvenik*), and it comes close by meaning to 'possessor' (Serb. *držalac*), though it is possible this 'partial mismatch' does not translate well in English. It requires further explanation. The liable party shall be the person who exercises control over the dangerous thing in question and uses this thing for his own purposes. This may be the owner, but under

187. Article 173 of LO: The damage caused in connection to a dangerous thing, or a dangerous activity, shall be considered as resulting from that thing or activity, unless it has been proved that the thing or activity in question was not the cause of the damage.

188. Article 174 of LO: The proprietor of a dangerous thing shall be liable for damage caused by it. The person performing a dangerous activity shall be liable for damage caused by it.

different circumstances, it may be the leaseholder, borrower, or the person otherwise entitled to possess/keep/hold/occupy the dangerous thing in question, to exercise his will over it, to use it for his own purposes, and, what is of the utmost importance, to exercise control and authority over the thing which is a source of elevated risk of damage to others.

250. When a proprietor is unlawfully deprived of a dangerous thing, the person who has unlawfully taken the thing from him shall be strictly liable for the resulting damage. However, the proprietor shall be jointly and severally liable with this person, if the proprietor is liable for the dispossession as such, that is, if he did not take all the measures needed to secure the dangerous thing from the unlawful taking.[189] In case of destruction of a thing (be it dangerous or not) which was unlawfully taken from its proprietor, the taker shall be liable even if the destruction was a consequence of force majeure.[190]

251. Where a proprietor entrusts another person with the use of a dangerous thing, or where another person (apart from the proprietor's employees) is in charge of watching over the dangerous thing (for instance, a repairer or serviceman), this person will be liable for the damage caused to others, instead of the proprietor, and under the same tortious regime as the proprietor. However, the proprietor shall be jointly and severally liable with this person if the damage originated from some hidden flaw or hidden characteristic of the dangerous thing in question, to which the proprietor failed to draw the other person's attention (i.e., to inform this other person of it). In that case, the person entrusted with the dangerous thing is entitled to seek reimbursement from the proprietor for the sum paid to the injured party. Where the proprietor hands over a dangerous object to a person who is not qualified or authorized to handle it, the proprietor shall be liable for the resulting damage.[191]

252. When it comes to the excuses from the general form of strict liability for dangerous things and dangerous activities, the foremost excuse is force majeure (*vis major*). The proprietor shall be excused from liability under the condition of rebutting the above-mentioned statutory presumption of causation, and this he may achieve by proving that, despite the fact the damage in question arose in connection to the dangerous thing (or dangerous activity), it was actually instigated by a cause *outside* the dangerous thing at issue, whose effects could not have been foreseen, avoided or eliminated.[192] For instance, the courts have held that the owner of the bus which slid off the road (no collision with other vehicles) may not be exempt from liability by pointing to another unidentified vehicle on a public road as *vis major*, even if this vehicle was improperly driven, as such occurrences on public roads are not unforeseeable.[193]

189. Article 175 of LO.
190. Article 187 of LO.
191. Article 176 of LO.
192. Article 177, para. 1 of LO.
193. SCS, Rev. 668/2003 of 19 Mar. 2003, *PLex*. The courts held the same with respect to a bustle and commotion in public transportation, as such activity of passengers is not unforeseeable. SC of Croatia, Gž. 622/1978 of 9 Jan. 1979, Comm LO BK, 1617. The same goes for a traffic accident

The cause which operated *inside* the dangerous thing, even if unforeseeable, unavoidable or inexorable, shall not be accepted as an excuse, because exactly the possibility of unforeseeable, unavoidable, inexorable internal or inner events, renders the thing at issue dangerous to the surroundings, and calls for the strict liability of its proprietor.[194]

The courts understand the term force majeure narrowly. For instance, a lightning strike in the mountain region, where the stormy weather with thunders and lightning strikes is frequent in summer, does not count as force majeure. The state is liable for damage suffered by the police officer hit by lightning, who was sent to provide security at an automobile race in the area known for the bad weather. The danger could have been avoided by removing the officer from the site while the storm was underway.[195]

253. Furthermore, the proprietor shall be excused from liability if he refutes the statutory presumption of causation by proving that, despite the fact the damage at issue occurred in connection to the dangerous thing (or dangerous activity), it was exclusively caused by the injured party, or by a third party. However, it is necessary that the injurious action in question was unforeseeable to the proprietor, and that he was not able to avoid or eliminate its consequences.[196]

254. Where the injured party has partially contributed to the damage he suffered, the proprietor shall be partially (and proportionally) excused from liability. And where a third party has partially contributed to the damage suffered by the injured party, the proprietor and the third party shall be jointly and severally liable towards the injured party. In the reimbursement proceedings, the third party shall incur the portion of the sum paid to the injured party, in proportion to the degree of his fault.[197] In other words, a proprietor of a dangerous thing and the third party who has partially contributed to the occurrence of damage shall be jointly and severally liable to the victim for the overall damage. If the proprietor pays the overall sum of compensation to the victim, he can recover a portion of it from the third party, and this portion shall be measured by the degree of the third party's fault.

255. However, a person being instrumental (implemental, subservient) in the proprietor's use of dangerous objects, or performance of dangerous activities, cannot be considered a third party for the purposes of the proprietor's partial or complete excuse from liability.[198] Also, a third party in this context cannot be a person for whose actions the proprietor is vicariously liable. So, when the minor child of the owner of a motor vehicle has taken the keys of the vehicle and caused a car

on a public road: it is not unforeseeable, so cannot be qualified as *vis major*. SC of Croatia, Rev. 233/1979 of 25 Jul. 1979, Comm LO BK, 1622.

194. M. Konstantinović, *Beleške s predavanja* (Beograd, 1969), 135.

195. SCS, Rev. 246/2001 of 17 Jan. 2002, *PLex*.

196. Article 177, para. 2 of LO.

197. Article 177, paras 3 and 4 of LO.

198. Article 170, para. 3 and Art. 177, para. 5 of LO. For example, an employee of the proprietor keeps, controls and uses a dangerous object for (the benefit of) his employer, and cannot be observed as a third party in this regard.

crash, the court held that the minor child cannot be observed as a third party for the purposes of releasing the owner from strict liability.[199]

256. Liability for damages caused by animals. In modern legal systems, animals are not regarded as tortfeasors or perpetrators of damage, but as the sources of risk, and possible causes of damage. Under a relatively new piece of legislation in Serbia, Law on Animal Welfare of 2009 (LAW), animals of certain species may have certain legally protected interests, and these interests the legislator identifies as 'welfare'. Yet, this concerns solely those animal species which are (deemed to be) capable of feeling pain, suffering, fear and stress.[200] In any case, animals do not possess delictual capacity and cannot be considered tortfeasors, either for the purposes of establishing their own tortious liability or for the purposes of establishing some person's vicarious liability for them.

257. As animals are considered to be items of property, hurting or killing an animal gives rise to a claim for damages. The owner of the animal may demand compensation for patrimonial loss (actual loss and lost profits) caused by the act of hurting or killing his animal. However, the owner cannot claim compensation for pain and suffering, since mental suffering due to destruction of an item of property does not constitute recoverable damage in Serbian tort law. Where the act of killing or hurting the animal qualifies as a criminal offence committed with premeditation, the court may determine the amount of indemnity against the value the animal used to have for its owner.[201]

258. Animals represent 'living dangerous things', as they generate an increased risk of damage to their surroundings. This does not have to come from their natural aggressiveness or forcefulness, but also from their unpredictability and impulsiveness. For example, the courts consider a roe deer to be a harmless animal and, when at rest, not dangerous at all. However, when a roe wanders around public roads, it becomes a source of elevated risk of damage due to its spontaneity, and thus it should be categorized as a dangerous thing.[202]

259. The situations at issue should be distinguished from the instances where an animal is used as a tool or instrument for causing damage (e.g., throwing an animal at someone), as well as from the cases of infection from improper disposal of dead animals. Liability for damage caused by animals presupposes active involvement of an animal (even if it was somehow induced) in the damaging event.

260. A special regime of liability for damages caused by animals was proposed to the Yugoslav legislator in *Skica*, the already-mentioned Draft Code on Obligations and Contracts of 1969. In brief, the proposal was as follows: A proprietor shall

---

199. SCS, Rev. 2288/2005 of 28 Sep. 2005, *Pravni informator* 12/2005. The same for a tractor: SC of Montenegro, Rev. 209/1987 of 21 Apr. 1989, *Ingpro*.
200. Articles 1 and 2 of Law.
201. Article 189, para. 4 of LO.
202. SCS, Rev. 3393/1992 of 26 Nov. 1992, *Ingpro*.

be strictly liable for damage caused by an animal. The same goes for the guardians, i.e., the persons entrusted with care and supervision over the animals, such as veterinary physicians, animal hospitals, trainers, dog pensions, etc. The proprietor shall be jointly and severally liable with the guardian, if the damage arose from some characteristics of, or flaw in the animal, of which the proprietor failed to warn the guardian. The injured party may keep the animal caught causing damage, as a pledge (*pignus*) for what is due to him, but has to inform the proprietor of the capturing, and if the proprietor is not known to him, then he needs to inform the municipality.[203] This proposal was never included in the then-federal LO of 1978. The Commission appointed by the Government to draft a new civil codex for Serbia is considering including these rules in the prospective codification.[204]

261. In the absence of special statutory rules on liability for damage caused by animals, the courts steadily apply the above-explained general rules on strict liability for dangerous things.[205] The courts have the power (i.e., authority under Article 154, paragraph 2 of LO) to categorize a type of thing as dangerous, for the purposes of establishing strict liability for damage caused by a thing of that kind. The courts will do so if the thing at issue meets the afore-analysed criteria (*see* paragraph 243). The proprietor shall be liable for the damage caused by the animal irrespective of the quality of care and supervision he has provided. His liability is not based on the deficiency of his actions, and he may not escape liability by proving that there was no fault on his side and that he supervised the animal in due manner. He may only invoke the general excuses from strict liability, and that includes force majeure or the fact that the damage was caused by the unforeseeable and inexorable actions of others (either the injured party or a third party). If the proprietor has entrusted an unqualified or otherwise inadequate person with the care and supervision of the animal, he should remain jointly and severally liable with the poorly chosen person, for the damage caused by the animal while under this person's guard.

262. The above-stated rules shall apply if the damage was caused by 'domestic animals'. This is a term with a specific meaning in the context of liability for damage caused by animals. It denotes animals which have owners or keepers and includes the animals belonging to domesticated, semi-domesticated and routinely captive-bred species, as well as the animals belonging to wild species that are held in captivity (i.e., animals of wild species held in zoos). In contrast, the term 'wild animals' stands for the animals living freely, not belonging to anyone and, in general, outside human settlements.

263. As a rule, no one is liable for damages caused by wild animals. However, there are certain exceptions to this. The state is not liable for damage caused by wild animal species unless otherwise prescribed by law. The state shall be liable for damage caused by an animal *of a protected species*, provided that the injured party has

---

203. Articles 142–144 of Skica.
204. Articles 314–317 of DCC.
205. For example, SCS, Rev. 5914/1999 of 9 May 2000, *Ingpro*; Decision of the Appellate Court in Novi Sad, Gž. 3545/2005 of 17 Nov. 2005, *PLex*; Comm LO BK, 685, Comm LO Per, 401.

taken the required preventive measures (which do not put animals in peril), such as driving away or repelling the animals, protecting the goods they might damage, building a fence.[206]

264. First, some wild species enjoy special protection under Law on Game and Hunting of 2010 (LGH, last changes in 2018). The protected wild animals may have one of the two different protection statuses under LGH.[207] The permanently protected animal species are safeguarded by 'permanent prohibition of hunting'. The animal species protected by 'close season' are covered by prohibition of hunting in certain periods of the year. The authority which has given a wildlife species a protected status, and either permanently, or temporarily prohibited its hunting, shall be liable for damages caused by an animal of this species.[208]

265. Therefore, a user of the hunting grounds, that is, a legal entity vested with the authority to manage the hunting grounds, shall be liable for damage caused by the species protected by close season on the hunting grounds in question. Likewise, the state (acting via the ministry in charge of environmental protection) shall be liable for damage caused by permanently protected animal species. Also, the state is liable for damage caused by a wolf, protected by close season on the hunting grounds, if both the injured party and the user of the hunting grounds have taken the required preventive measures against such damage. Besides, the state is liable for damage caused by wolfs in all areas where this species is permanently protected. In all of the aforesaid cases, tortious liability for both patrimonial and non-patrimonial damage caused by wild animals shall be strict.

However, the injured party which has failed to take the required preventive measures against damage from wild animals, shall not have the right to compensation. Where the conditions for strict liability under LGH are not met, the courts resort to the general rules on strict liability for dangerous objects, if possible.[209] In case the user of hunting grounds organizes a hunt on the grounds, and if during that time a participant in the organized hunting event causes damage to a third party, the user of the hunting grounds and the participant in the hunting event shall be jointly and severally liable.[210]

266. Second, in case of damage caused by stray dogs, or other animals belonging to no one, the city (or municipality) on whose territory the damaging event took place, shall be liable for both patrimonial and non-patrimonial damage suffered by

206. Articles 64–65 of the Law on the Protection of Nature of 2009 (last changes in 2021).
207. Article 20 of LGH.
208. Article 88 of LGH.
209. User of the hunting grounds is strictly liable for damage caused by an animal running into a motor vehicle in motion on the public road and outside the hunting grounds. Here, the court turned to Art. 174 of LO, because of the fact the damage was not caused 'on hunting grounds': SCS, Rev. 3393/1992 of 26 Nov. 1992, *Ingpro*. In a similar older case, a user of the hunting grounds and a company in charge of maintenance of public roads have been found jointly and severally liable. SC of Vojvodina, Rev. 10/1980, *see*: M. Počuča & R. Tepavac, 'Šteta koju prouzrokuje divljač i njena naknada', in *Savremeni aspekti održivog gazdovanja populacijama divljači* (Beograd, 2012), 155.
210. Article 90, para. 1 of LGH. This should, presumably, exclude damaging events that are not in connection with the activity of hunting.

the injured party. The courts sometimes find legal foundation of this liability in Article 154, paragraph 2 of LO (the most general norm on strict liability for dangerous things and dangerous activities), and at other times in Article 184 of LO (liability for damage caused by non-rendering, or by irregular rendering, of services of general interest).

Besides, the city (or municipality) on whose territory the damaging event took place cannot evade liability by showing that they have delegated this duty to either public or private utility companies. If the city (or municipality) has, in fact, assigned a company with taking care of stray dogs or other stray animals, and with the removal of such animals from public spaces, the city (or municipality) and the company in question shall be jointly and severally liable for the damage caused by such animals. The company shall be liable under Article 184 of LO.[211]

211. Decision of District Court in Novi Sad, Gž. 2669/2006 of 14 Feb. 2007, Decision of District Court in Novi Sad, Gž. 1687/2001 of 31 Oct. 2001, *PLex*.

Part III. Forms of Strict Liability

Chapter 1. Road and Traffic Accidents

267. A motor vehicle is a self-propelled road vehicle, such as a car, bus, motorcycle, off-road vehicle, light truck, regular truck, etc. It has an engine or motor of its own and may include towable semi-trailers, trailers and sidecars, as well as boxes, baskets or cargo bags.[212] In the long-standing practice of Serbian courts, a motor vehicle in motion meets the criteria of a 'dangerous thing' for the purposes of strict liability in tort. Therefore, the above-analysed general rules on strict liability for damage caused by dangerous things[213] apply in cases where either patrimonial or non-patrimonial damage was caused by a motor vehicle in motion.[214]

268. In a nutshell, a person who exercises control over the motor vehicle, and uses the vehicle for his own purposes ('the proprietor'), shall be liable for damages caused by the vehicle. A proprietor (Serb. *imalac*) may be the owner, leaseholder, borrower, or other person entitled to possess/keep/hold/occupy the vehicle at issue (as a source of elevated risk of damage to surroundings), to exercise his will over it, and to use it for his own purposes. The injured party must prove the existence of patrimonial or non-patrimonial damage, and the fact that damage occurred in connection to a source of an increased, abnormal, atypical risk of damage to surroundings – in this case, a motor vehicle in motion. Once the *connection* is proven, the court shall rebuttably presume that it was *causal*, and thenceforward, it will be up to the liable party to show that, notwithstanding the fact damage occurred in connection to his motor vehicle, the true cause of damage was something else. In other words, the liable party shall be excused from liability if he proves that the damage in question was instigated by force majeure[215] (a cause *outside* the motor vehicle at issue, whose effects could not have been foreseen, avoided or eliminated), or by an

212. Ž. Đorđević & V. Stanković, *Obligaciono pravo* (Beograd, 1987), 427.
213. Articles 173–177 of LO (*see* paras 238 et seq.).
214. For instance: SCS, Rev. 105/2006 of 10 May 2006, Decision of District Court in Niš, Gž. 1027/2006 of 25 May 2006, SCS, Rev. 668/2003 of 19 Mar. 2003, Decision of Higher Commercial Court, Pž. 226/2007 of 27 Dec. 2007, Decision of District Court in Valjevo, Gž. 1329/2001 of 14 Dec. 2001 (a bus is a dangerous object, Arts 173–174 of the LO apply), *PLex*. *See also*: P. Šulejić, 'Krivica vozača motornog vozila u sistemu građanske odgovornosti i osiguranja od odgovornosti', APFB 5–6/1969, 575–584, V. Jovanović, 'Odgovornost za štetu prouzrokovanu motornim vozilom', APFB 3–4/1953, 442–445 (court decisions).
215. *Vis major* is understood as qualified *casus*; the cause of damage which must have been unforeseeable, unavoidable and external: Severe wind along the Adriatic coast causing vehicles to skid is not

unforeseeable and unavoidable injurious action of either the injured party or a third party. However, a person being instrumental (subservient) in the liable party's use of the motor vehicle, such as the liable party's employee, cannot be considered a 'third party' for the purposes of the liable party's release from liability. Also, 'third party' in this context cannot be a person for whose actions the liable party is vicariously liable (e.g., his minor child).

269. The above-stated general rules on strict liability cover the accidents in which a motor vehicle has hit a pedestrian, or a person on a bicycle, a fence, a building, or a parked car. It is the courts' understanding that motor vehicle is not a dangerous thing when it is parked, i.e., not in motion. An unmoving motor vehicle may, however, qualify as a dangerous thing, by reason of the way it was parked (on a road covered in clay, or on a slope, for example), which increases the chance of the vehicle beginning to slide on its own.[216] In any event, the general rules on strict liability shall apply if and only if there was not more than one motor vehicle involved in the accident.

270. Where there were two or more motor vehicles involved in a road traffic accident, there is an explicit statutory rule on joint and several (strict) liability of the proprietors of the implicated vehicles towards an injured party.[217] The victim may be a pedestrian, a bicyclist, a passenger in either of the colliding vehicles, the owner of a parked car affected by the colliding vehicles, etc. Neither of the proprietors involved in the collision can invoke fault of another proprietor, of lack of his own fault, against the injured party. If the injured party has partially contributed to the damage, the compensation he may ask for shall be reduced in proportion to his involvement in the damaging event. The contribution of the injured party to the occurrence of damage shall be determined identically against all (jointly and severally liable) defendants.[218] In the reimbursement proceedings, that is, in the mutual relationship of the aforementioned defendants after the damage at issue has been redressed, their respective faults shall be relevant.

271. Special rules on liability apply in cases of collision of two or more motor vehicles in motion, concerning damage one of the involved parties inflicted on another.[219] These rules apply when there are at least two motor vehicles involved in an accident. Their purpose is to govern mutual liability of the two proprietors of dangerous things, who had inflicted damage to one another. As stated before, the proprietors of the collided motor vehicles shall be jointly and severally liable for damage inflicted upon third parties, and their liability shall be strict. The principle

unforeseeable, therefore, it is not force majeure. Tyre explosion, or detachment of a wheel from the vehicle, are not force majeure as they are not external (they are coming from within the vehicle). Comm LO Per, 407.

216. Comm LO BK, 641. Also: SCS, Rev. 344/2002 of 7 Feb. 2002, *PLex* (a passenger car parked on a slope is a dangerous object).
217. Article 178, para. 4 of LO.
218. The injured party's contribution is always the same, irrespective of the person from whom he seeks compensation: Decision of District Court in Valjevo, Gž. 323/2008(1) of 28 Feb. 2008, *PLex*.
219. Article 178, paras 1–3 of LO.

of fault comes into the equation solely for the purposes of regulating the relation between two (or more) proprietors of dangerous objects hurting or damaging one another.[220]

272. These rules are special as they exclude the application of the general rules on strict liability for dangerous things, which would normally be relevant. What is special here is that two dangerous things have damaged one another, and the two proprietors of dangerous things are potentially liable to one another. Both of the vehicles need to be in motion, in order for both of them to qualify as dangerous things. Both of the proprietors are members of the *risk community*, they increase the cumulative risk of damage from road traffic, benefit from the road traffic as a collective hazardous activity, participate in its financing, and stimulate its development.

Fault of each of the participants in a car crash shall be relevant in their reciprocal liability. Most commonly this would be either ordinary or gross negligence. Cases of intent are extremely rare in car crash situations, as they include self-inflicted harm. In contrast, bystanders (pedestrians, bicyclists, passengers in either of the colliding vehicles, owners of the parked cars affected by the colliding vehicles, etc.) should be firmly protected by a combination of the rules on strict liability and mandatory automobile liability insurance. Under Article 178, paragraph 4 of LO, and in line with the settled practice of the courts, the proprietors of the colliding vehicles shall be jointly and severally strictly liable (i.e., liable irrespective of their faults) for both patrimonial and non-patrimonial damages caused to a third party.

273. Under Article 178, paragraph 1 of LO, where a collision of two (or more) motor vehicles in motion is caused entirely by fault of the proprietor of one of the involved motor vehicles, the general rules of fault-based liability shall apply.[221] Plain or ordinary negligence of one of the participants in a car crash shall be sufficient for establishing his liability, and the scope of his liability shall not be dependent on the degree of his fault. Once the exclusive fault of one of the participants in a car crash is established, the principle of complete or full compensation (Article 190 of LO) shall apply, meaning that the injured party has the right to full recovery, irrespective of the degree of the liable party's fault. Be it negligence or intent on the side of the defendant, the compensation the injured party is entitled to is always the same.

However, there is one aspect of the general regime of fault-based liability which cannot apply in this situation, and that is the rebuttable statutory presumption of fault (Article 154, paragraph 1 of LO). Such presumption would work at the same time against all participants in a car crash, which would make it inoperable. Therefore, a proprietor of one of the motor vehicles involved in a traffic accident claiming that the accident was entirely caused by fault of another participant, cannot benefit from the statutory presumption of fault, and has to prove his assertion.

220. Comm LO Per, 409.

221. For instance, the driver of the tractor with the trailer is entirely at fault, because he took the turn left from a public road to his farm at the time when the vehicle behind him has already started overtaking. Decision of District Court in Novi Sad, Gž. 2345/2005 of 24 Nov. 2005, *PLex*.

274. Under Article 178, paragraph 2 of LO, where both sides are at fault, that is, where there is fault of each of the implicated proprietors, every proprietor shall be liable for the entire damage suffered by all of them, in proportion to the degree of his fault. In other words, the damages of both involved parties are added and then apportioned on the basis of their fault. However, if it is not possible to weigh out the shares in damages that should be attributed to each of their faults, the rules on reimbursement proceedings among the multiple tortfeasors shall apply.[222]

In any case, this rule cannot apply if only one of the participants in the car crash was at fault, while the other only physically contributed to the extent of damage.[223] Also, the above-mentioned principle of full compensation may not apply here, and each of the proprietors of the motor vehicles involved in a car crash shall only have the right to compensation in proportion to another participant's fault.

275. Under Article 178, paragraph 3 of LO, where neither party is at fault, the proprietors' liability shall be divided into equal shares, unless reasons of equity require differently. In other words, when none of the proprietors of the motor vehicles involved in the car crash is at fault, it shall be presumed that equity demands that they bear the damage in equal shares unless some special circumstances justify a different distribution of burdens.

222. Article 208, paras 2 and 3 of LO: When determining individual shares of each of the debtors in the recourse proceedings, the court shall take into account the degree of the debtors' respective faults, and the gravity of the consequences of their respective acts. If it is not possible to discern the individual shares, all jointly and severally liable debtors shall account for equal shares, unless equity requires otherwise.

223. Decision of District Court in Valjevo, Gž. 810/2005 of 14 Jul. 2005, *PLex*.

Chapter 2. Product Liability

276. Yugoslav LO of 1978 was one of the first statutes in Europe to lay down the rules on strict liability for defective products. Its provisions are still in force in Serbia. Where a producer puts into circulation a product which is dangerous to people or property because of a defect that was unknown to the producer at the time of release, the producer shall be liable regardless of his fault for damage caused by the aforesaid defect.[224] Furthermore, a producer shall be liable for damage caused by dangerous properties of his product (which do not make the product at issue defective), if he has failed to take all measures necessary to prevent the foreseeable damage, either by warning, user manuals, safe packaging, or by other appropriate procedures (*see* paragraph 281).[225] 'Other' measures include, for instance, natural gas odorization, i.e., ensuring that combustible gas in a distribution pipeline contains an odorant so that a leak can be detected by anyone who has a normal sense of smell.

277. The first paragraph of Article 179 of LO regulates a type of strict extra-contractual liability for damage caused by a thing which is not dangerous in itself, but which becomes dangerous by the fact that it has some flaw or defect. Because of this flaw or defect, the thing in question has become a source of atypical, abnormal, elevated risk of damage to others, when used in a way, or for the purpose, that could have been reasonably expected. The defectiveness or faultiness here is not the question of conformity to some previously agreed or implied attributes of the thing at issue (*see* paragraph 278). On the contrary, it is the question of legitimately expected safety of the said thing, when it is being used in a reasonably foreseeable manner. For the purposes of establishing product liability under the rules of LO, only material movable things may qualify as products. A product may also be a movable thing which is attached to an immovable object. Products include gas, electricity and thermal energy, water, human organs removed from the body, human blood, etc.[226]

278. The law of contracts plays a very limited role in product liability litigation. The rules on liability for non-conformity of the goods with a contract, or with the specific contractual provisions on guarantee, are limited to the situations where a manufacturer or distributor has a direct contractual relationship with the consumer (which, when it comes to consumer products, happens very rarely). In Serbian law of contracts, the acquirer may claim the transferor's liability under the rules of liability for non-conformity of goods with the sales contract, or with another synallagmatic contract (Articles of 578–500 LO). The purchaser may also claim the

224. Article 179, para. 1 of LO. For example, a plumbing pipe, which was not thermally insulated, freezes and bursts. The manufacturer is strictly liable. Decision of the Appellate Court in Belgrade, Pž. 6423/2013 of 17 Oct. 2013, *PLex.*

225. Article 179, para. 2 of LO.

226. J. Radišić, 'Odgovornost za štetu koju uzrokuje stvar s nedostatkom', *PZ* 1/1989, 467–468, Comm LO Per, 410.

seller's and producer's joint and several liability for non-conformity of the electronics and appliances ('technical goods') with the specific provisions of the producer's guarantee (Articles 501–507 of LO).

279. A producer of a defective product shall be liable in damages only if the defect was present in the product at the time the product was released from the producer's control of the producer's own accord, i.e., at the time it was willingly put into circulation. The producer will also be liable where the defect came about later, but *the source* of the defect at issue was already in existence in the product at the time the product left the producer's control. The notion of 'producer' includes producers of raw materials and components, as well as manufacturers of finished goods or end-products. Importers shall be liable for damage caused by defective imported products, under the same conditions as the producer. If the importer is not known (not identified on the product), the seller or supplier shall be liable, as if they were the importers.[227]

280. The injured party may be either a natural or a juridical person. Namely, the application of the rules of LO in the matters of product liability has never been restricted to the consumer context, and it remained unrestricted even after the Product Liability Directive of 1985 was implemented in Serbian law in 2005, in a separate piece of legislation, which will be addressed later. The injured party must prove that he has suffered damage, that this damage was caused by a defect in the product, and that it is more likely than not that the defect existed at the time of putting the product into circulation. Recoverable damages include both patrimonial and non-patrimonial damage. A producer may plead general excuses from strict liability, which include force majeure, or that the damage was caused by the unforeseeable and inexorable actions of either the injured party or a third party. He cannot escape liability by proving that the defect was objectively undiscoverable while the product was under his control.

281. Article 179, paragraph 2 of LO regulates a type of extra-contractual liability for substandard behaviour of a producer, or, to be more precise, for his failure to take all measures necessary to prevent damage from the dangerous characteristics of his product. A producer shall be liable for omission, that is, for not acting in line with an objective, depersonalized and highly set standard of socially desirable behaviour. The injured party needs to prove he has incurred (patrimonial or non-patrimonial) damage which was reasonably foreseeable to the producer at the time the producer willingly put the product into circulation. The injured party also needs to prove that the damage suffered was caused by some dangerous property or attribute of the product in question. However, the circumstance that the product bears such a feature or characteristic does not make it 'faulty' or 'defective', but 'dangerous'. The fact that the damage at issue was predictable at the time the product was willingly released from the producer's control, and the fact that such damage actually came about, gives rise to the factual presumption that the producer

227. Comm LO Per, 411.

failed to take all measures necessary for its prevention.[228] It is then up to the producer to show the foreseeable damage occurred in spite of the fact that he has taken all the necessary preventive measures, such as adequate and visible warnings with reference to full user instructions, directions for safe use, safe packaging,[229] product specific user manuals, etc.

282. The above-stated rules of general tort law regarding producer's liability exceed the consumer context. They date back to the year of 1978 and are much older than the first piece of consumer legislation in Serbia. Thus, the plaintiff may be either a natural, or a juridical person, and the same goes for the defendant,[230] all types of legally recognized damage are recoverable, all other general rules of tortious liability apply, such as the principle of complete or full compensation (Article 190 of LO), the rules on the injured party's contribution to causation of the damage (Article 192 of LO), the provisions on limitation periods for tort claims (Article 376 of LO), etc.

283. The first piece of consumer legislation in Serbia, which at the time was one of the two federal units of the FRY, was enacted at the federal level in 2002 (*Law of Consumer Protection of 2002*). Prior to 2002, there were no separate laws concerning the issues of consumer protection. As already stated, LO of 1978 contained (and still contains) certain provisions on the seller's liability for non-conformity of goods and services with the contract in both B2B and B2C transactions, as well as the here-explained general provisions on the producer's liability for damage caused by a defective product. The next attempt to regulate consumer matters in Serbia ensued in 2005 (*Law of Consumer Protection of 2005*), after the dissolution of the federal state. This piece of legislation was soon replaced by the next umbrella LCP in 2010 (*Law of Consumer Protection of 2010*), yet another one in four years' time (*Law of Consumer Protection of 2014*), and finally the most recent *LCP of 2021*. Serbian authorities have been facing the challenges of making the new legal framework operative. While consumer legislation is fairly harmonized with the EU acquis as of 2010, national standards of consumer protection still lag behind those in the EU.[231]

284. The first attempt to implement the Product Liability Directive 85/374/EEC into Serbian law took place in 2005, through a separate legislative act (*Law on*

228. This applies to importers as well. SCS, Pzz. 34/1997 of 20 May 1998, *PLex*.
229. Decision of the Federal Court of Yugoslavia, Gzs. 45/1998 of 19 Nov. 1998, *PLex* (liability of the authorized representative of the foreign manufacturer for damage caused by herbicide T 101 sold in unlabelled packaging).
230. Where a director of a company, acting in his private capacity (as a natural person and not in the course of the company's business), developed and sold a 'cure' for multiple sclerosis, and where the plaintiff's medical condition worsened after submitting to this treatment, the court has found the company not liable. The director's liability was not at issue, because he died in the meantime. SCS, Rev. 351/2007 of 21 Feb. 2007, *PLex*.
231. In detail, M. Karanikić Mirić, *Understanding the Enforcement Malfunction of Consumer Legislation in Serbia*, Journal of Consumer Policy 231–246 (3/2013).

Product Liability). However, the later modifications concerning agricultural products, particularly the concept of 'product' after the 'BSE/mad-cow-disease' crisis, introduced by Directive 99/34/EC, were omitted from this act. The provisions of the said law have been incorporated, with necessary changes, into the subsequent umbrella laws on consumer protection (of 2010, 2014 and 2021). The said changes were intended to correct certain imprecisions and to bring Serbian consumer law closer to the tortious regime envisaged by the Directive.[232]

285. At present, Serbia has two sets of statutory provisions on product liability: (a) the aforesaid Article 179 of LO, and (b) Article 5, paragraph 1, lines 14, 16 and 22, and Articles 58–64 of LCP of 2021. The courts are yet to consider and clarify the relationship between them.[233]

286. Under the rules of LCP of 2021, the product is taken to mean all movables, including a movable incorporated into another movable or into an immovable, and including energy produced or collected to provide light, heat or movement.[234] The producer is taken to mean the producer (the manufacturer), or the importer, of a raw material, a component part or a finished product for sale, hire, leasing or any form of distribution; any person putting their name, trade mark or other distinguishing feature on the product and thus presenting himself as the producer; any person supplying a product whose producer cannot be identified on the product, unless he informs the injured person, within a reasonable time, of the identity of the producer or of the person who supplied him with the product; any person supplying an imported product whose importer cannot be identified from the product.[235] Where two or more persons are liable for the same damage, they shall be liable jointly and severally.[236]

287. The notion of damage under LCP is restricted to damage caused by death or personal injuries, damage to, or destruction of, an item of property which was used by the injured party mainly for his own private use or consumption.[237] The injured party maintains the right to compensation for non-patrimonial damage (psychological pain, physical pain, fear) under the general rules of tortious liability.[238] A limit for the total liability of a producer in the case of death or personal injury caused by identical items with the same defect is not set by LCP.

232. Under Art. 78 of Stabilization and Association Agreement between the European Communities and their Member States of the one part, and the Republic of Serbia, of the other part (OJ EU L278 of 18 Oct. 2013, 16), the parties to the SAA have agreed to the harmonization of legislation of consumer protection in Serbia on that in force in the Community. Serbia passed the Law on ratification of the SAA in 2008.
233. For instance, it will be open for debate whether a consumer may seek protection under the more generous rules of LO, having in mind the full or maximum harmonization heralded by the European Court of Justice in relation to Product Liability Directive (despite its fragmented nature).
234. Article 5, para. 1 (14) of LCP.
235. Article 5, para. 1 (16) of LCP.
236. Article 62 of LCP.
237. Article 5, para. 1 (22) of LCP.
238. Article 59, para. 2 LCP.

288. No contractual clause may allow the producer to exclude or limit his liability for damage caused by his defective products.[239] A product is considered 'defective' when it does not provide the safety which is legitimately expected, taking all circumstances into account, including the presentation of the product, the reasonable use of the product, and the time when the product was put into circulation. It shall not be considered defective just because a better product is later put into circulation.[240] The producer shall be strictly liable for damage caused by his defective product, irrespective of whether he was aware of the defect at the time he put the product into circulation. To that end, the injured party must prove the actual damage, the defect in the product, and the causal link between defect and damage.[241]

289. Under Article 63 of LCP, a limitation period of three years applies to the injured party's right to damages, starting from the day on which the injured party became aware of the damage, the defect, and the identity of the producer (the so-called subjective prescription period). In any case, the right to damages shall become unenforceable ten years after the date the product was put into circulation (the so-called objective prescription period). The latter prescription period is two times longer than under the general provision of Article 376, paragraph 2 of LO. Namely, under the general rule of Serbian tort law regarding the objective prescription period for claims in damages, the right to damages expires five years from the manifestation of the damage in question. Apparently, the injured party benefits from a two times longer limitation period in the consumer context. However, the objective prescription period under LCP starts running when the product is put in circulation, while under LO it does not start before the damage manifests itself completely. This means that in some cases of latent damage, where the period of time between the release of the product and the occurrence of damage may be very long, the rules of LO may be more favourable to the consumer. Besides, the reception of the EU rule on the preclusive term (a cut-off period) of ten years into Serbian LCP is faulty, to begin with. Namely, Article 63 of LCP states that 'in any case, the claim for damages shall expire in ten years from the day the manufacturer put the defective product on the market.' However, under Article 11 of the Product Liability Directive, the rights of the injured party shall be extinguished upon the expiry of a period of ten years from the date on which the producer put into circulation the actual product which caused the damage. In other words, Serbian law stipulates the ten-year statute of limitation (after which the injured party's position depends on whether or not the producer raises the objection of limitation), while the EU Directive sets the time limit for complete extinguishment of the injured party's right to compensation (the so-called cut-off period or *preclusion*, regardless of whether the producer has raised any objection).

239. Article 64 of LCP.
240. Article 58 of LCP.
241. Articles 59–60 of LCP.

290. Under Article 61, paragraph 1 of LCP, the producer shall be excused from liability if he proves either of the following: he did not put the product into circulation; the defect did not exist at the time the producer put the product into circulation, or the defect appeared after the product was put into circulation; the product was not manufactured to be sold or distributed for profit *and* the product was not manufactured in the course of his business; the defect is due to compliance of the product with mandatory regulations issued by the public authorities. Similarly to some (but not all) EU countries, the so-called state-of-the-art (development risk) defence has not been integrated into Article 61 of LCP. In other words, the producer cannot exempt himself from liability by proving the state of scientific and technical knowledge at the time the product was put into circulation was insufficient to identify the defect.

291. A manufacturer of a component shall be exempt from liability if he proves that the defect is attributable to the design of the final product in which the component has been fitted, or to the instructions given by the manufacturer of the final product.[242] The producer may be partially or completely exempt from liability if he proves contributory negligence of the injured party or a person for whom the injured party is vicariously liable.[243] In contrast, the producer shall remain exclusively liable if a third party has partially contributed to the occurrence of damage.[244]

242. Article 61, para. 2 of LCP.
243. Article 61, para. 3 of LCP.
244. Article 61, para. 4 of LCP.

Chapter 3. Liability for Services

292. As already stated, there are two sets of statutory provisions on product liability in Serbian tort law: the general regime of producers' liability under Article 179 of LO, and the rules pertaining to the consumer context of Articles 58–64 of LCP of 2021. Contrary to the producers of raw materials and component parts, neither the providers of maintenance services nor the repairers, may qualify as 'producers' for purposes of establishing product liability. In consequence, suppliers of maintenance and repair services cannot be held liable under the above-mentioned rules on product liability. Still, a repairer can incur liability in a capacity of a 'producer of a component part' (under either of the two product liability regimes), if he has replaced a component in a product in need of repair, with a new part which was of his own production.

293. In addition, suppliers of services (including the repair and maintenance services) may be liable under the general rules of extra-contractual liability for damage caused to others by negligent performance of their work. Considering that suppliers of services normally act in a professional role, i.e., in their capacity as experts, they are supposed to have some special professional knowledge that could not be legitimately expected from a hypothetical reasonable and careful man. Therefore, their conduct is measured against a special yardstick, that is, against the conduct of a reasonable and careful expert (professional) under the given circumstances.

294. Furthermore, a supplier of services shall be liable for the breach of contract for services to another contracting party under the general rules of contractual liability, or, to be more precise, under the rules of liability for damage caused by violation of a pre-existent duty (Article 262 and Article 266 of LO): The client may demand compensation for the foreseeable patrimonial damage caused by the breach, and if the supplier has acted with gross negligence, intention or fraudulently, the client may seek compensation for total patrimonial damage, irrespective of its foreseeability. The supplier may not release himself from liability by proving that partial performance, non-performance or late performance was not his fault. However, a qualified degree of fault shall extend the scope of his liability to include the unforeseeable (though still solely patrimonial) damage.

295. Where the supplier's work, i.e., the service he renders, meets the requirements of a 'dangerous activity', the general rules on strict extra-contractual liability for dangerous activities shall apply (*see* paragraphs 238 et seq.)[245] Under Article 154, paragraphs 2 and 3 of LO, strict liability in tort shall be imposed where damage results from (things or) activities representing an increased source of danger for the surroundings. There is no statutory definition of a 'dangerous activity'. An activity may be labelled as dangerous either by the legislator or by the courts. Some dangerous activities simply boil down to the use of a dangerous thing (such as operating

245. Article 154, paras 2 and 3, and Arts 173–177 of LO. N.B. The rules on strict liability for dangerous things and dangerous activities are the same, both situations fall under the same tortious regime.

a motor vehicle). However, both the legislator and the courts accept the possibility of human activity being abnormally dangerous when performed as a reasonable and careful man would, even when it does not involve any dangerous object (diving, skydiving, felling trees, gathering a large group of people in a limited space, extracting gravel from a riverbed, using ladder sling, etc.)

296. The first condition of strict liability for damage caused by performing a dangerous activity is the existence of recoverable damage, be it patrimonial or non-patrimonial. The second condition is causation, and here, the rebuttable statutory presumption of causation applies. The injured party must prove material, physical involvement of an abnormally dangerous activity in the occurrence of damage. Once it is proved that the damage at issue occurred in connection to an activity which is a source of an increased, abnormal, atypical risk of damage to surroundings, the court shall rebuttably presume that it was *a causal* connection. In other words, the court will take that the damage which arose in connection to a dangerous activity was produced by this very activity. From then on, it will be up to the defendant to show that, irrespective of the fact that damage occurred in connection to his dangerous activity, the true cause of damage was some external event that amounts to force majeure.

297. The central question is whether a service rendered by a potentially liable party meets the criteria of a 'dangerous activity'. As early as 1948, the highest court of Yugoslavia held:[246]

> A legal rule has been adopted in the practice of the courts, that businesses, associations and persons, whose activity generates an increased danger of damage to their surroundings, shall be liable for the so caused damage, unless they prove that the damage at issue resulted from force majeure, or fault of the injured party.

This rule was very strict, in fact. Today, the liable party shall be excused from liability for damages caused by dangerous activity under condition of proving force majeure, or the fact that the damage was caused by the unforeseeable and inexorable actions of either the injured party or a third party.[247] It is not required to prove fault of either of them.

298. As previously elaborated, a 'dangerous activity' is a human activity which generates an abnormal, atypical, elevated risk of damage to others, when carried out in a legitimately expected manner, that is, in a way a hypothetical reasonable and careful man would perform it under the given circumstances. This may be, but does not have to be, a business activity, in a sense of an aggregate economic activity of the liable party. It may also be, but does not have to be, a regulated profession. For the purposes of establishing strict liability for dangerous activities, an 'activity' may

246. Supreme Court of FNRJ, Gz. 25/1948 of 31 May 1948, in M. Konstantinović, *Beleške s predavanja* (Beograd, 1969), 134.
247. Article 177 of LO.

be any human pursuit or engagement which is recognized in society as a coherent and rounded human effort. If the activity in question is such that a reasonable and careful man would not engage in it, unless he is specially educated and trained for it, then the activity qualifies as 'dangerous' if it generates an abnormal, atypical, elevated risk of damage to others when performed in a way a hypothetical reasonable and careful professional (expert) would, under the given circumstances.

299. In addition to what was already said, a juridical person providing services of general (economic) interest, such as postal services, energy supply, telecommunications or public transport, shall be liable for damage if they cease to perform, or irregularly perform their activity for no justified reason (Article 184 of LO). The courts understand the excuses for this type of liability in a very narrow and restrictive manner. This is a type of extra-contractual liability, strict in nature, as the courts accept only those excuses or justifications from the providers that amount to force majeure.[248]

248. For instance, electric company remains liable for suspended delivery of electricity even if it proves that the power lines were cut-off by a third party. The same goes for the water supply companies. Comm LO Per, 425.

Chapter 4. Environmental Liability

300. Environmental rights enjoy constitutional protection in Serbia. Under Article 74 of CRS of 2006, everyone shall have the right to a healthy environment and the right to timely and full information about the state of the environment; everyone, and especially the Republic of Serbia and its autonomous provinces, shall be accountable for the protection of the environment; everyone shall be obliged to preserve and improve the environment. These provisions guarantee a right to a healthy environment and a right to be informed about the state of the environment; standardize, in the most general way, the behaviour of all natural persons and legal entities with regards to the environment; and prescribe, at the level of principle, a positive obligation to protect the environment.

301. The LEP of 2004 (LEP, last changes in 2018) regulates the integral system of environmental protection, with the purpose of ensuring human rights to life and development in a healthy environment and establishing balance between economic growth and environmental protection.[249] In other words, the exercise of the constitutional right of every person to a healthy environment is not the only purpose of an integrated system of environmental protection. The second objective of this system is reflected in balancing the two often opposing interests: economic development of the country, and the preservation of a healthy environment. A certain level of environmental pollution in modern conditions is considered to be a necessary concession to economic development.

302. Natural and legal persons have a fundamental constitutional obligation, and more specific statutory duties regarding the prevention and improvement of the environment, as well as statutory obligations to reduce and redress the pollution which occurs. A single episode of environmental pollution may qualify as a criminal act, an economic offence or a misdemeanour, it may give rise to civil obligation to compensate for the damage caused by pollution, and to a series of public law duties to mitigate and repair the pollution.

303. Environmental pollution happens when either human activities, or natural processes, introduce pollutants or energy into the environment, which has or may have adverse effects towards the quality of the environment and human health. LEP defines a 'polluter' as either a legal or natural entity that is polluting the environment by his actions or omissions,[250] and 'pollutants' as substances whose discharge into the environment affects or may affect the environment's natural composition,

249. Article 1 of LEP. In detail, M. Karanikić Mirić, 'Odgovornost za zagađivanje životne sredine', *PZ* 9/2007, 455–479.

250. A polluter whose facility, plant, installations or activities generate high risk of environmental damage, shall be obliged to take out insurance against liability towards the third parties. Art. 106 of LEP.

properties and integrity. 'Risk' is defined as a certain level of probability that an activity will directly or indirectly cause adverse effects on the environment, life and human health.[251]

304. In the course of their activities, both natural persons and legal entities are obliged to ensure environmental protection (personally or through an authorized organization), by means of abiding by the rules and regulations on environmental protection; sustainable use of natural resources, goods and energy; introducing the energy-efficient technologies and use of renewable natural resources; opting for the products, processes, technologies and practices that are less harmful to the environment; taking preventive and restorative measures with respect to threats to the environment or ecological damage; keeping records and informing the authorities on the raw materials and energy consumption, pollutants and energy release, waste, and the like; controlling the facilities, plants and installations which generate or may generate risk to the environment and human health; and other measures prescribed by law.[252]

305. LEP makes a distinction (though sometimes not clearly enough) between the two concepts: 'damage to the environment' or 'environmental damage', on the one hand, and 'damage' in the traditional (tort law) sense, on the other hand. The environmental or ecological damage should be understood as a measurable adverse change in natural resources, where the environment or natural resources in themselves are legally protected goods. A polluter is obliged to reduce the damage to the environment, eliminate further risks of such damage, and restore and regenerate the damaged environment under *the polluter-pays principle*.[253]

However, the pollution of the environment may also result in damage in the tort law sense, i.e., further material or moral damage from the (polluted) environment. The polluter and his legal successor shall be liable for this type of damage as well,[254] if the polluter has contributed to its occurrence by his unlawful or otherwise wrongful or improper conduct. The polluter is obliged to take out insurance against this kind of liability.

Finally, under the principle of subsidiary liability, the state shall eliminate the consequences of environmental pollution and redress the damage, within its financial abilities, when the polluter is unknown, and also when the pollution originates from sources outside the state territory.[255]

306. A polluter shall be strictly liable for environmental damage. If environmental damage occurs, the polluter shall be obliged to undertake all the required preventive and restorative measures, in order to reduce the damage to the environment, eliminate further risks of such damage, and restore and regenerate the damaged environment. Where rehabilitation is not possible, the polluter shall have to

251. Article 3, para. 1 (11), (14), (15) and (23) of LEP.
252. Article 102 of LEP.
253. Article 9, para. 1 (6) of LEP.
254. Under the principle of polluters' and legal successors' liability, Art. 9, para. 1 (5) of LEP.
255. Article 9, para. 1 (8) of LEP.

pay full compensation for the value of the destroyed goods. The polluter cannot evade liability for the environmental damage by proving that he has exercised the highest level of prudence and care: he shall be liable regardless of any fault on his side. The polluter shall bear the costs of evaluation and elimination of the damage to the environment, especially the costs of urgent preventive interventions; direct and indirect costs of rehabilitation of the environment; the costs of monitoring (of rehabilitation and of further damaging effects of the pollution); the costs of prevention of the same or similar environmental damage; and the costs of redress to the injured parties. The polluter is also obliged to ensure financial or other guarantees for payment of these costs.[256]

307. When it comes to liability for material and moral damages from the pollution,[257] LEP reaffirms the injured party's right to damages and further stipulates that the injured party may file a claim for damages (in summary proceedings) against the polluter, and also against the polluter's insurer, or the issuer of the financial guarantee. Where more than one polluter participated in or contributed to the occurrence of damage, and their respective shares in, or contributions to the damage cannot be discerned, they will be jointly and severally liable. A prescription period of three years starts from the day on which the injured party became aware of the damage and the identity of the polluter (the so-called subjective limitation period). In any case, the right to damages shall become unenforceable twenty years after the occurrence of damage (so-called objective limitation period). Under the general rule of Serbian tort law regarding the objective period of limitation for claims in damages, the right to damages expires five years from the manifestation of the damage in question. In contrast, here the objective limitation period is five times longer. The state reserves the right to compensation where there are no other claimants.[258] This provision should be understood as restricted to the aforementioned 'environmental damage' (damage to the environment), and not including 'damage' in the traditional (tort law) sense. For example, this could relate to the measurable adverse change in a natural resource beyond any rehabilitation.

308. Under Article 108 of LEP, the general rules of LO on tortious liability shall apply in the absence of special provisions of LEP. For instance, under Article 156 of LO, any person may demand from another to eliminate a source of danger, where this source threatens to cause considerable damage to him, or to an unspecified number of persons. Along the same lines, each person may demand from another to refrain from an activity which causes disturbance or generates risk of damage, if disturbance or damage cannot be prevented by appropriate measures. Should the keeper of the said source of danger fail to take the appropriate measures for preventing damage or disturbance, or should he fail to eliminate the source of danger in question, the court shall, at the request of the interested party, order the keeper to do so at his own expense. Damage caused by an activity which was performed in public interest and authorized by the public authorities shall be recoverable only if

256. Articles 103–105 of LEP.
257. Article 107 of LEP.
258. Article 107, para. 6 of LEP.

it exceeds the normal scope of damage under the circumstances. The potentially injured party can, however, demand socially justified measures to be taken, in order to prevent or mitigate the impending damage.

Chapter 5. Others

§1. Strict Liabilities under the General Civil Code

309. The 1844 Civil Code of the Kingdom of Serbia was among the oldest European codifications of civil law. It was predominantly based on the model of the Austrian codification of civil law. The Code went out of effect in 1946. However, the courts were left with the possibility of using the rules originating from the pre-WWII laws, if there was no applicable law for a given case, and if the old rule did not contradict the values of the new constitutional order. Still, the rules on strict liability for dangerous things and dangerous activities were not included in the codification, so the possibility of invoking the pre-WWII rules could not have been used as a mechanism for introducing strict liability into the post-WWII legal system. So, as previously elaborated, in the period after WWII, the courts in Yugoslavia slowly developed a general norm on liability regardless of fault, for both material and moral damage coming from a source of abnormal, atypical, elevated risk of damage to others (*see* paragraphs 238 et seq.).

310. A source of abnormal risk may present itself either as a dangerous thing (under the liable party's guard) or as a dangerous activity (conducted by the liable party). The general norm on strict liability for dangerous objects under one's guard, initially created by the courts, was at one point proposed for codification to the Yugoslav legislator. The proposal was made by professor Mihailo Konstantinović, the author of *Skica* of 1969. One version of the proposed legislative solution found its way to Yugoslav LO of 1978 and is still in force in Serbia. Under Article 154, paragraphs 2 and 3 of LO, where damage results from things or activities representing an increased source of danger for the surroundings, as well as in other cases prescribed by law, liability shall be imposed regardless of the fault. There is no statutory definition of either a dangerous thing or a dangerous activity. Both things and activities (or, to be more precise, *the types of* things and *the types of* activities) may be labelled as dangerous by the legislator, or by the courts.

311. In addition to the general regime of strict liability, LO also establishes 'special regimes' of strict liability, all of which have already been mentioned. The derivative forms of non-contractual strict liability under LO are strict liability of producers for material and moral damage caused by defective products (Article 179, paragraph 1 LO); joint and several strict liability of the proprietors' of motor vehicles involved in a collision, for material and moral damage suffered by third persons (passengers, commuters, pedestrians, bicyclists, etc.) as a result of the collision (Article 178, paragraph 4 LO); strict liability of the state for patrimonial and non-patrimonial damage resulting from death, or bodily injury, or from impairment or destruction of property which belongs to a natural person, where such damage was caused by an act of public violence or terror, or during mass public demonstrations (Article 180 of LO); strict liability of organizers of large gatherings in either enclosed, or open-air spaces, for material and moral damage resulting from death, or bodily injury due to extraordinary circumstances such as disorderly crowd behaviour, general turmoil, etc. (Article 181 of LO); joint strict liability of parents (or adopters) for damage caused to another by their child, if the child in question was under 7 years of age and under the care and supervision of his parents at the time of damaging event (Article 165, paragraphs 1 and 2 of LO); strict liability of an employer for damage caused by an employee to a third party in the course of work or in connection to the work (Articles 170 and 171 of LO).

§2. Other Strict Liabilities for Dangerous Activities

312. According to the LRNSS of 2018 (LRNSS, last changes in 2019), legal persons and entrepreneurs licenced to engage in nuclear activity shall be strictly liable, i.e., liable irrespective of their fault, for nuclear damage caused by 'nuclear emergency event' that may arise as a result of an extraordinary or unexpected happening, human error, equipment failure and other irregularities, including malicious acts. 'Nuclear activities' are phases of a lifetime of nuclear facility, namely: siting, design, construction, trial run, commissioning, operation, decommissioning or closure of nuclear facilities, and remediation of their sites.[259]

313. Serbia has ratified the Vienna Convention on Civil Liability for Nuclear Damage of 1963. Under the Convention, liability of the operators of the nuclear installations for nuclear damage is absolute, i.e., the operator is held liable irrespective of fault. The LRVC was passed in 1977. Under Article 16 of CRS, generally accepted rules of international law and ratified international treaties form an integral part of the national legal system and shall apply directly. However, LRNSS contains some additional rules on liability for damage caused in a nuclear accident.[260] It prescribes that holder of a licence to carry out nuclear activity shall be liable for nuclear damage caused by a nuclear emergency in accordance with LRVC and LRNSS, based on evidence that such damage was caused in the licence holder's nuclear facility. It remains for the courts to resolve the relationship between the two pieces of legislation, having in mind that LRNSS restricts, in certain aspects and to a certain extent, the protection guaranteed under LRVC and the Convention.[261]

314. Under the provisions of LRNSS, the licence holder's liability in tort shall be limited to the amount of USD 5 million for each nuclear accident, exclusive of the interest and the costs awarded by the court in disputes on compensation for nuclear damage. The licence holder shall also be liable for nuclear damage caused by the nuclear material that was stolen, lost, discarded from a ship, or abandoned if he was the last one to have control over that material. The holder of a licence to carry out nuclear activities must acquire and maintain liability insurance for nuclear damage (another financial security is not mentioned). The insurer may suspend or

259. Nuclear activities may also include import, export, use, transport and exploitation of ores, radioactive waste management, etc.
260. Article 5 and Arts 207–210 of LRNSS.
261. Under LRVC and the Convention, the state shall ensure the payment of claims for compensation by providing the necessary funds to the extent that the yield of insurance or other financial security is inadequate to satisfy such claims. There is no such provision in LRNSS.

cancel the insurance only if he has duly notified the holder of the licence for carrying out nuclear activities (in writing and at least six months in advance). The right to compensation for nuclear damage shall be extinguished if an action is not brought within ten years from the date of the nuclear incident. If nuclear damage was caused by the nuclear material that was stolen, lost, discarded from a ship, or abandoned, the right to compensation shall be extinguished if an action is not brought within twenty years from the date of theft, loss, discarding or abandonment of nuclear material. Within the aforesaid objective time limits, the action for compensation of nuclear damage may be brought within three years from the day the injured party has learned or should have learned about the nuclear damage and the identity of the licence holder. The decision on nuclear damages shall be subject to the territorial jurisdiction of the court that the nuclear facility belongs to, and if nuclear damage occurs during transport of nuclear material, it shall be subject to the territorial jurisdiction of the court where the nuclear emergency event occurred. All persons entitled to nuclear damages in accordance with the Vienna Convention on Civil Liability for Nuclear Damage and the LRNSS can lodge their claims against the licence holder or directly against the insurer or any other person providing financial resources for the nuclear damage compensation.

315. Serbia has signed the Convention concerning International Carriage by Rail (COTIF) without reservations and with all its appendices and has passed the laws on their ratifications. The rules on liability for damage in the LCTR of 2015 (LCTR, last changes in 2021) follow, to some extent, the lines of Uniform Rules concerning the Contract of International Carriage of Passengers by Rail (CIV – Appendix A to the Convention). Under LCTR, the carrier shall be liable for damage resulting from the death of, bodily injury to, or impairment of health of a passenger, caused by an accident arising out of the operation of the railway and happening while the passenger is in, entering or alighting from railway vehicles, as well as for the damage resulting from cancellation or the late running of a train which may be attributed to the carrier.[262]

316. The carrier shall be partially or completely relieved of this liability: if the accident has been caused by circumstances not connected with the operation of the railway and which the carrier, in spite of having taken the care required in the particular circumstances of the case, could not avoid and the consequences of which he was unable to prevent, if the accident is due to the fault of the passenger, if the accident is due to the behaviour of a third party which the carrier, in spite of having taken the care required in the particular circumstances of the case, could not avoid and the consequences of which he was unable to prevent.

317. The carrier shall be liable for damage caused to a passenger by the carrier's employees and other persons on whose services the carrier relies, including the operator of the railway infrastructure. Furthermore, the carrier shall be liable to the

262. Articles 18–22 of LCTR. As of 2021, Art. 22a of LCTR stipulates that the provisions of Parts II-VII of the Uniform Rules (CIV – Appendix A to COTIF), with subsequent ratified amendments, shall apply to the issues that are not regulated by LCTR.

passenger for loss or damage resulting from the fact that, by reason of cancellation, the late running of a train or a missed connection, his journey cannot be continued on the same day. The damages shall comprise the reasonable costs of accommodation as well as the reasonable costs occasioned by having to notify persons expecting the passenger.

318. The carrier shall be relieved of this liability, when the cancellation, late running or missed connection is attributable to one of the following causes: circumstances not connected with the operation of the railway which the carrier, in spite of having taken the care required in the particular circumstances of the case, could not avoid and the consequences of which he was unable to prevent, fault on the part of the passenger, the behaviour of a third party which the carrier, in spite of having taken the care required in the particular circumstances of the case, could not avoid and the consequences of which he was unable to prevent. Another undertaking using the same railway infrastructure shall not be considered a third party.

319. When this service has been provided by more than one carrier, they shall be jointly and severally liable, unless it can be clearly and unquestionably determined which one of them has caused the damage in question. The upper limit of the carrier's liability for damage resulting from the death of, bodily injury to, or impairment of health of a passenger caused by an accident arising out of the operation of the railway, is set at EUR 175,000 (in RSD, at the middle exchange rate of the NBS, on the day of payment).

320. LCTR does not state this limit relates to the upper limit of the carrier's liability *per passenger*. The upper limit of the carrier's liability for the damage resulting from cancellation or the discontinuation of a train which may be attributed to the carrier is set at the amount of the paid costs of transportation Even if the railway undertaking contests its responsibility for physical injury to a passenger whom it conveys, it shall make every reasonable effort to assist a passenger in claiming compensation for damage from third parties.[263]

321. Under Article 26, paragraph 1 of the Law on Obligations and the Basics of Property Relations in Air Transport of 2011 (LOPAT, last changes in 2015),[264] the air carriers' liability shall be governed by LOPAT and by the Montreal Convention for the Unification of Certain Rules for International Carriage by Air of 1999, which was ratified by the National Assembly of Serbia in 2009. The same rules apply in respect of carriage by air within the airspace of the Republic of Serbia. The carrier is liable for damage sustained in case of death or bodily injury of a passenger. If the carrier proves that the damage was caused or contributed to by the negligence or other wrongful act or omission of the injured party, or the person from whom the

263. The rule on contestation of liability is obviously based on the wording of Art. 14 of Regulation (EC) No. 1371/2007 on rail passengers' rights and obligations.

264. Regulation (EC) No. 261/2004 on compensation and assistance to passengers in the event of denied boarding and of cancellation or long delay of flights is adjusted to Serbian law and to a large extent incorporated in LOPAT.

injured party derives her rights, the carrier shall be wholly or partly exonerated from liability to the extent the said negligence or wrongful act or omission caused or contributed to the damage. When by reason of death or injury of a passenger compensation is claimed by a person other than the passenger, the carrier shall be wholly or partly exonerated from liability to the extent that he proves that the damage was caused or contributed to by the negligence or other wrongful act or omission of the passenger in question.[265]

265. Article 26, paras 2 and 3 of LOPAT. Art. 27, para. 1 of LOPAT refers to the Montreal Convention with respect to the carriers' liability for damage to baggage.

Part IV. Defences and Exception Clauses

322. There are different means of limiting liability in Serbian tort law, that is, various instruments which in some way reduce or exclude the tortfeasor's liability, despite the fact that the general conditions of his liability are met. For instance, where the prescription period has lapsed, the tortfeasor shall be excused from liability if he invokes provisions on prescription, even though the prerequisites of his fault-based liability (damage, causation and fault) are satisfied.

323. There is a range of instruments for limiting liability. They may be set up by the statutes (like prescription, necessity, self-help, self-defence, contributory negligence, etc.), or created by the will of the parties (consent, exemption clauses). Besides, the fundamental concepts of tort law, like responsibility, fault, causation, reasonableness and the rest, are socially construed and have movable limits. The ways in which the courts shape, understand, use or change these concepts, may also be regarded as instances of limitation (or expansion) of tortious liability. However, this is outside the scope of this study.

324. The justifications for different means of limiting liability are diverse. For instance, contributory negligence and self-defence consider the fact that the victim has played a factor in his own injury, prescription periods are intended to control the length of the proceedings and to sanction a creditor holding a passive attitude regarding his own claim. Some of the mechanisms of keeping tortious liability within reasonable limits are used as tools for fine corrections of the effects of the principle of full compensation (Article 190 of LO), with a view to ensuring the fair balance of interests of the parties concerned, as admittedly the principle of full compensation fails to produce fair and reasonable results in some cases. For instance, depending on the conditions of the case, the courts may take into account that the tortfeasor is deprived of the financial means necessary for his own maintenance. Or, the fact that the tortfeasor has acted in the sole interest of the injured party may also be relevant. The purpose of these mechanisms is to make certain that, taking all circumstances into account, liability is not unjustifiably burdensome for the tortfeasor. However, the issue of *what is justified* with respect to the limits of liability is one of the hardest questions of tort law.

Chapter 1. Limitation of Action (Suspension and Interruption)

325. 'Extinctive' prescription generally stands for a limitation period after which the creditor's claim can no longer be enforced by legal action. Namely, where the creditor has had a fair chance to pursue his claim, but he remained passive, such behaviour indicates his indifference towards his own right, or at least that he does not mind prolonging the uncertainty. The debtor may rightfully read this passivity as if the creditor has given up his claim. Also, it is in the public interest to prevent prolonged litigation and to terminate the uncertainty arising from creditors' indifference to their own matters.

326. In Serbian law, prescription is considered to be a matter of substantive law, that is, prescription is not procedural in its nature. After the expiry of the period of prescription, the debtor shall be entitled to refuse performance.[266] Yet, the creditor's claim as such shall not be extinguished. In other words, the creditor's claim shall become unenforceable, but the debtor's payment shall remain unrecoverable. If the debtor makes an 'erroneous' payment, in the sense that he pays his debt after the expiration of the prescription period, no claim for restitution shall be available to him, as the payment he made was actually his *obligatio naturalis*. The court may not consider the prescription time-limits of its own accord. Where the debtor has failed to invoke prescription, the courts may not consider the fact that the period of prescription has expired,[267] nor they may advise any of the parties on this issue. In other words, the debtor must invoke the expiry of the prescription period, as the courts cannot take this fact into account ex officio. Periods of prescription are set by statutes, and they cannot be modified by agreement in Serbian law, that is, the parties may not agree on shorter or longer prescription periods than the ones prescribed by statute. The same goes for suspension: the parties may not agree to temporarily suspend the period of prescription.[268]

327. A period of prescription generally starts to run from the first day after the day the creditor was entitled to seek performance. In case of a negative obligation (an obligation to abstain from what the debtor would otherwise have a right to) the period of prescription runs from the first day after the day the debtor breached the obligation in question. The claim shall become unenforceable after the last day of the prescription period, i.e., following the ending of the period specified by statute during which the creditor was entitled to request performance. The prescription period includes the time which has run in favour of the debtor's predecessors.

328. The debtor may not renounce the prescription in advance, that is, before the prescription period expires: the time limits may not be waived in advance. Where after expiry of the period of prescription the debtor acknowledges the creditor's claim in writing, gives an object as a pledge to the creditor, or provides another

266. The same goes for accessory rights: When the principal claim becomes time-barred, so too do all claims for interest and other accessory claims. Art. 369 of LO.
267. Article 360, para. 3 of LO.
268. Article 364 of LO.

security for the payment of his debt, it shall be considered that the debtor has renounced the prescription. Payment of an expired debt may not give rise to *condictio indebiti*: the debtor does not have the right to recover what he paid, even if he was not aware that he could invoke a prescription. The rules on extinctive prescription shall not apply where the cut-off periods, which extinguish the right to claim, are prescribed by statute, that is, where the statute sets up a time limit for filing a claim or undertaking a specific action, under the threat of losing the right to do so.[269]

329. All claims shall become time-barred (i.e., unenforceable due to lapse of time) if ten years have passed since their maturity unless otherwise provided by law.[270] And, LO provides differently for the claims for damages brought on grounds of the general rules of tortious liability.[271] There are two periods of prescription concerning the injured party's right to damages.

330. *First of all*, a claim for damages shall become time-barred (i.e., unenforceable due to lapse of time), if three years have passed since the injured party learned of the damage and the tortfeasor's identity. The injured party is deemed to have 'learned of the damage', only when they become aware of the final extent of the overall damage. Therefore, the three-year prescription period cannot start running before the end of medical treatment.[272]

331. To offer some further explanation: a period of prescription for the right to seek compensation for non-patrimonial damage in cases of personal injury starts running separately for different types of damage, and for each of them this would be from the day after the damage of a certain type has taken its full and final form. For the physical pain or fear this shall be the day after the pain or fear ends, and for the psychological pain due to impairment of life activities the prescription period shall start the day after the medical treatment ends and the injured party realizes the full extent of the impairment.[273]

When it comes to future patrimonial damage, such as loss of earnings or support, or expenses for future care and treatment, the injured party may claim compensation consecutively, that is, in sequence for each period of time that has passed, and the prescription shall run separately for each consecutive claim.[274]

The prescription period for the loss of earnings starts when the loss occurs, i.e., when the injured party's earnings were due, regardless of the time of injury.[275] The other, more convincing, opinion is that the prescription period should start running

269. Articles 361–370 of LO.
270. Article 371 of LO.
271. Article 376, paras 1 and 2 of LO. Under para. 3 of the same article: A claim for damages for breach of contract shall become time-barred (i.e., unenforceable due to lapse of time) in the same time as the breached contractual obligation.
272. SCS, Rev. 148/2006 of 22 Mar. 2006, *PLex.*
273. SCS, Rev. 260/2005 of 16 Feb. 2005, *PLex.*
274. Conclusion of the Joint session of the Federal Court, state Supreme Courts and the Supreme Military Court of 25 and 26 Nov. 1986, *Bilten sudske prakse Vrhovnog suda BiH* 4/1986, 40–41.
275. SC of BIH, Pž. 23/1989 of 14 Jul. 1989, *Bilten sudske prakse VS BIH* 4/1989, 71.

from the moment the injured party may seek compensation, and that is from the time of injury, i.e., when the earnings were lost for certain, which may be well before they were due.

A delayed consequence of an injury, which was *foreseeable* at the time of the injury, shall not be regarded as a new injury. Yet, if blindness occurs a long time after the injury to the eye, but as a consequence of this injury which was *unforeseeable* at the time of injury, it shall be regarded as a new injury, so the prescription period shall start to run when the blindness occurs.[276]

332. *Second*, a claim for damages shall become time-barred *in any case* (even if the said three years have not passed yet), if five years have lapsed since the occurrence of damage. However, where the injured party's right to damages is recognized by a court decision with final force and effect, or by a settlement before a court or other competent body, the claim arising from the decision of the court, or from the written settlement, shall expire only after ten years have passed.[277] A direct claim of the injured party against the tortfeasor's insurer shall become time-barred (i.e., unenforceable due to lapse of time) at the same time as the injured party's claim against the tortfeasor.[278]

333. Where damage has been caused by a criminal offence and where a longer period of prescription is provided for criminal prosecution, the claim for damages against the liable party shall become unenforceable when the longer prescription period for criminal prosecution also expires. Interruption and suspension of the prescription period for criminal prosecution shall have an effect on the claim for damages as well.[279] The practice of the courts was extremely uneven for more than a half of century on the matter of whether the prolonged prescription period in case of damage caused by a criminal act runs solely against the tortfeasor, or also against a person vicariously liable for him. The Constitutional Court has recently held that the extended prescription period should run against both the tortfeasor and the vicariously liable person, even if the criminal proceedings against the tortfeasor were discontinued, or the tortfeasor died before the criminal proceedings were initiated, or an amnesty or a pardon were granted to the tortfeasor.[280] Finally, if the criminal prosecution does not expire, then the right to compensation for the damage caused by the commission of that criminal offence does not expire either. For example, criminal prosecution and execution of sentences do not expire for crimes against sexual freedom committed by adult perpetrators against minors (as per

276. SC of BIH, Rev. 233/1986, 30 Jul. 1986, *Bilten sudske prakse VS BIH* 3/1986, 37.
277. Article 379, para. 1 of LO. Under para. 2 of the same article: Still, all periodic claims that have yet to mature and that arise from the said decisions or settlements, shall expire within the time limit set for prescription of periodic claims.
278. Article 380, para. 5 of LO.
279. Article 377 of LO.
280. Opinion of the Constitutional Court of Serbia, Su. I-400/1/3-11 of 14 Jul. 2011, *PLex*. In detail: M. Karanikić Mirić, 'Zastarelost potraživanja naknade štete prouzrokovane krivičnim delom', *A PFB* 1/2011, 178–204. The Supreme Court held that the extended period of prescription (in case of liability for damage caused by a criminal offence) applies to the insurer as well. SCS, Rev. 1335/05 of 30 Nov. 2005, *PLex*.

Article 5 of the Law on Special Measures for Preventing the Commission of Sex Crimes against Minors of 2013). In such cases, the claim for damages does not expire as well, both against the perpetrator of the crime, and against the person who may be vicariously liable for damage caused by that perpetrator.

334. In the product liability context, a prescription period of three years applies to the injured party's right to damages, starting from the day on which the injured party became aware of the damage, the defect, and the identity of the producer. In any case, the right to damages shall become unenforceable ten years after the date the product was put into circulation.[281] Apparently, the injured party benefits from a two times longer objective limitation period in the product liability context. Namely, under the general rule on prescription of claims for damages (Article 376, paragraph 2 of LO), a claim for damages shall become time-barred in any case, if five years have lapsed since the occurrence of damage. However, the prolonged objective prescription period under LCP starts running when the product is put in circulation, whereas the five-years-objective prescription period under LO does not start before the damage manifests itself completely. This means that in some cases of latent damage, where the period of time between the release of the product and the occurrence of damage may be very long, the rules of LO may be more favourable to the consumer.

335. Suspension. The prescription period does not commence and, if it has begun, is suspended in respect of the claims between spouses, for the duration of the marriage; children and their parents, for the duration of parental custody; cohabitants[282] for the duration of their cohabitation; guardians, wards and guardianship authorities, for the duration of guardianship and until the accounts are passed. The same applies to claims of an employee against his employer (and against the members of the employer's family) with whom the employee shares a household, for the duration of the employment relationship; claims of persons in military service at the time of mobilization, imminent danger of war, or war. Also, the prescription period does not run for as long as the claim cannot be brought before the court due to insurmountable obstacles.

The prescription period begins or resumes when the cause for its suspension ceases to exist. If the prescription period has been running before the period of suspension, the time which has lapsed prior to suspension shall be counted in the total prescription period.[283] The prescription shall run against incompetent creditors, that is, against minors and other persons lacking capacity to enter into legally binding relations.[284] However, where a creditor lacks legal competence, and where he also lacks legal representation, the period of prescription shall only commence two years

281. Article 63 of LCP. N.B. Serbian LCP erroneously stipulates the ten year statute of limitation, while the corresponding Product Liability Directive sets the ten year cut-off period for complete extinguishment of the injured party's right to compensation.
282. Unmarried couples who live together on a long-term or permanent basis without formally registering their relation as a marriage.
283. Articles 381–384 of LO.
284. Here we distinguish legal personhood and legal competence.

after he gains full legal competence (e.g., in case of minors as creditors, two years after their age of majority), or two years after he gets legal representation.[285]

336. Interruption. Running of the prescription period shall be interrupted if the debtor acknowledges the claim, either by an outright statement to the creditor or indirectly (for instance, by making a partial payment, paying the interest on debt, giving an item in pledge or providing surety). The prescription period shall also be interrupted if the creditor files a claim against the debtor, or if he undertakes any other action before a court or other competent authority with a view to ascertain, secure or enforce his right against the debtor. However, should the creditor file a withdrawal of such claim or action, or should the proceedings initiated by the creditor be discontinued, dismissed or rejected, there will be no interruption of the prescription period.[286] The prescription period may not be interrupted by a mere creditor's request for payment addressed to the debtor, be it spoken or in writing.[287]

A new prescription period commences as of the date of the interruption, that is, when the debtor acknowledges the claim, or, where the prescription period was interrupted by way of initiating certain proceedings, when the proceedings in question end. The time that lapsed prior to the interruption shall not count. The new prescription period shall last as long as the interrupted period should have lasted, was it not for the interruption. However, where the initial prescription period is interrupted by the debtor's acknowledgement, and the parties have agreed on novation (i.e., replacing an obligation to perform with a new obligation), the length of the new prescription period shall be the one that is prescribed by statute for the new obligation.[288]

337. A waiver of prescription by one of the jointly and severally liable debtors may not be invoked against other debtors. Where the prescription period is interrupted, or it does not run for one of the jointly and severally liable debtors, it continues to run for others. However, the debtor who did not benefit from the expiry of the prescription period and who has paid the debt shall be entitled to recourse against other jointly and severally liable debtors whose obligations were time-barred. (Article 422 of LO).

And, when obligation is solidary for the creditors, that is, when it gives each creditor the right to demand the whole performance from the common debtor, all creditors shall benefit from the debtor's waiver of prescription directed to one of

285. Article 385, paras 1 and 2 of LO. Under para. 3 of the same article: Where the prescription period is shorter than two years, it shall start running when the creditor gains full legal competence, or when he gets legal representation. Also, under Art. 386 of LO, if the creditor is summoned for military training, the prescription period against him starts running three months after the end of the training.

286. Articles 387–389 of LO. Also, under Art. 390, para. 1 of LO, where the proceedings have been dismissed due to lack of competence of the court, or for some other reason with no bearing on the essence of the dispute, and if the creditor files a new claim within three months from the dismissal, it shall be deemed that the prescription period was interrupted when the claim was filed for the first time.

287. Article 391 of LO.

288. Articles 392 and 393 of LO.

them. However, if one of the creditors interrupts the prescription period, or if prescription does not run against him, other creditors shall not benefit from it, i.e., the prescription periods running against them shall not be affected (Article 433 of LO).

Chapter 2. Grounds of Justification

§1. Consent

338. Under the rules of Serbian tort law, a person who has allowed, to his own detriment, another person to take a certain action, i.e., to behave in a certain manner, shall not be entitled to compensation for damage caused by such action. However, if the injuring conduct of another person, to which the injured party has consented, is prohibited by law, the injured party's statement of consent shall be null and void.[289]

Consent may be either express or implied, and it may exclude the tortfeasor's liability (regardless of whether it is fault-based or strict) under several requirements: the general conditions for validity of unilateral declarations of will must be met; the injured party must be aware of the risk of damage; and the infringed good must be of a type that is at the injured party's disposal; the consent to the infringement in question must be clearly within the limits of public order (*ordre public*).

339. Consent may justify a medical intervention or other socially acceptable activities that generate risk of damage to a person's body or health, such as hitchhiking or participating in competitive sports.[290] The injured party's consent may also justify actions causing damage to that person's property, or pain and suffering due to infringement of the person's reputation, honour, freedom or personal rights. In recent years, the courts also consider the consent of the injured party in the fields of contractual liability and employment relations.[291]

340. The injured party's consent must be given in advance, that is, prior to the damaging event. Once the injuring conduct has resulted in damage, the obligation of the tortfeasor has arisen. The remission of the injurer's debt (his release from the obligation to redress the damage) cannot occur one-sidedly, that is, by the creditor's unilateral statement. Namely, remission or cancellation of debt is a type of contract in Serbian law, meaning that a debtor cannot be released from his obligations unless he agrees to it.[292]

The consent of the injured party is a form of voluntary limitation of liability of another person, which may take place solely in the context of another, pre-existing legally relevant relationship between the two (the potentially injured party and the potential injurer).

289. Article 163 of LO. *Volenti non fit injuria.*
290. Comm LO BK, 588–589.
291. SCS, Rev. 5310/2002 of 16 Jun. 2003, SCS, Rev. 6380/1998 of 3 Dec. 1998, SCS, Rev. II 1039/2004 of 23 Feb. 2005, *PLex.*
292. Article 344, para. 1 of LO: An obligation shall be terminated when the creditor states to the debtor that he will not demand performance, and the debtor agrees to it.

§2. NECESSITY

341. Under Article 161, paragraph 2 of LO, where damage is caused in the state of necessity, the injured party (i.e., a third person who was injured in the event of averting the approaching damage) is entitled to seek compensation from the person who is at fault for the state of necessity, that is, from the one who has wrongfully created the danger. If the impending damage was averted from someone, the injured party may seek compensation from them as well. In such cases, the amount of compensation awarded may not exceed the benefits the persons from whom the impending damage was diverted accrued from this event. Under Article 161, paragraph 3, the rescuer may seek compensation for the damage he suffered in an effort to avert the impending harm from another, provided that he reasonably exposed himself to this type of damage (i.e., provided that it was reasonable to subject oneself to the risk of such damage under the circumstances).

342. These are the situations where one person (the 'rescuer') has taken measures to protect himself or others from imminent danger, that is, from the impending harm to property, life, body, health, etc. In the course of this action, the rescuer has sustained damage or has caused damage to another. The rescuer may be excused from liability, under the conditions that (1) the impending harm could not have been avoided in any other way than by the damaging conduct in question; and that (2) the damage he has caused is still smaller or less significant than the damage which was averted. In other words, a tortfeasor shall be excused from liability if he proves that he has caused damage in a state of emergency, with a view of escaping an imminent danger of an even more serious and significant forthcoming damage to self or others.[293]

343. Liability shall lie with the person who has created the hazard, or the risk of damage, that is, with the one who is at fault for the state of necessity. This person shall be liable for damages originating from the attempts to overcome the state of necessity and suffered by the rescuer, or by the persons in need of rescue. In addition, if the persons from whom damage was averted profited in some way from the incident at hand, they may be liable for the damage suffered by another, but only to the extent of their benefits. Finally, the rescuer may seek compensation from them as well, but only for the damage he has reasonably exposed himself to, as he was averting damage from them.

§3. SELF-HELP AND SELF-DEFENCE

344. Under Article 161, paragraph 1 of LO, a person who was acting in self-defence shall not be liable to pay compensation for loss or damage caused to the

293. For instance, the tortfeasor was found liable for killing the injured party's dog. The necessity defence was rejected, as the dog in question was not threatening and did not pose imminent danger to others. Decision of District Court in Valjevo, Gž. 170/2006 of 27 Jan. 2006, *PLex*.

person or property of the aggressor, unless the measures of self-defence were excessive. To act in self-defence means to act with the purpose of countering an ongoing or imminently ensuing unlawful attack on self or others, by using necessary and proportionate countermeasures against the aggressor. The measures of self-defence must be assumed simultaneously with the illicit attack, i.e., against the unlawful aggression that is under way, or imminently about to happen. Also, the countermeasures must be proportionate and reasonable under the given circumstances, that is, sufficient to avert the impending injury to self or others.[294] Excessive self-defence shall not serve as a ground for justification. The same goes for the beforehand self-defence and after-the-event self-defence.

345. A countermeasure is not proportionate, for instance, if someone punches a person smoking in a non-smoking wagon, or if he kills a person attacking his property. However, it would be an instance of self-defence if the defender kills an attacker trying to rob him of a wristwatch, as this is also an assault on the defender's person.[295] Self-defence may only be invoked against the aggressor. In other words, the defender shall not be liable to the attacker for the damage inflicted on him by acting in legitimate self-defence, but he may not be excused from tortious liability to third persons on the grounds of legitimate self-defence against the attacker.

346. Under Article 162, paragraphs 1 and 2 of LO, a person who resorts to the permitted self-help, and thereby causes damage to the person who has created the need for self-help, shall not be liable to redress it. Permitted self-help refers to the right of every person to eliminate the infringement, or to ward off an impending violation of his right, should such protection be necessary, and should the way in which the person defends against the infringement correspond to the circumstances of the emerging danger.

347. Generally speaking, self-help is not allowed. A person whose legally protected interests have been infringed is obliged to bring his case before a court or other competent authority, that is, to submit his complaint to the legal authorities in charge, and to try to protect and enforce his rights in proper legal proceedings. Therefore, self-help is only permitted where it is not possible to address the competent legal authority and request and obtain legal protection in due time, and it may last only for the time the assistance of the authorities is unavailable.[296]

294. The defender's countermeasure was adequate, since he merely pushed the attacker who had punched him in the face. The case that the attacker fell on a wire fence and suffered injuries was a matter of the environment in which the attack took place, and which the defender did not choose. SCS, Rev. 1797/2002/1 of 9 May 2002, *PLex*.

295. J. Radišić, *Obligaciono pravo* (Beograd, 2004), 226–227. Radišić adds there can be no legitimate self-defence if the defender has wrongfully provoked the aggression, that is, if he is at fault for the attack.

296. Moreover, no one can profit from failing to protect their own rights. Thus, the owner who never asked for an item of property to be handed over to him by a person who was keeping and using it

348. Under Article 286, paragraph 1 of LO, a creditor of a claim that has fallen due, who is in possession of an item of the debtor's movable property, shall have the right to retain this item in his possession, until his claim is paid off. The courts consider this to be an instance of permitted self-help, therefore, the creditor who resorts to retain the debtor's item of the property until his claims are paid off, shall not be under obligation to compensate for the damage caused thereby.[297]

§4. Others

349. The instruments of keeping tortuous liability within reasonable limits are numerous and hard to classify. Some of these mechanisms of limiting or excluding liability of the tortfeasor are set up by the legislator, others may be used by the courts, or agreed upon by the parties. In addition to the already-mentioned categories of statutory, judicial and voluntary limitations of liability, and limitations in time, there are limitations with respect to the grounds of liability (e.g., under Article 171, paragraph 2 of LO, an injured party shall have a direct claim for damages against an employee-tortfeasor, if he proves the employee's intent: negligence, which is normally sufficient, is not enough); limitations concerning the identities of injured party and tortfeasor (e.g., under Article 180 of LO, the state is strictly liable to *natural* persons for damage caused by public acts of violence, the producer's liability under LCP is restricted to *natural* persons as injured parties); limitations regarding the heads of damages (e.g., under Article 181 of LO strict liability of event organizers in cases of disorderly crowd behaviour, general turmoil and the like, is restricted to the damage resulting from death or bodily injury), as well as those in respect of the amounts of compensation (cases where the courts, in determining the amount of compensation, consider the values of the property of the injurer and of the injured party, e.g., Article 169 LO), and some special instances of the exclusion of liability, including the situations where the breach of information duties may lead to the loss of the right to compensation (in the sphere of contractual liability and especially liability for non-conformity).[298]

350. Some authors cite exercise of the public duties, and exercise of one's own rights as grounds for justification, alongside necessity, consent, self-defence and the rest.[299] However, the courts do not follow this line of thought, and they never quote these two excuses outright, the reasoning of the courts is structured differently, they inspect, as they otherwise do, whether the tortfeasor has acted in accordance with the legitimate social expectations (even if the damage occurred in exercising the public duties, or one's own rights).

without grounds, cannot seek compensation for lost profits, if he was in position to protect his own rights, and has failed to do so without a justified reason. Decision of the Commercial Appellate Court, Pž. 6634/2010(1) of 3 Feb. 2011, *PLex*.

297. SCS, Prev. 406/2005 of 23 Nov. 2005, *PLex*.

298. In detail, M. Karanikić Mirić, 'Ograničenja odgovornosti za štetu u srpskom pravu', *APFB* 1/2012, 244–273.

299. J. Radišić, *Obligaciono pravo* (Beograd, 2004), 224 and 229.

Chapter 3. Contributory Fault

351. Under Article 192 of LO, where the injured party has contributed to the occurrence of damage, or caused damage to be higher than it would otherwise be, he shall be entitled only to a proportionally reduced compensation. Where it is not possible to establish how much did the injured party contribute to the harm he suffered, that is, which part of the damage comes from the injured party's action, the court shall award compensation while taking into account the circumstances of each particular case. These rules can be applied by the court irrespective of whether the defendant has pleaded the injured party's contribution as a defence.

The title of this article is 'Divided liability', implicating that the liability is shared or split among the liable party and the victim. This is clearly inadequate, as a person cannot bear tortious liability to self, only to others. Liability in tort is a legal relationship between two parties, it presupposes the existence of another person to whom damage was caused, and to whom compensation is owed.

Article 192 of LO applies to liability for both patrimonial and non-patrimonial losses (as per Article 205 of LO).

352. The contribution of the injured party to the happening of damage, or to its scope or gravity or extent, does not have to be negligent in order to be legally relevant. In other words, the injured party's contribution shall be determined as a matter of causation, and it shall be taken into account irrespective of whether there was any fault on the injured party's side. A person lacking capacity of discernment may contribute to the occurrence of damage, or to the extent of damage caused to him by another, and it such cases the compensation to which the incapacitated injured party is entitled shall be reduced in proportion to his contribution to the harm he suffered.

353. However, the question of causation is inevitably joined up with the question of fault, and with some broader policy considerations. If an erroneous human conduct preceded damage, people will have a tendency to single it out as the cause of the following unwelcome events. And also, human conduct which caused undesirable consequences will be easily categorized as erroneous or mistaken. The courts also bear in mind the qualities of the injured party's conduct when deciding on the percentage of their contribution to the damage in question.[300] SCS stated that in these cases the courts do not determine the injured party's fault, but solely inspect if his actions were unusual, i.e., different from the standard behaviour of other people in situations alike.[301]

300. For example: SCS confirmed the decisions of the lower courts determining that a person who was driving a car slightly above the speed limit and ignored the sign 'Children on the Road', but reacted properly (by promptly hitting the breaks), has contributed 70% to the occurrence of the damage, while the injured children contributed 30% to the incident, as they were *running near the pedestrian crossing and being incautious*. SCS, Rev. 1364/05 of 10 Nov. 2005, *PLex*.

301. SCS, Rev. II 507/2003 of 3 Jul. 2003, *PLex*.

354. When it comes to the general rules of strict liability, as elaborated earlier, the injured party must prove material, physical involvement of an abnormally dangerous thing, or an abnormally dangerous activity in the occurrence of damage. Once this connection has been established, the court shall rebuttably presume that the involvement of the said thing or activity in the damaging event amounts to *causation* (Article 173 of LO). From then onwards, it will be up to the defendant to show that, irrespective of the fact that damage occurred in connection to his dangerous object or activity, the true cause of damage was something else (Article 177 of LO). Among other ways to refute the statutory presumption of causation, the liable party may prove that, even though the damaging event entailed the source of abnormal risk under the liable party's guard, it was the injured party's behaviour that caused, or contributed to the damage in question. The liable party shall be released from liability under the condition of proving that the true cause of damage was the injured party's action, which was unforeseeable to the liable party, and whose consequences the liable party was not able to avoid or eliminate. However, where the injured party has only partially contributed to the damage he suffered, the liable party shall be partially (and proportionally) excused from liability. The existence of fault on the victim's side is not required. The liable party may use the victim's contribution as an excuse even if there was no fault on the victim's side, and even if the victim is lacking capacity of discernment, meaning that she is not capable of being at fault.

355. In case of a collision of two (or more) motor vehicles in motion, and where both sides are at fault, both parties shall be liable for the entire damage, in proportion to the degrees of their respective faults. In other words, the damages of both involved parties are added and then apportioned on the basis of their fault.[302] Where it is not possible to weigh out the shares in damages that should be attributed to each of the parties, the rules on reimbursement proceedings among the multiple tortfeasors shall apply *mutatis mutandis* (Article 208, paragraphs 2 and 3 of LO), meaning that where it is not possible to discern the individual shares (in proportion to the individual faults and the gravity of the consequences of individual actions), the participants shall account for equal shares, unless equity requires otherwise. However, this rule cannot apply if only one of the participants in the car crash was at fault, while the other has only contributed to the extent of damage.[303] There, the general rules of fault-based liability shall apply, and when it comes to one party's contribution to the extent of damage, it shall be determined as a matter of causation.

356. In any case, that is, irrespective of whether tortious liability at issue is fault-based or strict, the compensation the victim is entitled to shall be proportionally reduced if force majeure (an external cause whose effects could not have been foreseen, avoided or eliminated) has contributed to the occurrence of damage.

302. Article 178, para. 2 of LO.
303. Decision of District Court in Valjevo, Gž. 810/2005 of 14 Jul. 2005, *PLex*.

Chapter 4. Exemption Clauses

357. The possibility to extend, limit or exclude one's liability for damage to another may exist only in the context of an older, pre-existing legally relevant relationship between the two parties. Therefore, extension, limitation or exclusion of liability for damage, which is effectuated by an agreement between the potentially liable and the potentially injured party, should be viewed rather as an instrument of contractual then tortious liability. The codified principle of *neminem laedere* (Article 16 of LO: general duty to refrain from actions that may result in damage to others) should be understood as a general rule of behaviour in society, and not as a pre-existing legal obligation of the tortfeasor towards the injured party. Thus, it does not create a context in which the exemption clauses could easily apply.

358. Where there is a contractual or other pre-existing legal relationship between the parties, and one of them causes damage to another by breach of an obligation arising from this relationship, Articles 264 and 265 of LO shall apply: The liability of a debtor for the damage caused by non-performance or late performance may be extended in advance by agreement, so as to cover the cases in which he would otherwise not be liable unless it would be contrary to good faith and fair dealing to invoke such extension. Liability for intention or gross negligence can be neither excluded nor limited in advance by agreement. Where liability for plain negligence is limited or excluded in advance by agreement, the court may, at the request of the interested party, annul the exemption clause, if such clause has resulted from the monopoly position of the debtor, or otherwise from inequality of bargaining powers and imbalance of the parties. A limitation clause, i.e., a clause which places a limit on the amount of compensation that can be claimed for a breach of contract, regardless of the actual loss, shall not be valid if such limit is in obvious disproportion to the damage, as well as in other cases where it contravenes the law. And in any case, where the impossibility of performance is caused by intent or gross negligence of the debtor, the limitation clause shall not apply and the creditor shall be entitled to full redress.

359. The rules on exemption clauses are more stringent in the consumer context. Exemption clauses as such are forbidden to the producers, a producer cannot exclude or limit his strict liability for damage caused by defective products.[304] Furthermore, under the already-mentioned LCP of 2021, and not restricted to the product liability issues: the consumer may not waive the rights guaranteed to him by statute, and a contract term derogating from the statutory provisions to the detriment of the consumer shall be null and void.[305]

304. Article 64 of LCP. The producer may try do so (to no effect) on the packaging, in the contract (if he is also the seller), in the commercial guarantee statement, etc.
305. Article 3, paras 1 and 2 of LCP.

Part V. Causation

360. Damage and causation are considered the two universal and essential conditions of liability in Serbian tort law. Tortious liability cannot be established in the absence of either damage or causal link, irrespective of the grounds of liability. The causation requirement is met if it is determined that the damage in question was occasioned by the defendant's conduct, or by the conduct of a person for whom the defendant is liable under the rules of vicarious liability, or by other cause which may be attributed to the defendant, such as position, use, or the very existence of an abnormally dangerous thing, or engagement in an abnormally dangerous activity.

361. Under the rules of fault-based liability, a person who has caused damage to another shall be liable to redress it, unless he proves absence of fault on his part (Article 154, paragraph 1 of LO). Thus, the injured party must prove that he suffered legally recognized damage and that the damage he suffered occurred as a consequence of the injurer's conduct. Only then will the court rebuttably presume that there was fault on the injurer's side. Under the general rules on strict liability, the injured party must prove the existence of damage, and the fact that damage occurred in connection to a source of an increased, abnormal, atypical risk of damage to surroundings (Article 173 of LO). In other words, the injured party must prove material, physical involvement of an abnormally dangerous thing, or an abnormally dangerous activity in the occurrence of damage. Once the link or the connection is proven, the court shall rebuttably presume that it was *a causal* link or connection, i.e., that the involvement of abnormally dangerous properties of the said thing or the said activity in the damaging event amounts to *causation*. That is to say, the court will take that damage was occasioned by a dangerous thing which participated in the occurrence of damage, or that damage which arose in connection to a dangerous activity was produced by this very activity, and then, it will be up to the defendant to show that, irrespective of the fact that damage occurred in connection to his dangerous object or activity, the true cause of damage was something else.

362. To sum up, under the general rules of fault-based liability, the burden of proof of causation lies with the victim. The court's decision on whether the facts in question are sufficiently proven shall be based on the conscientious and careful assessment of each piece of evidence separately, all the evidence as a whole, and on the results of the entire proceedings (Article 8 of CPA). The court must form a clear conviction that the causal link exists. This conviction shall be formed freely but must be based on the rules of logic and life experience.[306] Under the general rules of strict liability, there is a rebuttable statutory presumption of causation, which will stand if the victim proves the connection between the occurrence of damage, and a source of abnormal risk of damage, which is attributed to the tortfeasor. However, the idea of what it really means in law *to cause a consequence* does not depend on the type of tortious regime in question. The concept of causation will not change depending on the grounds of liability under consideration.

363. To cause means to alter the existing or the expected state or situation. A person shall be liable if he has intervened in the regular course of things and turned the normal sequence of events for the worse. The underlying idea is that of *an agent causing an effect*, in default of another event that is the cause of that very event (and in itself the effect of an earlier cause, and so on). In other words, law presumes that events necessarily have causes, but takes that the chain of causation may have its beginning in the tortfeasor's conduct, without there being a legally relevant cause of the injurious conduct itself. The causes that precede the injuring behaviour (in the chain of causes and effects) shall not be examined. The sole question will be: can it be taken, *for the purposes of establishing the tortfeasor's liability*, that the injury or loss suffered by the injured party was occasioned by the tortfeasor' conduct?

This question is normative, of course, and it is a binary question, as well. The court will never ask an open question of what could have been the cause of certain damage. The question will rather be: can we take the defendant's conduct as the cause of damage, in order to ascertain if he should bear the final patrimonial consequences of the damaging event? The objective of this reasoning is *not* to discover connections between the classes of events, or to verbalize laws of invariable connection between the two types of events, but to apply the existing generalizations to a particular case in order to identify, in a complex factual situation, a condition (among numerous conditions under which damaging event occurred) which deserves to be considered causally related to damage, for the purposes of attribution of liability. The defendant will not be liable if his conduct, though it preceded the occurrence of damage, was not more than a part of the given circumstances or, to put it differently, one of the conditions under which damage arose.

364. As stated before, the question of causation is inevitably joined up with the questions of wrongfulness and fault, and with some broader policy considerations. If an erroneous human conduct preceded damage, people will have the tendency to single it out as the cause of the following undesirable events. Also, human conduct which caused undesirable consequences will be easily categorized as erroneous or mistaken. And even when the defendant's behaviour clearly belongs to the factual setup of the case, the court needs a mechanism for recognizing the consequences for which it would be unreasonable or undesirable to impose liability.

306. Comm CPA Poz, 32.

365. Over the last several decades, Serbian courts have adhered to the concept of 'adequate causation'.[307] The same goes for legal scholarship.[308] The tortfeasor's conduct is considered to be an 'adequate cause' of damage sustained by the injured party, if in the normal course of events, and in accordance with the experience of life, such conduct would adequately, normally, regularly cause the damage in question.

366. This is a generalizing theory, as it derives the status of the injuring conduct as a cause, from the fact that it is of a kind of action believed to be generally causally connected to damage of the kind in question. In other words, one from among a set of conditions of the occurrence of damage is selected as the cause of that damage, because it is of a kind which adequately, normally, regularly leads to damage of the given type. This may include cases where the damaging consequences of the injurious conduct were unforeseeable for the actual tortfeasor.

367. The causal link will not be 'adequate' if the behaviours *like the one in question* usually, typically, normally do not bring about or result in the consequences *as those in question* (i.e., the damage as the one under discussion). The requirements of 'adequate causation' are not met when damage originates from an objectively unforeseeable intervening factor, or, in other words, when the damage in question seems like an absurd, abnormal, atypical consequence of the tortfeasor's activity.

368. However, even under the theory of adequate causation, a causal connection will be denied, if the allegedly injurious conduct does not meet one prior condition: it must pass the 'but-for' test (the '*conditio sine qua non*' test), to begin with. If the damage would have occurred irrespective of the conduct of a person whose liability is under consideration, then there is no causation whatsoever. Only if it is established that but for the allegedly injurious conduct, the injury would not have happened, the next step should be to examine whether this conduct qualifies, under the adequacy theory, as the cause of the given damage.

369. There are also two instances of statutory reliance on the '*conditio sine qua non*' theory of causation, and they both pertain to the field of liability for acts of others. If a minor, who is under the supervision of a tutor, school or other institution, inflicts damage to someone, the person in charge to oversee this minor may be exonerated from liability for the consequences of the acts of the supervised minor, if it is proved that he has exercised supervision in due manner, or that damage would have occurred irrespective of the quality of the supervisor's conduct. The same excuses are available to those in charge of supervising persons lacking capacity of

307. SCS, Rev. 1479/1994 of 13 Apr. 1994, Sudska praksa 6/1995: If the damage results from several conditions, the condition which is typical for the occurrence of such damage shall be considered its cause. Also, for example: SCS, Rev. 514/2012 of 20 Jun. 2012; Decision of Higher Commercial Court in Belgrade, V Pž. 1275/2006 of 1 Jun. 2006; Decision of District Court in Valjevo, Gž. 359/2003 of 20 Feb. 2003; Decision of District Court in Kraljevo, Gž. 724/2003 of 16 Jan. 2004, *PLex*. In detail, M. Karanikić Mirić, *Krivica kao osnov deliktne odgovornosti u građanskom pravu* (Beograd, 2009), 230–256.

308. J. Radišić, *Obligaciono pravo* (Beograd, 2004), 208.

discernment due to mental illness or intellectual disability. The second exonerating reason boils down to the application of the but-for test: would damages of the same type and scope occur but for the supervisor's omission? In other words, if we imagine that the supervisor acted like a reasonable and very careful person in performing his responsibilities, would the damage still come to pass? If the answer to this question is affirmative, then the supervisor's omission may not be taken as the cause of the damaging event.

370. Human conduct can be described alternatively in terms of acts or omissions, and damage may be caused by both. However, the case of causing damage by omission is somewhat specific. According to one view, an omission may qualify as an injuring conduct, only if the liable party was bound by the pre-existing duty to act in a certain way. Such duty may originate from a statute, custom, contract, morals, others' trust, etc.[309] To phrase it more in keeping with the rest of the system of tortious liability in Serbia, which does not count unlawfulness of the injurious conduct among the conditions of liability in tort: If a hypothetical reasonable and very careful man under the given circumstances *would have acted*, then there are legitimate social expectations to act, not to refrain from action. These legitimate expectations run towards the tortfeasor. His omission to act as a reasonable and careful man would under the circumstances give rise to his fault-based liability for the damage caused by omission. The adequacy of the established causal link shall still be required.

371. In the cases of the so-called *multiple tortfeasors*, that is, when more than one person acted as a wrongdoer in a single damaging event, special rules apply. First of all, if the contributions of every tortfeasor to the damage suffered by the victim can be told apart, the tortfeasors' liabilities will be limited to their respective contributions, i.e., each of them will be liable solely for the portion of the total damage which came from the cause that can be attributed to him. Here, the damage in question originated from several sources, and none of them was sufficient to cause the whole damage. Still, the contributions of all of the sources can be differentiated one from another, and thus, the liability of the wrongdoers shall be *several* or *proportionate*.

372. If the multiple tortfeasors acted independently of one another and coincidentally caused damage to the victim, and if their respective shares in, or contributions to, the damage may not be discerned, then they will be jointly and severally liable to the victim (Article 206, paragraph 3 of LO).

373. There are no special statutory provisions concerning the so-called minimal causation, that is, the case when damage was caused by a vast number of tortfeasors, but the contributions of each one of them were minor and insignificant. Here, the general rules of Serbian tort law on multiple tortfeasors shall apply. If their contributions to the whole damage in question may be discerned, their liability should

309. *Ibid.*, 209–210 (based on the writings of Erwin Deutsch).

be proportionate. In contrast, if their contributions are undistinguishable (though each one of those contributions is negligible), the tortfeasors should be liable jointly and severally.

374. Instigators and accomplices, as well as those who have helped the tortfeasor after the fact to escape from being identified, shall be jointly and severally liable with the tortfeasor (Article 206, paragraph 2 of LO). However, it is possible that an instigator causes damage by inducing another to inflict damage upon a third person, while there is no fault on the side of the direct injurer. In such a case, the instigator may be solely liable under the condition that there was fault on his side.

375. Cumulative causation. If more than one person participated in the damaging event, and they together caused damage to the injured party, all of them will be jointly and severally liable to the victim (Article 206, paragraph 1 of LO). This is the case where each and every one of the multiple causes was sufficient to cause the whole damage in question: each of the tortfeasors' conducts alone would have been sufficient to cause the damage at hand. The injured party may recover all the damages from any of the tortfeasors, regardless of their individual share of the liability.[310] If the injured party pursues one tortfeasor and receives compensation, that tortfeasor must then pursue other tortfeasors for a contribution to their share of the liability. Here, it is irrelevant whether the tortfeasors acted in concert, or separately one from another. The theory of adequate causation applies, albeit none of the conducts meets the preceding requirements of the '*conditio sine qua non*' test.

376. Alternative causation. Where there are two or more wrongdoers who are mutually connected in a certain way, and there is no doubt that only one of them could have caused the damage in question, but the person who caused the damage cannot be identified, all of the wrongdoers shall be jointly and severally liable to the victim (Article 206, paragraph 4 of LO). Here, it is clear that the injury suffered by the victim was caused by only one of the persons involved, but it is not possible to ascertain which one. The '*conditio sine qua non*' test is obviously disregarded in these types of cases.

310. Article 208, paras 2 and 3 of LO: When determining individual shares of each of the debtors in the recourse proceedings, the court shall take into account the degree of the debtors' respective faults, and the gravity of the consequences of their respective acts. If it is not possible to discern the individual shares, all jointly and severally liable debtors shall account for equal shares, unless equity requires otherwise.

Part VI. Remedies

Chapter 1. General Principles

377. Under Serbian tort law the regular remedy of an injured party is the full or complete recovery of the losses suffered. The injured party is entitled to full compensation, and nothing but the full compensation, for the legally recognized, i.e., 'recoverable', losses inflicted on him. Consequently, punitive damages are not available under Serbian law. The purpose of compensation is neither to punish the liable party, to better the financial position of the injured party, nor to deter the liable party and others from engaging in certain conduct. The extent of compensation the injured party is entitled to does not depend on the degree of the liable party's fault. Irrespective of the gravity of the tortfeasor's fault, the amount of compensation to which the victim shall have the right shall be the same, and it shall be equal to the loss the victim has suffered. The injured party is entitled to a financial position in which he would have been, was it not for the injuring conduct of the tortfeasor. Hence, while also taking into account the circumstances that have ensued following the occurrence of damage, the court shall award damages in the amount necessary for the recovery of the injured party's financial situation, i.e., the amount necessary in order to place the injured party into the financial position in which he would have been, was it not for the injuring action or omission.[311] The courts and legal doctrine recognize this principle as the general principle of *full* or *integral compensation*: the amount of compensation awarded should put the victim in the position he or she would have been in, had the injuring action not been committed. This includes the recovery of the lost profits.

378. When it comes to the compensation for non-patrimonial harm, the purpose of the remedy is understood differently. The argument is not that the awarded sum of money should compensate for the victim's loss in the moral sphere. It is undisputed that such losses are final, they cannot be recompensed by awarding a sum of money, and the awarded sum is not, and never can be, an equivalent of the suffering the victim has experienced in their intimate personal sphere.

The purpose of the awarded amount is to allow the victim to acquire some source of personal contentment or relief that will alleviate their suffering and ease their definitive loss in the moral sphere. Thus, after finding that the circumstances of the case at hand, and particularly the duration and the intensity of the pain and fear sustained by the injured party, justify such a decision, the court shall award equitable

311. Article 190 of LO.

monetary compensation to the injured party, irrespective of compensation for patrimonial damage, and in the absence of any patrimonial harm. In deciding on the merits of the claim, and on the amount of equitable compensation for non-patrimonial damage in question, the court shall take into account the importance of the violated non-patrimonial interests, the purpose of the equitable compensation for non-patrimonial losses, and also make sure the awarded equitable amount does not favour the goals which are otherwise incompatible with its nature and social purpose.[312]

The courts and legal doctrine understand the purpose of awarding equitable compensation for non-patrimonial damage to be *satisfaction*, i.e., reinstatement of the injured party's moral and psychological equilibrium.

379. As a matter of principle, the recovery of the losses suffered is awarded *in natura*: the courts shall order *compensation in kind*, that is, in goods or services as opposed to money. The liable party shall be instructed to make a loss good by returning the same or identical item to the victim instead of paying damages.

Under Article 185 of LO, the regular remedy shall be a 'return to the former state' so the liable party must re-establish the situation which existed prior to the occurrence of damage. Where the restitution in kind fails to provide complete recovery, that is, where the compensation *in natura* cannot put the victim in the position they would have been in, had the injuring action not been committed, the court shall award the rest of the compensation to be paid in money. This will always be the case if the victim has suffered lost profits. The court shall award full monetary compensation if the restitution in kind is not possible; if the court finds that it is not necessary; or if the injured party requests compensation to be paid in money and the circumstances of the case so justify. With this number of exceptions, it is clear that compensation in kind (*in natura*) has lost much of the importance it may have had before, but it still remains the governing principle of compensation for material damage.

Under the explicit rule of Article 187 of LO, in case of destruction of a thing which was unlawfully taken from its proprietor, the taker shall be liable to pay monetary compensation, even if the destruction was a consequence of force majeure.

380. In contrast, and as a matter of principle, the courts award equitable compensation for non-patrimonial harm as a sum of money. Some other remedies are available to victims in cases of violation of their personal rights. As these remedies may be pursued irrespective of whether the violation of the personal right in question has resulted in pain and suffering of the victim, they are available also to juridical persons. Under Article 199 of LO, in cases of violation of personal rights, the court *may* order, at the expense of the injurer, a decision of the court to be published, or a published information to be corrected, or a statement of the injurer to be retracted, or another remedy by which the purposes of redress may be achieved.

312. Article 200 of LO.

Chapter 2. Kinds of Damage

§1. Individual and Collective Damage

381. A distinction between individual and collective damage has not been made in LO. Serbian tort law adheres to the principle of individuality of damage. This principle is not explicitly stated by the legislator. However, damage is clearly understood as a legally recognized form of either patrimonial or non-patrimonial loss or harm to an individual, be it a natural or a juridical person, and the right to compensation for the damage is comprehended as a subjective right of the person to whom the damage in question has been caused. The same applies even in multiple-victim situations, where there is a number of injured parties from a single damaging event. Along the same lines, the duty to compensate the damage lies with the tortfeasor alone, or in some situations with the vicariously liable person.

382. This stance may generate procedural and substantive problems in situations where a large number of persons have individually suffered (often minor, but at times even considerable) damage by a single tortfeasor, and also in situations where it is not simple for the traditional rules of tort law to identify a single person that should be entitled to compensation (e g., the cases of environmental damage and the like).

There are, however, some instruments of the socialization of risk of tortious liability, such as the rules on mandatory (or voluntary) third-party insurance, i.e., the insurance against liability to others. In addition, there are some instruments on the side of the (potentially) injured party, like popular action, which at least to some extent depart from the aforesaid principle of individuality.

383. First of all, there is an *actio popularis* in Serbian tort law. Under Article 156, paragraphs 1–3 of LO, any person may demand from another to eliminate a source of danger, where this source threatens to cause considerable damage to him, or to an unspecified number of persons. Along the same lines, each person may demand from another to refrain from an activity which causes disturbance or generates risk of damage, if disturbance or damage cannot be prevented by appropriate measures. If the keeper of a source of danger fails to take the appropriate measures for preventing damage or disturbance, or if he fails to eliminate the source of danger in question, the court shall, at the request of the interested party, order him to do so at his own expense.

Hence, there is a possibility of a preventive civil law claim to be pursued by a member of the public in the interest of public order. The provisions of LO are so wide they may be used for the purposes of environmental protection, against prohibited emissions, as a general instrument of legal protection against impending damage, but also against all sorts of disturbances and intrusions.[313]

313. Comm LO BK, 545.

384. Second, there are some procedural mechanisms for the aggregation of claims for damages under Serbian law. Where a number of litigation proceedings are pending before the same court, between the same parties, or when one party has multiple proceedings against different plaintiffs or different defendants, the court has the discretion to order a joinder of proceedings, should the joinder accelerate the proceedings, or save the costs of it.[314]

385. Third, the first legislative attempt to regulate horizontal judicial collective redress in Serbia was made in 2011. Namely, the organizational claim was introduced by the already-mentioned CPA of 2011, with a view of transposing the elements of the Injunctions Directive, the Unfair Contract Terms Directive and the Unfair Commercial Practices Directive into Serbian law. The horizontal collective redress available under the CPA was injunctive and declaratory, CPA did not provide for compensatory collective redress. Nonetheless, where the violation of collective rights was determined in the collective declaratory proceedings, the affected individuals were entitled to file individual claims for compensation, and the violation in question could not have been disputed in their individual proceedings. However, the Constitutional Court ruled the aforementioned provisions of CPA on horizontal collective judicial redress unconstitutional due to a lack of clarity, soundness and coherence.[315]

386. The first sectoral collective redress mechanism in Serbia was introduced in 2010, and it was related specifically to the collective interests of the consumers. The LCP of 2010 contained some limited and insufficient provisions on judicial injunction procedure against unfair terms and unfair commercial practices, as well as an underdeveloped rule on skimming-off procedure in relation to ill-gotten gains. These statutory provisions were abrogated in July 2014, when the National Assembly passed the then-new LCP. The legislator exempted sectoral collective redress from the jurisdiction of the courts and placed *injunctive collective redress* under the jurisdiction of the Ministry in charge of consumer protection.[316] The latest LCP of 2021 also contains some limited provisions on collective administrative *injunction* procedure against the unfair terms in consumer contracts and against the violations of statutory rights of a total number of at least ten consumers by the same trader and in the same manner.[317] There are no rules on consumer compensatory collective redress in Serbia at this moment.

---

314. Article 328 of CPA.
315. Decision of the Constitutional Court, IUz-51/2012 of 23 May 2013, *OG RS* 49/2013.
316. Sectoral collective *injunctive* redress before the courts is available, at present, under the provisions of the Law on Prohibition of Discrimination of 2009 (LPD, last changes in 2021, *see*: Art. 46), and the Law on Gender Equality of 2021 (LGE). When it comes to judicial protection of persons and groups of persons who are exposed to discrimination on the basis of sex, sexual characteristics, or gender, Art. 4, para. 9 of LGE refers to the more general rules of LPD.
317. Articles 170–180 LCP.

§2. Direct and Indirect Damage

387. There is no explicit provision in LO with regard to direct and indirect damage. The proximity of damage is not explicitly analysed by the courts when inspecting if the requirements of liability are met. Irrespective of the type of tortious liability, i.e., whether the liability is strict or based on fault, the injured party has to prove the existence of legally recognized damage. The issue of proximity of damage is generally not examined at that point: neither does the plaintiff has to prove that the damage in question was direct in order to prove that it is in fact recognized by law as recoverable, nor the defendant may escape liability by proving that the damage at issue is far too removed from his action.

388. Nevertheless, the courts sometimes do show interest in the proximity in discussions on causation. In other words, when observed, and that would be rarely, the proximity is regarded as a matter of causation, and not as an attribute of recoverable damage. For several decades now the courts have been consistent in using the doctrine of adequate causation (*see* paragraphs 365 et seq.). Normally the courts use the concept of adequacy (and not proximity) of the causal link, in order to set the limits of tortious liability. The distinction between 'direct damage' and 'indirect damage' should rather be one between the adequate, normal, typical consequences of the tortfeasor's conduct, and those which are not.

389. Only occasionally do the lower courts employ the theory of proximate causation, for obvious reasons of wanting to limit the scope of liability. For instance, according to the facts established in a number of court decisions during the armed conflict in Croatia and Bosnia and Herzegovina, the authorities in charge of internal affairs of the Republic of Serbia have had a practice of repeatedly unlawfully detaining citizens of the Republic of Srpska Krajina (RSK) and unlawfully transferring them across the border on the Drina river and into the territory affected by the ongoing war, where they were then forcefully recruited. A lot of these persons or their close relatives have filed claims for damages against Serbia. The Civil Chamber of SCS took a position that Serbia should be liable for psychological pain due to the violation of freedom and personal rights to the persons who were unlawfully detained by Serbian authorities and then surrendered to the authorities of RSK, but the damage these plaintiffs had suffered once on the foreign territory was not a direct consequence of their unlawful detainment, the proximate causation was interrupted there, and Serbia should not be held liable.[318]

390. Not only that LO does not exclude the possibility of extra-contractual liability for indirect losses, but it also contains some provisions explicitly allowing for such liability to be established. For example, there is an explicit rule granting

318. Legal position of the Civil Chamber of SCS of 5 Feb. 2001, *Bilten sudske prakse VSS* 1/2002, 80, *PLex*. N.B. This legal position was changed shortly thereafter, and the Civil Chamber of SCS took the opposite stance. *See*: Legal position of the Civil Chamber of SCS of 25 Jun. 2001, *Bilten sudske prakse VSS* 1/2002, 81, *PLex*.

close relatives of a victim the right to compensation for their own mental suffering due to the victim's death or severe disability (Article 202 of LO).

391. When it comes to the scope of liability for the breach of contract, the promisor is generally only liable for patrimonial damage foreseen or which could have been reasonably foreseen (by him) at the time when the agreement was made (Article 266, paragraph 1 of LO). In other words, damages are not normally recoverable for loss that the party in breach did not have reason to foresee at the time the contract was made. The scope of contractual liability is controlled through the concept of foreseeability (and not proximity) of damage. Here, the distinction between 'direct' and 'indirect damage' should rather be one between 'foreseeable' and 'unforeseeable' damage at the time of contract formation.

§3. Pecuniary and Non-pecuniary Losses

392. The existence of damage that is recoverable under law serves as an indispensable condition of liability in damages. Serbian tort law recognizes neither the concept of harmless wrongs nor that of nominal damages.[319] Damage is a detrimental consequence of the tortfeasor's action, which affects the injured party's person or property. There can be no tortious liability where there is no loss which legally qualifies as damage, and where such loss exists, the principle of complete or full compensation applies. The burden of proof of the existence of recoverable damage rests with the injured party.

The recoverable damage may be either patrimonial (pecuniary, material) or non-patrimonial (non-pecuniary, moral). This is maybe the most important legal classification of damage from the standpoint of the Serbian legislator. There are two sorts of patrimonial damage: direct loss (actual or positive damage or *damnum emergens*) and loss of expected gain or profits (*lucrum cessans*). In addition, there are three kinds of non-patrimonial or moral damage: physical pain, psychological pain and fear, each of sufficient duration and intensity.[320]

393. Pecuniary or material damage may consist of a decrease in the value of the victim's property (actual loss), or in a profit which the injurer prevented the victim from making (loss of profits). The injured party is entitled to compensation for both types of material damage regardless of the degree of the injurer's fault.

394. Actual loss is also known as simple, ordinary, or positive damage, which is an *impairment of the victim's existing assets*. It may come about as loss or diminishing of, or a burden on, the victim's property or another real right (*ius in re*), or as any other restriction thereof. Actual loss may also manifest itself as an *increase*

319. However, under Art. 194, para. 4 of CPA, an action for declaratory judgment (declaratory relief), asking a court to conclusively rule on and affirm (ascertain) the infringement of a personal right, may be filed irrespective of whether the plaintiff has also filed the claim for damages, or any other claim.
320. Article 155 of LO.

in the victim's liabilities. For instance, the injurer may create risk of damage and expose the victim to the costs of eliminating the risk and prevention of damage. These costs are also detrimental to the victim's proprietary interests. They represent recoverable damage, inasmuch as the victim has reasonably assessed the risk of damage and taken preventive measures in proportion to the impending harm.

395. Loss of profits (lost profits, *lucrum cessans*) encompasses both consequential and pure economic loss. Namely, under Serbian tort law, the victim's lost profits are recoverable even if there was no physical damage whatsoever, irrespective of the degree of the tortfeasor's fault. In cases of strict liability, lost profits shall be recoverable regardless of the liable party's fault as such. Typical cases of loss of profits are loss of earnings; loss of production by a company whose electricity supply is interrupted; lost profit on the thing that has been physically damaged; loss of income suffered by a family whose principal earner dies in an accident; etc.

Loss of profit is a frustrated income; it is a profit which could have been reasonably expected, in view of the normal course of events, or considering the extraordinary circumstances at hand, whose realization was hindered by the tortfeasor's action or omission.[321]

396. Loss of profits is a projection of the future. Frustrated profits shall be recoverable solely if the probability of their acquiring was very high, i.e., if it was reasonable to expect them, considering the circumstances at hand.[322] The chance of making the frustrated income must have been close to certainty, was it not for the tortfeasor's behaviour.[323] The courts' comprehension of lost profits is restrictive. They do not award compensation where the probability of income was lesser than stated above, or where the activity which was expected to bring profit to the injured party was unlawful in the broader sense (contrary to mandatory legal norms, 'ordre public' or *bonos mores*).

397. Moral (non-patrimonial) damage in Serbian law includes physical and psychological pain and suffering, and fear, each of sufficient duration and intensity. For a short period of time after WWII, presumably under the influence of Soviet legal doctrine, Yugoslav legal scholars have questioned the moral, ethical and legal validity of awarding monetary compensation for moral (non-patrimonial) damage.[324] This discussion ended in favour of awarding such compensation and, for several decades now, the moral and ethical appropriateness of monetary compensation for pain and suffering has not been seriously challenged.

398. Serbian tort law accepts a purely subjective concept of moral damage: the mere infringement of non-patrimonial rights, or violation of personal goods as

321. Article 189, paras 1 and 3 of LO.
322. The fact that the impeccable career of the injured esteemed national football referee shows that he could have one day end up on the FIFA list of the international football referees, does not suffice for treating the injury as an event which has prevented him from the profits from international career. SCS, Rev2. 120/2014 of 15 May 2014, *PLex*.
323. SCS, Rev. 1545/2010 of 30 Mar. 2011, *PLex*.
324. In detail: O. Stanković, *Novčana naknada neimovinske štete* (Beograd, 1968), 26–29.

objects of these rights, does not constitute moral damage, unless they caused physical or psychological pain (mental suffering), or fear, to the plaintiff, and disturbed his or her mental equilibrium.

399. Moreover, recoverable moral damage may exist even if none of the injured party's personal rights was violated, as in the cases of mental suffering of the injured party due to the death or particularly severe disability of his or her close relative. Under Article 201 of LO, in case of the death of a person, the court may award equitable compensation for psychological pain (mental suffering) to the members of the deceased's immediate family: his spouse or cohabitant;[325] parents; children; brothers and sisters who have lived with the deceased in a shared household. In case of a particularly serious disability of a person, the court may award equitable compensation for psychological pain to his spouse or cohabitant, parents and children.

400. Objectivization of moral damage is a change in this paradigm, towards the understanding of moral damage as an abstract infringement of a non-patrimonial right of the injured party, irrespective of any pain or fear caused by such infringement: Moral damage exists if personal (non-patrimonial) right, or personal good or legally protected personal interest is violated, even if the injured party did not suffer any pain or fear due to this violation. The Commission appointed to draft the new Civil Code of Serbia considers partial objectivization of the concept of moral damage in the prospective codification.[326]

401. Under Article 200 of LO, after finding that the circumstances of the case at hand, and particularly the duration and the intensity of the pain and fear sustained by the injured party, justify such a decision, the court shall award equitable monetary compensation for the following heads of damage: (1) psychological pain (mental suffering) due to the impairment of life activities, severe disfigurement, violation of reputation, honour, freedom or personal rights, or death or severe disability of a close relative; (2) physical pain; (3) fear; irrespective of compensation for patrimonial damage, and also in the absence of any patrimonial damage. This is an all-in list. Thus, psychological pain (mental suffering) due to the loss of an item of property, even if the item in question is a piece of artwork, does not represent recoverable moral damage.[327]

In addition, a victim of a criminal offence against sexual freedom has a special right to equitable compensation for psychological pain.[328]

---

325. 'Cohabitation' should be understood here as an arrangement where two people of opposite sexes who are not married live together in a sexually intimate relationship on a long-term basis.
326. DCC, Arts 287 and 346. The new Law on Trade of 2019 contains a rule under which a trader who suffers damage due to an act of unfair market competition shall be entitled to compensation for both material damage, and for non-material (moral) damage due to injury to business reputation (Art. 41). There are no court decisions based on this as of yet. Outside this unusual example, legal entities do not have the right to compensation for non-material damage in Serbian tort law, as they are considered not capable to experience pain and suffering.
327. SCS, Rev. I 2749/2004 of 25 Nov. 2004, *PLex*.
328. Article 202 of LO (*Satisfaction in Special Cases*).

In deciding on the merits of the claim, and on the amount of equitable compensation for non-patrimonial damage, the court shall take into account the importance of the violated interests, the purpose of the equitable compensation for non-patrimonial losses, but also that it does not favour goals otherwise incompatible with its nature and social purpose.

402. Claims for compensation of non-pecuniary damage are generally uninheritable unless they are settled by a *written* agreement between the parties, or *confirmed* by a non-appealable court decision. They can be subject to cession, offsetting and forced execution under the same conditions.[329] The Commission appointed to draft a new civil code for Serbia is considering eliminating the existing rule, and introducing the new one, under which these claims would be inheritable and transferable *inter vivos* if they are settled by an agreement between the parties (not necessarily in writing), or if the proceedings have been initiated before the court during the lifetime of the injured party.[330]

§4. Pure Economic Loss

403. Serbian tort law provides wide-ranging protection against this type of damage. The injured party shall have the right to compensation for lost profits (*lucrum cessans*) irrespective of whether they have also suffered actual patrimonial loss (*damnum emergens*), or any kind of physical damage. Lost profits are recoverable under the rules of both contractual and tortious liability (the latter also including pre-contractual liability, i.e., *culpa in contrahendo*).

404. Moreover, lost profits are recoverable irrespective of the degree of the injurer's fault: even if the tortfeasor has acted with plain or ordinary negligence, he shall be liable to compensate for the lost profits he has inflicted on the injured party. And in cases of strict liability, the liable party shall be obliged to compensate for the profits lost, irrespective of any fault on their side. Serbian tort law is more interested in treating all injured parties in the same manner than in adequately punishing the tortfeasor (in proportion to the gravity of his fault), or differentiating between tortfeasors who acted with plain negligence and those who acted with recklessness or malice. The victim should be entitled to integral compensation irrespective of the gravity of the tortfeasor's fault, because the victim had no influence on this, and because the victim's interest to obtain full compensation does not change depending on the degree of the tortfeasor's fault.

405. There is one restriction here: concerning liability for breach of contract, the promisor is generally only liable for patrimonial damage (including the profits lost) foreseen or which could have been reasonably foreseen (by him) at the time when the agreement was made. In other words, under the rules on contractual liability, lost

329. Article 204 of LO.
330. Article 350 of DCC.

profits are recoverable solely if they were foreseeable at the time of contract formation. Then again, in case of intentional, grossly negligent or fraudulent breach of contractual obligation (or any other pre-existent duty), the injured party shall have the right to compensation for both foreseeable and unforeseeable patrimonial damage (lost profits included).[331]

406. However, the courts' understanding of what 'lost profits' actually are, is quite narrow and restrictive. As previously stated, loss of profit is a patrimonial gain which could have been reasonably expected, in view of the normal course of events, or considering the extraordinary circumstances at hand, whose realization was hindered by the tortfeasor's action or omission.[332] Frustrated profits shall be recoverable solely if the probability of their acquiring was very high, i.e., if it was reasonable to expect them considering the circumstances at hand. The chance of making the frustrated income must have been close to certainty. The courts shall not award compensation where the probability of income was lesser than stated, or where the activity which was expected to bring profit to the injured party was unlawful in the broader sense (contrary to mandatory legal norms, 'ordre public' or *bonos mores*).[333]

§5. Actual and Future Damage

407. Under the principle of full or integral compensation an injured party is entitled to be put into the position in which he would have been, was it not for the damaging event. The amount of compensation awarded should place the victim in the position he or she would have been in, had the injuring action not been committed. This includes the recovery of lost profits (which has already been discussed), other future patrimonial damage (e.g., expenses for future care and treatment), as well as future non-patrimonial (moral) damage.

408. At the request of the injured party, the court shall award equitable compensation for future moral (non-patrimonial) damage, i.e., for physical and psychological pain and fear the injured party is going to experience in the future, where it is *certain*, in view of the normal course of events, that the moral damage in question will also last in the future.[334] In order for future damage to be recoverable, it must be highly likely that it will happen, it is not sufficient that the occurrence of future damage cannot be excluded.

331. Article 266, paras 1 and 2 of LO.
332. Article 189, paras 1 and 3 of LO. As stated before, typical cases are: loss of earnings; loss of production by a company whose electricity supply is interrupted; lost profit on the thing that has been physically damaged; loss of income suffered by a family whose principal earner dies in an accident; etc.
333. The owner of a vehicle cannot claim compensation for loss of earnings from performing commercial transportation services, if he was not registered for performing this type of services at the time of damaging event. SCS, Rev. 1149/2007 of 28 May 2008, *PLex.*
334. Article 203 of LO.

The courts have held that moral damage (such as psychological or physical pain, or fear) which occurs repeatedly, that is, which recurrently comes about, represents *one (single) damage*, and therefore, *one (single) amount of compensation* needs to be awarded for such damage, taking into account its past and future occurrences. For instance, physical pain before, during and after medical treatment represents a single damage. The decisive moment for determining if the damage in question is 'future damage' shall be the ending of the principal hearings before the Court of First Instance.[335]

409. When it comes to future patrimonial damage, such as loss of earnings or support, or expenses for future care and treatment, the injured party may claim compensation consecutively, i.e., in sequence, for each period that has passed, and the prescription shall run separately for each consecutive claim.[336] The prescription period for the loss of earnings starts when the loss occurs, i.e., when the injured party's earnings were due, regardless of the time of injury.[337]

410. Where it is certain that damage is going to last or reoccur in the future, the court may award annuity payments. The court must be convinced, in view of normal course of events, there will certainly be some further detrimental consequences of the damaging event in question. Hence, the future negative consequences must be foreseeable at the time of adjudication

411. In cases of death, bodily injury or harm to health the court shall, as a rule, determine indemnity in the form of annuities, for the duration of life of the injured person, or for a definite period of time. An awarded annuity as a form of damages shall be paid in advance in monthly instalments, except if the court decides differently. The injured party may request a guarantee for the payment of annuities unless such demand would be unjustified under the circumstances of the case. Should the liable party fail to produce a guarantee for the payment of annuities, as per the order of the court, the injured party may demand a lump sum to be paid instead of the annuities. In determining the appropriate lump sum, the court shall consider the amount of the annuities and the injured party's life expectancy and shall deduct the corresponding interest. The injured party may demand a lump sum to be paid instead of the annuities whenever it is justified.[338]

412. In case of loss of support, the court shall award indemnity in the form of annuities to a person who was supported, or entitled to demand support from the

335. Conclusion of the Joint session of the Federal Court, state Supreme Courts and the Supreme Military Court of 15 and 16 Oct. 1986, *Bilten sudske prakse Vrhovnog suda BiH* 1/1987, 12 and 55.
336. Conclusion of the Joint session of the Federal Court, state Supreme Courts and the Supreme Military Court of 25 and 26 Nov. 1986, *Bilten sudske prakse Vrhovnog suda BiH* 4/1986, 40–41.
337. SC of BIH, Pž. 23/1989 of 14 Jul. 1989, *Bilten sudske prakse VS BIH* 4/1989, 71. The other, more convincing, opinion is that the prescription period should start running from the moment the injured party may seek compensation, and that is from the time of injury, i.e., when the earnings were lost for certain, which may be well before they were due (*see* para. 331).
338. Article 188 of LO.

deceased. When deciding on the amount of the annuities, the court shall take all circumstances of the case into account, but in any case, the awarded sum cannot exceed the amount the injured party would have been receiving from the deceased, had he not died.[339]

413. In cases of bodily injury or harm to health, should the injured party, due to total or partial inability to work, suffer the loss of his earnings, or should his needs become permanently increased (including support by relatives and loss of home maintenance capacity), or should possibilities of his further development and advancement be destroyed or reduced, the court shall award compensation for these future losses in the form of annuities (in regular intervals).[340] Loss of housekeeping capacities may be qualified as a permanent increase in the defendant's needs. This may include costs of specific diet, nursing, domestic help, treatment, etc.[341]

414. Under Article 196 of LO the court may raise the amount of the future annuities at the request of the injured party, or may reduce or cancel the future annuities at the request of the tortfeasor, in case of a considerable change in the circumstances previously taken into account. This goes both for the annuities awarded for material and moral (non-material) damage.[342]

§6. Other Costs

415. Costs of assessing damage and liability. Under the principle of full or integral compensation an injured party is entitled to be put into the position in which he would have been, was it not for the damaging event. The amount of compensation awarded should put the victim in the position he or she would have been in, had the injuring action not been committed. This includes compensation for actual patrimonial loss incurred by the injured party. One of the ways in which actual loss may manifest itself is an *increase in the victim's liabilities*. For instance, the injurer may create risk of damage and expose the victim to the costs of eliminating the risk and prevention of damage. These costs are also detrimental to the victim's proprietary interests. They represent recoverable damage, inasmuch as the victim has reasonably assessed the risk of damage and taken preventive measures in proportion to the impending harm.

416. The principle of integral compensation leaves open the possibility of the victim fixing the damage on his own and charging the injurer with the reasonable costs of repair. If the victim chooses to alleviate the detriment by himself, he will sustain additional costs relating to damage assessment, analysis of the possible methods of repair, repair check on an item in question, supervising the professional

339. Article 194 of LO.
340. Article 195, para. 2 of LO.
341. Comm LO Per, 458.
342. Conclusion of the Joint session of the Federal Court, state Supreme Courts and the Supreme Military Court of 15 and 16 Oct. 1986, *Bilten sudske prakse Vrhovnog suda BiH* 1/1987, 55.

employed to repair the damaged item, etc. These expenditures represent an increase in the victim's liabilities caused by the tortfeasor, hence they qualify as recoverable damage.

However, if the victim decides to cure the detriment on his own, he shall be entitled to the costs of assessing damage and the costs of repair solely to the extent these costs were kept within reasonable limits.

417. Costs in obtaining judicial or extra-judicial payment. Under Serbian civil procedure law,[343] 'costs of litigation' include expenses incurred in the course of, or in relation to the civil proceedings, as well as remuneration for the work of attorneys and other persons entitled to remuneration pursuant to law. 'Costs of litigation' also include the costs of failed attempts of court settlement, as well as the costs of the failed mediation (where the parties have agreed to attempt mediation, or the court has directed them to mediation).

418. Each party to the proceedings shall individually and in advance bear the costs of litigation incurred by her actions. The party that has lost the lawsuit in its entirety will have to reimburse the costs of litigation to the successful party, including the expenses for legal counsel and the costs of presentation of evidence. However, the successful party may recover solely the costs that were required for the litigation in question and not the expenses it has unnecessarily assumed. The costs of the winning party's legal counsel shall be remunerated to the extent they do not exceed the official schedule. When deciding on the amount of the successful party's litigation costs to be remunerated, the court shall take into account all circumstances at hand.

419. Where the claim of one party has been only partially honoured, that is, where one party has not succeeded in the lawsuit in its entirety, the court shall distribute the costs among the parties proportionally to their respective successes in the litigation, or order each party to bear its own costs. Where one party to the proceedings has not succeeded in a proportionally insignificant part of its claim, and where this failure was negligible, in the sense that it did not generate additional costs, the court may decide the litigation costs of this party to be refunded in full. If civil dispute is resolved by a court settlement, or by a settlement after mediation, each party to the proceedings shall bear its own costs of litigation, unless they agree otherwise.

420. Where litigation costs are imposed on one party by fault of the opposing party or by an event which has befallen the opposing party, the opposing party shall reimburse these costs irrespective of the outcome of the proceedings. The court may order a legal counsel or a legal representative of one party, to reimburse litigation costs of the opposing party, if these costs were caused by the counsel's or representative's fault. A party having needlessly launched a lawsuit, despite the other party's willingness to perform, shall bear the other party's litigation costs, provided that the

343. Articles 150–173 of CPA.

other party recognizes the claim at the preliminary hearing or, if no preliminary hearing is scheduled, at the trial hearing before the discussion on the merits of the case.

§7. Mitigation of Damages

421. Under the general rules of Serbian contract law or, to be more precise, under the general rules on liability for breach of obligation, the party claiming damages for breach of obligation has a statutory duty to mitigate the damage he has suffered. Namely, under Article 266, paragraphs 4 and 5 of LO, a party claiming damages for breach of contract shall take all reasonable measures to mitigate damage, or else the other party may seek reduction of damages, the same rule applies in cases of breach of non-contractual obligations unless otherwise prescribed by law.

422. This is actually an elaboration of the general principle of Article 18 of LO. However, the relevance of Article 18 and Article 266, paragraphs 4 and 5 is restricted to creditor-debtor relationships in the already existing obligations. Under Article 18 of LO parties to the obligation must exercise due care in performing their commitments. In general, parties to the obligation have to observe the standard of a careful man, a careful businessperson, or a careful professional – depending on the context. Also, a party to the obligation has a duty to refrain, in exercising his or her rights, from actions that would impede or aggravate the performance of the other party. This principle applies only if the parties are already legally bound one to another, that is, once there is a legal obligation between them (for instance, a contractual one) which, from that point on, needs to be performed.

423. Insofar as tortious liability under Serbian law is concerned, it is considered that there are no pre-existing obligations between the parties and that the obligation (to redress the damage) arises from the very fact that damage to one was caused by the fault of another. Oddly enough, one could consider the existence of the injured party's duty to mitigate additional damage caused by the tortfeasor's failure to compensate for the damage previously caused to the injured party.

424. When it comes to extra-contractual liability, and as it has already been discussed, where the injured party has contributed to the occurrence of damage, or caused damage to be higher than it would otherwise be, he shall be entitled only to a proportionally reduced compensation. Where it is not possible to establish how much the injured party contributed to the harm they suffered, that is, which part of the damage comes from the injured party's action, the court shall award compensation while taking into account the circumstances of each particular case.[344] These rules can be applied by the court irrespective of whether the injured party's contribution was pleaded as a defence.

The injured party's contribution shall be determined as a matter of causation, and it shall be taken into account irrespective of whether there was any fault on the

344. Article 192 of LO.

injured party's side. And as it has been stated: the question of causation is, still, inevitably joined up with the question of fault, and with some broader policy considerations. So, despite the fact that they are not bound to, the courts do keep qualities of the injured party's conduct in mind, when deciding on the percentage of their contribution to the damage in question.[345]

425. The question is, then, if the injured party may have contributed to the damage in a legally relevant way, by omission to take reasonable action that would have mitigated the damage in question. The Supreme Court answered affirmatively.[346]

The idea that the victim's legal position could deteriorate if he does not take action to mitigate the damage he has sustained, may also be drawn from the principle of good faith and fair dealing (Article 12 of LO).

426. The victim has a 'duty in her own interest' to mitigate the damage he has suffered, but cannot be legally coerced to take the necessary mitigating measures. The injurer has no claim against the injured party with a view of compelling her to alleviate the loss. However, the injured party's failure to undertake necessary measures to mitigate the loss, may set another civil law sanction in motion, and that is the proportionate reduction of damages the victim would otherwise be entitled to (Article 192 of LO).

427. The injured party may not be compelled to take mitigating measures, but if he fails to reasonably do so, the assumption would be that he has contributed to the extent of damage he suffered. For instance, the victim may not be coerced to mitigate unlawful loss of earnings by seeking another job, but if he fails to reasonably do so, the rules on the proportionate reduction of damages (due to the victim's contribution to the extent of damage) shall apply.[347]

The courts held that the victim cannot be sanctioned for not taking the mitigating measures to the detriment of his constitutional rights. For example, the injured party may not be compelled to submit to a medical treatment or undergo surgery in order to avoid future disability. Victim's refusal to submit to a treatment or surgery may be qualified as contribution to damage he has suffered, only if the treatment or the surgery in question was of the kind that normally does not present a risk of additional damage, and that a reasonable man would submit to under the normal course of things.[348]

---

345. A girl did not contribute (in the sense of Art. 192 of LO) to the bodily injury she has suffered, by trying to defend her dog from another person's dog that bit her. Decision of Higher Court in Požarevac, Gž. 402/2013(2012) of 5 Jun. 2013, *PLex*.
346. SCS, Prev. 105/2005 of 24 Mar. 2005, *PLex*. Also, e.g., Decision of Higher Commercial Court, Pž. 969/2008(2) of 11 Nov. 2008; Decision of Higher Commercial Court, Pž. 9910/2004 of 31 Jan. 2005, *PLex*.
347. Legal position of the Civil Chamber of SCS of 16 Feb. 1998, *PLex*.
348. Conclusion of the Joint session of the Federal Court, state Supreme Courts and the Supreme Military Court of 15 and 16 Oct. 1986, *PLex*. Also, the injured party has contributed to the extent of damage by refusing to undergo a medical procedure which in the ordinary course of things bears no risk of additional harm. Decision of District Court in Valjevo, Gž. 1799/2005 of 21 Nov. 2005, *PLex*.

Chapter 3. Assessment and Compensation of Damages

§1. Objective Versus Subjective

428. The purpose of damages in Serbian law is compensatory. The goal of awarding compensation is to put the injured party in a position he or she would have been in, was it not for the damaging event under consideration. The victim shall be compensated both for the actual losses and for the lost profit, irrespective of the degree of the injurer's fault. Moreover, the ways in which damage will be assessed and compensated are not governed by the gravity of the injurer's fault.

429. In general, compensation shall be given in kind (*in natura*), which means replacement of that which was destroyed or removed by the tortfeasor. Rather than restoring the injured party's loss with money, the loss shall be repaired by restitution of the thing injured or removed. The injured party may decide to take care of the restoration of the former state of affairs himself. For instance, a farmer whose crop was lost may purchase grain and claim the sum spent from the tortfeasor, and an owner of a motor vehicle may take it for repair. In these cases, the restoration of the former state of affairs must be actually performed, either by the victim or by someone else the victim has engaged to do so. For instance, the injured person is entitled to the actual expenses of the medical treatment: to what was really (de facto) spent on the medical treatment, and not to what should have been spent.[349]

430. Where the restitution in kind fails to provide complete recovery, the court shall award the rest of the compensation to be paid in money. This will always be the case if the victim has suffered lost profits. Also, the court shall award full monetary compensation if the restitution in kind is not possible, or if the court finds that it is not necessary, or if the injured party requests compensation to be paid in money and the circumstances of the case so justify. In case of destruction of an item of property unlawfully taken from the owner, the taker shall be liable to pay monetary compensation (even if the destruction was a consequence of force majeure).[350]

431. The assessment shall be performed objectively. The amount of damages shall be determined according to the market prices at the time of rendering a court decision unless otherwise provided by law.[351] The crucial moment for assessment of damages is the moment when the court renders a decision in the case at hand, and not the time when the damage was caused. The court shall award compensation in line with the economic price for which a good (or service) is offered in the marketplace. Where the price is regulated by law, damages shall be awarded in accordance with stipulated prices at the time of rendering a decision by a court. Where there is no such thing as a current market price for an item of property (e.g., a work

349. SC of BIH, Pž. 265/1990 of 25 Feb. 1991, *Bilten sudske prakse VS BiH* 2/1991, 61.
350. Article 185 and Art. 187 of LO.
351. Article 189, para. 2 of LO; SCS, Rev. 3618/2004 of 26 Jan. 2005, *PLex*.

of art), damages shall be determined on the ground of factors which are usually taken into account when pricing the items of the same kind.[352]

432. As stated before, the amount of damages shall be determined according to the market prices at the time of adjudication. To that end, the court must compare the market price of the damaged item at the moment of the giving of a decision, with the market price at the same time (the time of adjudication) of the item as it was prior to the damaging event. For instance, the injured party was unlawfully deprived of his vehicle for a longer period of time and demands full monetary compensation. The court needs to establish the condition of the vehicle at the time of its seizure (taking into account its depreciation by the time of seizure) and to award the injured party damages in the market price of a vehicle in such condition, but as of the time of adjudication. Further depreciation of the vehicle (for the time it was used by the liable party) is not a damage-reducing factor.[353]

The same goes for the assessment of the lost profits. For example, where an injured party was deprived of the possibility to continue renting out the goods, the court shall take into account rental prices at the time of rendering a decision (minus the expenses the owner would have incurred in relation to renting out the goods in question).[354]

The time of 'the giving of a decision by a court' also comprises a short period of time between the day the extent of damage was determined (e.g., the date of an expert witness opinion) and the day of rendering the decision in the first instance.[355]

433. There is no legal relevance to the fact that the victim has subjectively valued the item more than it would be priced in the market. The victim's personal appraisal of the value of the damaged item is generally irrelevant. However, where an item of property was destroyed by a criminal offence committed with premeditation, the court may determine the amount of damages against the value the item has had for the injured party (*pretium affectionis*).[356] In these cases, the court may, by way of exception, award monetary compensation of the specific value the damaged item of property subjectively bears for the victim.

434. The courts and legal doctrine understand the purpose of awarding equitable compensation for non-patrimonial damage to be *satisfaction*, i.e., reinstatement of the injured party's psychological equilibrium. After finding that the circumstances of the case at hand, and particularly the duration and the intensity of the pain and fear sustained by the injured party justify such a decision, the court shall award equitable monetary compensation to the injured party, irrespective of compensation for patrimonial damage, and in the absence of any patrimonial harm. In deciding on the merits of the claim, and on the amount of equitable compensation for non-patrimonial damage in question, the court shall take into account the

352. Comm LO Per, 438.
353. SCS, Rev. 3551/2004 of 6 Jul. 2005, *PLex.*
354. SCS, Rev. 1639/2006 of 12 Apr. 2007, *PLex.*
355. SCS, Rev. 3618/2004 of 26 Jan. 2005, *PLex.*
356. Article 189, para. 4 of LO.

importance of the violated non-patrimonial interests, the purpose of the equitable compensation for non-patrimonial losses (i.e., *satisfaction*), but also that the awarded equitable compensation does not favour the goals which are otherwise incompatible with its nature and social purpose.[357]

435. In the assessment of moral damage and of the equitable compensation for it, the principle of free evaluation of the evidence by the court applies. There are no firm rules according to which certain types of evidence are, or are not, convincing. The court has the freedom of unfettered consideration of all the evidence produced with regard to the existence and the extent of non-patrimonial damage.[358]

436. In spite of this, the assessment is quite mechanical. The official guidelines exist, as to the amount of equitable damages for pain and fear, depending on their intensity and duration. More precisely, there is a document called *Approximate criteria for determining equitable compensation for non-patrimonial damage*, adopted by the Civil Chamber of the Supreme Court of Serbia, on 8 February 1999. The document contains an outline of the recommended approximate amounts of compensation for different types of non-patrimonial damage. The recommended sums are regularly adjusted to the consumer price index, which measures changes in the price level of a market basket of consumer goods and services purchased by households.[359]

The lower courts are not legally bound to abide by these criteria issued by the highest court. The criteria are a sort of recommendation, not an order to the lower courts. However, the courts do award damages within the recommended sums, hoping for such decisions to be confirmed on appeal.

§2. Concrete Versus Abstract

437. The terms 'concrete' and 'abstract' are generally not used in Serbian tort law to describe damage assessment and compensation. Some scholars differentiate between abstract and concrete *damage*, on the one hand, and abstract and concrete *assessment of damage*, on the other.[360] However, the relevance of these categorizations for extra-contractual liability is only theoretical.

357. Article 200 of LO.
358. The amount of compensation for mental suffering and fear shall be determined by the court's free evaluation of the evidence. Decision of Higher Commercial Court, V Pž. 3250/2006(2) of 10 Oct. 2006, *PLex*.
359. On date 30 Apr. 2015, these amounts (expressed in *euros*) were: *for physical pain* (strong 7.376, medium 3.688, slight 1.229); *for fear* (strong 4.917, medium 2.459, slight 615); *for different types of recoverable psychological pain due to*: reduction of general lifetime activities 24.590, disfigurement (very severe 12.294, grave 7.376, medium 3.688, slight 1.229), death of a close person (to parent 8.605, to child 8.605, to spouse or cohabitant 6.146, to brother/sister 4.917), severe disability of a close person (to parent 4.917, to child 4.917, to spouse 3.688), injury to reputation and honour (via media 6.147–12.294, in other ways 1.229–6.147).
360. J. Radišić, *Obligaciono pravo* (Beograd, 2004), 204.

438. Concrete damage is actual loss, tangible harm, or real detriment to a legally protected good, i.e., loss or damage to property. Abstract damage is an intangible detriment, i.e., pure economic loss caused by late delivery of goods. The concrete approach to damage assessment is based on the injured party's actual circumstances, intended to fully compensate the injured party for the loss she actually suffered, while the abstract approach is based on a fixed formula which is presumed to constitute the injured party's loss, with a view to provide the certainty regarding the extent of potential liability for breach. The latter may be relevant in commercial contracts (e.g., the difference between the price fixed by the contract and the current price at the time of avoidance of the contract).[361]

§3. Methods of Assessing Damage

439. Irrespective of the type of tortious liability in question, be it strict or based on fault, the burden of proving, by a preponderance of the evidence, the existence and the extent of damage lie with the injured party in his role as 'plaintiff'. However, under the well-established rules on evidence in civil proceedings, sometimes it will be sufficient to prove the existence of damage and leave it to the court to determine the extent of damage and the amount of due compensation, namely, if it is determined that a party is entitled to damages, but the amount of damages cannot be established, or could be established only with disproportionate difficulties, the court shall establish the amount of due compensation at its own discretion, that is, as per the principle of free evaluation of the evidence.[362] Also, where the defendant has proved that the injured party has contributed to the occurrence of damage, but the extent of such contribution is not possible to establish, the court shall determine the amount of damages taking into account all circumstances at hand.[363]

440. When proving actual loss, the plaintiff must show the presence and the measure of the impairment of his existing assets: loss or diminishing of, or a burden on, the plaintiff's property or another real right (*ius in re*), or increase in his liabilities, caused by the injuring conduct. Concerning loss of profits, the plaintiff must present a very high probability of realization of the frustrated income in view of the normal course of events, or considering the extraordinary circumstances at hand. In any case, the assessment of damage shall focus on establishing the difference in values of the injured party's property as it is now (at the moment of rendering the court's decision), and as it would have been at the same point in time, was it not for the injuring conduct.

441. As has been previously stated, the assessment shall be performed objectively. The amount of damages shall be determined according to the market prices at the time of rendering a court decision unless otherwise provided by law. The crucial moment for assessment of damages is the moment when the court renders a

361. *See* Art. 76 of the UN Convention on Contracts for the International Sale of Goods (CISG).
362. Article 232 of CPA.
363. Article 192, para. 2 of LO.

decision in the case at hand, and not the time when the damage was caused. The time of 'rendering a decision' includes a short period between the day the scope of damage was determined (e.g., the date of an expert witness opinion) and the day of rendering the decision in the first instance. Damages shall be awarded in line with the economic price for which a good (or service) is offered in the marketplace. There is no legal relevance to the fact that the victim has subjectively valued the item more than it would be priced in the market. However, where an item of property was destroyed by a criminal offence committed with premeditation, the court may determine the amount of damages against the value the item has had for the injured party.

442. The plaintiff also has to prove the existence of non-patrimonial damage, that is, of mental suffering, physical pain, or fear, of sufficient duration and intensity. The court has the freedom of unfettered consideration of all the evidence produced with regard to the existence and the extent of non-patrimonial damage. In deciding on the merits of the claim, and on the amount of equitable compensation, the court shall consider the importance of the violated non-patrimonial interests, the purpose of the equitable compensation (*satisfaction*, i.e., reinstatement of the victim's psychological balance), but also make sure the awarded amount does not further the goals which are otherwise incompatible with its nature and social purpose.[364] After finding that the circumstances of the case, and particularly the duration and the intensity of mental suffering, physical pain, or fear, as proven by the plaintiff, justify such a decision, the court shall award equitable monetary compensation, irrespective of compensation for patrimonial damage, and in the absence of any patrimonial harm.

443. As mentioned earlier, the assessment is quite mechanical (*see* paragraph 436). The courts rely on the official guidelines for deciding on the amount of equitable damages for non-material losses (*Approximate criteria for determining equitable compensation for non-patrimonial damage*, adopted by the Civil Chamber of the Supreme Court in 1999, and regularly adjusted to the consumer price index).

§4. Equitable Limitation of Damages

444. There are some situations where, in determining the amount of damages the injured party should be awarded, the courts are allowed to consider and compare the respective values of the victim's and the tortfeasor's properties, or to take into account that the tortfeasor is deprived of the financial means necessary for his own maintenance. In addition, a reduction of liability is sometimes possible on the grounds of equity.

445. First of all, the court *may* reduce the amount of damages the tortfeasor is obliged to pay to the injured party and order him to pay the amount which does not provide for full compensation. In this instance, the court must take into account the

364. Article 200 of LO.

financial status of the injured party. Also, two requirements must be met: First, it is necessary that the tortfeasor did not cause damage by intent or gross negligence. Secondly, the tortfeasor's financial status must be so bad, that paying the full amount of compensation would deprive him of the financial means necessary for his own maintenance.[365] This is a departure from the principle of integral compensation, under which an injured party is entitled to be put into the position in which he would have been, was it not for the damaging event. The degree of the tortfeasor's fault does not generally dictate the amount of damages the victim is entitled to under Serbian tort law. Nevertheless, qualified fault of the tortfeasor (intent or gross negligence) excludes the possibility of equitable limitation of damages due to his poor financial situation.

446. Second, where the tortfeasor has caused damage while performing an activity for the benefit of the injured party, the court *may* reduce the amount of damages the tortfeasor would otherwise have to pay. Here, the court shall take into account the degree of care the tortfeasor demonstrates in his own affairs.[366] In other words, when acting for the benefit of the victim, the injurer may be held to a lesser standard of care, that is, he is expected to behave as diligently as he usually does in his own affairs (*diligentia quam in suis/rebus*).

447. Furthermore, when it comes to the case of tortious liability in emergency cases (Article 182 of LO), the court may exonerate the tortfeasor from duty to compensate, or reduce the awarded compensation, on the grounds of equity. This is a type of fault-based liability of a person who causes foreseeable damage, by omitting to render help to another person whose life or bodily integrity was in an obvious peril. Liability for failure to rescue may be established if the help that was needed could have been rendered without risk to oneself or to others. Equitable exoneration from liability or equitable limitation of damages may come into play, for instance, where the liable party was able to help only some of the injured, as there were too many of them and not enough time, or he had phobia, or he made an erroneous decision under time pressure, etc.

448. In addition, in case of collision of two (or more) motor vehicles in motion in which neither of the participants in a traffic accident is at fault, liability of the proprietors of motor vehicles shall be divided into equal shares unless reasons of equity require differently (Article 178, paragraph 3 of LO). In other words, when none of the proprietors of the motor vehicles involved in a car crash is at fault, it is presumed that equity would command that they bear the damage in equal shares unless special circumstances justify different distribution of burdens.

449. There are some other cases where the courts, in determining the amount of damages, consider the values of the property of the injurer and of the injured party.

365. Article 191, para. 1 of LO. Applies to liability for both patrimonial and non-patrimonial losses (Art. 205 of LO).
366. Article 191, para. 2 of LO. Applies to liability for both patrimonial and non-patrimonial losses (Art. 205 of LO).

Under Article 169, paragraph 1 of LO, if damage was caused by a person who cannot be liable as he or she lacks capacity of discernment because of young age, mental illness or mental disability, and if compensation cannot be obtained from the person who had a duty to supervise the incapacitated tortfeasor, the court may award either full compensation or a part thereof to be paid by the tortfeasor, if the reasons of equity demand such a decision, especially when the values of the property of the injurer and of the injured party are taken into consideration. Furthermore, if damage was caused by the minor who is fully capable of discernment but unable to redress the damage he inflicted upon the injured party, the court may award either full compensation or a part thereof to be paid by the minor's parents, if the reasons of equity demand such a decision, especially when the values of the property of the minor's parents and of the injured party are taken into consideration (Article 169, paragraph 2 of LO).

450. In addition, where there are two or more persons liable for the same damage, and where their individual shares in the damage in question should be determined in the recourse proceedings, the court shall take into account the degree of their respective faults and the gravity of the consequences of their respective acts. If it is not possible to discern their individual shares, all jointly and severally liable tortfeasors shall account for equal shares, unless equity requires otherwise.[367]

§5. METHODS OF PAYMENT

I. Lump Sum

451. As a matter of principle, actual or positive patrimonial loss (*damnum emergens*) is awarded *in natura* in Serbian law: the courts normally order *compensation in kind*, that is, in goods or services as opposed to money. Exceptionally, the courts may award pecuniary compensation: if full recovery cannot be achieved by compensation in kind; if compensation in kind is not possible or the court finds it not necessary; or if the injured party requests pecuniary compensation and the circumstances at hand so justify.[368] With these many exceptions, it is clear that compensation in kind has lost much of the importance it may have had before, however, it remains the governing principle of compensation for positive material damage.

452. In contrast, the courts normally award pecuniary compensation for lost profits (*lucrum cessans*). Also, as a matter of principle, the courts award equitable *pecuniary* compensation for non-patrimonial harm. Furthermore, in cases of destruction of things that are unlawfully taken from their proprietors, takers shall be liable to pay monetary compensation, even if the destruction resulted from force majeure.[369] In all of the cases where compensation is awarded as a sum of money,

367. Article 208, paras 2 and 3 of LO.
368. Article 187 of LO.
369. *Ibid.*

the courts shall, as a rule, order pecuniary compensation to be paid as a lump sum, determined as of the date of rendering of a court decision.

453. As a rule, equitable pecuniary compensation for non-patrimonial (moral) damage shall be determined as individual sums of money, separately for each type of moral damage (physical pain, fear, different types of recoverable psychological pain). In very hard cases, where sufferings of the victim are closely interrelated and cannot be estimated separately, the court shall determine one amount of compensation for non-pecuniary damage as such, in its totality.[370] As stated before, the courts generally award equitable pecuniary compensation for non-patrimonial damage as a lump sum. Once the said separate amounts of compensation for each type of moral damage are determined, their aggregate shall be awarded to the defendant in the form of one payment. However, the court may order, on the plaintiff's request, this (aggregate) pecuniary sum to be paid in annuities, should the annuities better serve the purpose of equitable compensation, considering the circumstances of the case at hand.[371]

II. Annuities

454. As previously stated, where it is certain that damage is going to last or reoccur in the future, the court may award annuity payments. The court must be convinced, in view of the normal course of events, there will certainly be some further detrimental consequences of the damaging event in question. Therefore, the future negative consequences must be foreseeable at the time of adjudication.

455. In cases of death, bodily injury or harm to health the court shall, as a rule, determine indemnity in the form of annuities, for the duration of life of the injured person, or for a definite period of time. An awarded annuity as a form of damages shall be paid in advance in monthly instalments, except if the court decides differently. The injured party may request a guarantee for the payment of annuities unless such demand would be unjustified under the circumstances of the case. Should the liable party fail to produce a guarantee for the payment of annuities, as per the order of the court, the injured party may demand a lump sum to be paid instead of the annuities. In determining the appropriate lump sum, the court shall consider the amount of the annuities and the injured party's life expectancy and shall deduct the corresponding interest. The injured party may demand a lump sum to be paid instead of the annuities whenever it is justified.[372]

456. In case of loss of support, the court shall award indemnity in the form of annuities to a person who was supported, or entitled to demand support from the

370. Conclusion of the Joint session of the Federal Court, state Supreme Courts and the Supreme Military Court of 15 and 16 Oct. 1986, *Bilten sudske prakse Vrhovnog suda BiH* 1/1987, 72.
371. Conclusion of the Joint session of the Federal Court, state Supreme Courts and the Supreme Military Court of 7 and 8 May 1981, *Bilten sudske prakse Saveznog suda* 14/1981, 14.
372. Article 188 of LO.

deceased. When deciding on the amount of the annuities, the court shall take all circumstances of the case into account, but in any case, the awarded sum cannot exceed the amount the injured party would have been receiving from the deceased, had he not died.[373]

457. In cases of bodily injury or harm to health, should the injured party, due to total or partial inability to work, suffer the loss of his earnings, or should his needs become permanently increased (including support by relatives and loss of home maintenance capacity), or should possibilities of his further development and advancement be destroyed or reduced, the court shall award compensation for these future losses in the form of annuities (in regular intervals).[374] Loss of housekeeping capacities may qualify as a permanent increase in the defendant's needs. This may include costs of specific diet, nursing, domestic help, treatment, etc.[375]

458. Under Article 196 of LO the court may raise the amount of the future annuities at the request of the injured party, or may reduce or cancel the future annuities at the request of the tortfeasor, in case of a considerable change in the circumstances previously taken into account. This goes both for the annuities awarded for material and moral (non-material) damage.[376]

III. Others

459. The basic form of compensation under Serbian tort law is *compensation in kind*, that is, in goods or services as opposed to money. The liable party shall be instructed to make a loss good by returning the same or identical item to the victim instead of paying damages. As mentioned before, the primary remedy is a 'return to the former state:' liable party must re-establish the situation which existed prior to the occurrence of damage. Rather than restoring the injured party's loss with money, the liable party shall repair the loss by restitution of the thing injured or removed, i.e., by carrying out the reinstatement of the situation as it was before the damage occurred. Another possibility would be for the injured party to decide to take care of the restoration of the former state of affairs by himself. In that case, the liable party shall be obliged to reimburse the money the injured party had to spend, on the condition that these expenditures were reasonable.

373. Article 194 of LO.
374. Article 195, para. 2 of LO.
375. Comm LO Per, 458.
376. Conclusion of the Joint session of the Federal Court, state Supreme Courts and the Supreme Military Court of 15 and 16 Oct. 1986, *Bilten sudske prakse Vrhovnog suda BiH* 1/1987, 55.

Chapter 4. Personal Injury and Death

§1. Pecuniary Losses

460. Pecuniary losses arising from personal injury or death may include actual patrimonial loss (such as costs of medical treatment and care, funeral, etc.), as well as lost profits (such as loss of earnings or loss of support).

461. Under Article 193 of LO, whoever causes someone's death shall be liable for the usual expenses of the funeral. According to the well-established practice of the courts, this includes the costs of funeral, tombstone and mourning gathering as per the customs of the place, obituary, mourning attire and travel to the place of funeral for the closest relatives, but not the costs of further preservation of the grave. He shall also be liable for the costs of the victim's medical care and treatment, increased needs, and other related necessary expenses for the time from injury to death, including the loss of earnings due to the victim's inability to work.

'Other related necessary expenses' include the costs of support by the victim's relatives, costs of transportation to the hospital, loss of income suffered by the person who has escorted the victim to the hospital, travel costs for the family paying visits to the victim while at the hospital, etc.[377] The costs of a pre-trial *medical expert opinion* are not litigation costs. However, the costs of *medical assistance* the victim receives before the trial shall be regarded as patrimonial damage resulting from the injury.

The notion of 'earnings' is expanded to include not only the injured party's salary but also the allowances the injured party would have been entitled to as an employee if, by missing out on these allowances, the plaintiff misses out on an increase in his property.[378] Where compensation for loss of earnings is calculated as a difference between the frustrated salary and the disability benefits, the compensation cannot be reduced for the 'advantages' of the victim not having to work anymore.[379]

462. Under Article 194 of LO, a person who was financially supported, or entitled to demand support from the deceased, may claim compensation for the loss of support from the injurer. When deciding on the amount of the annuities, the court shall take all circumstances of the case into account, but in any case, the awarded sum cannot exceed the amount the injured party would have been receiving from the deceased, had he not died.

463. In cases of bodily injury or harm to health the victim shall be entitled to the costs of medical treatment, the expenses incurred in relation to the medical treatment, as well as the loss of earnings due to inability to work during medical treatment and recovery. Should the injured party, due to total or partial inability to work, suffer the loss of his earnings, or should his needs become permanently increased

377. Comm LO Per, 456.
378. SC of BIH, Rev. 496/90 of 21 Mar. 1991, *Bilten sudske prakse Vrhovnog suda BiH* 2/1991, 68.
379. SC of BIH Rev. 686/86 of 9 Jul. 1987, *Bilten sudske prakse Vrhovnog suda BiH* 4/1987, 45.

(including support by relatives and loss of home maintenance capacity), or should possibilities of his further development and advancement be destroyed or reduced, the court shall award compensation for these future losses in the form of annuities (in regular intervals).[380] Loss of housekeeping capacities may be qualified as a permanent increase in the defendant's needs. This may include the costs of specific diet, nursing, domestic help, treatment, etc.[381]

As it was mentioned before, the court may raise the amount of the future annuities at the request of the injured party, or may reduce or cancel the future annuities at the request of the tortfeasor, in case of a considerable change in the circumstances previously taken into account.[382]

464. The right to compensation in the form of annuities in cases of bodily injury, harm to health, or death of a close person, shall be non-transferable. This equally relates to transfers *inter vivos* and *mortis causa* (cession, offsetting, testamentary dispositions). However, a matured annuity of compensation for these types of losses shall be transferrable, provided that the amount of compensation is settled by a written agreement between the parties, or confirmed by a non-appealable court decision.[383]

§2. Non-pecuniary Losses

465. In cases of bodily injury or harm to health the victim shall be entitled to equitable pecuniary compensation for psychological pain due to impairment of life activities, severe disfigurement, physical pain and fear, irrespective of whether he has suffered any kind of patrimonial damage. In deciding on the merits of the claim, and on the amount of equitable compensation, the court shall take into account the importance of the violated interests and the purpose of equitable compensation and shall make sure the compensation awarded does not favour the goals that are otherwise incompatible with its nature and social purpose.[384] At the request of the injured party, the court shall also award equitable compensation for the physical and psychological pain and fear the injured party is going to experience in the future, where it is *certain*, in view of the normal course of events, that pain or fear are going to persist in the future.[385]

466. In case of death, the court may award equitable compensation for psychological pain (mental suffering) to the members of the deceased's immediate family:

380. Article 195, para. 2 of LO.
381. Comm LO Per, 458.
382. Article 196 of LO. Also, this goes both for the annuities awarded for material and moral (non-material) damage. Conclusion of the Joint session of the Federal Court, state Supreme Courts and the Supreme Military Court of 15 and 16 Oct. 1986, *Bilten sudske prakse Vrhovnog suda BiH* 1/1987, 55.
383. Article 197 of LO.
384. As per Art. 200 of LO.
385. Article 203 of LO.

his spouse or cohabitant;[386] parents; children; brothers and sisters who have lived with the deceased in a shared household. In case of particularly serious disability, the court may award equitable compensation for psychological pain to his spouse or cohabitant, parents and children.[387]

467. As mentioned before, claims for compensation of non-pecuniary damage are generally uninheritable, unless they are settled by a written agreement between the parties, or confirmed by a non-appealable court decision. They can be subject to cession, offsetting and forced execution under the same conditions.[388]

468. The court shall award equitable compensation for non-patrimonial loss arising from bodily injury provided that duration and intensity of the pain or fear sustained by the injured party so justify.

Physical pain is estimated not only by its intensity and duration but also by the accompanying inconveniences such as immobilization and other kinds of restraint, number of surgical procedures, physical therapy, transfusions, injections, etc.[389]

Psychological pain (mental suffering) in cases of bodily injury is recoverable when resulting from the impairment of life activities or severe disfigurement.

Impairment of life activities is a limitation in regular, normal activities of the victim, including the activities the victim used to perform before the injury, as well as the activities he would have been reasonably expected to perform in future, was it not for the injury. It includes the case where the victim can still carry out the activities he used to engage in, and would under normal circumstances continue to engage in, but after the injury, he can carry them out only under some special conditions, with increased efforts, or with difficulties. Impairment of life activities also includes the victim's discontinuation of education.[390] The courts are inclined to award higher amounts of compensation for psychological pain due to impairment of life activities, where the injured party is a younger person.[391]

469. When deciding on the amount of equitable compensation for psychological pain due to impairment of life activities, the court takes into account benefits the victim may claim under the laws and regulations on health, pension and disability insurance. The court freely estimates whether such benefits influence the indemnity the victim should be entitled to. If the victim fails to initiate the proceedings for disability benefits, the court shall decide on a preliminary question of the victim's right to disability benefits under relevant regulations and considering the nature and gravity of the injury.[392]

386. 'Cohabitation' should be understood here of an arrangement where two people of opposite sexes who are not married live together in a sexually intimate relationship on a long-term basis.
387. Article 201 of LO.
388. Article 204 of LO.
389. Conclusion of the Joint session of the Federal Court, state Supreme Courts and the Supreme Military Court of 15 and 16 Oct. 1986, *Bilten sudske prakse Vrhovnog suda BiH* 1/1987, 58.
390. *Ibid.*, 60–61.
391. Comm LO Per, 468–469.
392. Conclusion of the Joint session of the Federal Court, state Supreme Courts and the Supreme Military Court of 6 and 7 Nov. 1986, *Bilten Saveznog suda 23/1986*, 1.

The courts have awarded equitable compensation for the victim's psychological pain due to impairment of life activities in cases of loss of sexual abilities;[393] long-term reoccurring headaches;[394] small farmer having to put more effort into his everyday work after the injury in order to achieve the same economic results.[395]

Psychological pain because of *temporary* impairment of life activities is generally not recoverable. However, the courts have held that very severe intensity and prolonged duration of mental suffering because of *temporary* impairment of life activities may justify awarding equitable compensation.[396]

470. When deciding on the amount of equitable compensation for psychological pain due to *severe disfigurement*, the court shall reasonably take into account the personal traits of the victim, and shall consider relevant: to which extent the disfigurement in question causes pity and revulsion in a social context, and to which extent it disturbs mental stability and psychological wellbeing of the victim.[397]

471. Equitable compensation for psychological pain due to *fear* shall be awarded provided that the fear was intensive and lasted longer. The kinds of fear that are recoverable are *primal fear*, i.e., intensive and lasting fear induced by the damaging event in question, which causes psychological shock and trauma to the victim; *secondary fear*, i.e., delayed fear of death and grave consequences of the injury in question. Damages for minor or short-lasting fear are generally not recoverable. However, the courts are awarding damages for short-lasting, but very intense fear, provided that it has caused a long-lasting psychological instability of the victim.[398]

393. SC of Croatia, Rev. 643/1983 of 21 Sep. 1983.
394. SC of Slovenia, Rev. 208/1980 of 4 Dec. 1980.
395. SC of Slovenia, Rev. 9/1985 of 14 Feb. 1985.
396. Conclusion of the Joint session of the Federal Court, state Supreme Courts and the Supreme Military Court of 15 and 16 Oct. 1986, *Bilten sudske prakse Vrhovnog suda BiH* 1/1987, 60.
397. *Ibid.*, 61.
398. *Ibid.*, 59.

Chapter 5. Various Damages (Property)

472. Under the explicit rule of Article 187 of LO, in case of destruction of a thing unlawfully taken from the owner, the taker shall be liable to pay monetary compensation, even if the destruction resulted from force majeure.

Chapter 6. Interference with Collateral Benefits

§1. Insurance

473. Third-party insurance and indemnity insurance are the widespread forms of insurance coverage. In addition to *voluntary* insurance against liability to others, third-party liability is *mandatory* for certain professions, as well as for some dangerous activities.

474. For instance, professional liability insurance of the attorneys is compulsory and may be purchased individually, or as a bar association collective scheme;[399] notaries are bound by statutory duty to take out insurance against professional liability, individually or through their chamber;[400] bankruptcy administrators are obliged under the statute to insure against professional liability.[401] Health professional liability insurance is not mandatory in Serbia as yet. And when it comes to environmental liability, a polluter whose facilities or activities create a high risk of damage to human health and the environment shall be obliged under law to take out insurance against liability to others.[402]

475. Besides, the LCTI of 2009 (LCTI, last changes in 2013) lays down four types of mandatory traffic insurance: accident insurance for passengers in public transport; third-party liability insurance for owners of motor vehicles; aircraft passenger and third-party liability insurance for aircraft owners; third-party liability insurance for boat owners. Insurance against liability for damage caused to third parties purchased by the owner (or the keeper) of the means of transportation shall cover the damages to third persons made by the means of transportation, irrespective of the identity of the operator (the driver) at the time of the accident at issue.[403] A passenger, or a person specified in the insurance policy as an insurance beneficiary in case of the passenger's death, shall be entitled to request payment under the insurance contract directly from the insurance company. If the owner of the means of transportation did not purchase mandatory insurance, or if bankruptcy proceedings are initiated against the insurance company, the payment of the sum assured may be requested from the Guarantee Fund, which was established by LCTI.[404] The same goes for cases where the damage has been caused by the use of unidentified means of transportation.

---

399. Article 37 of the Attorney Profession Act of 2011 (last changes in 2012).
400. Article 59 of the Notaries Act of 2011 (last changes in 2015).
401. Articles 30 and 31 of Law on Bankruptcy of 2009 (last changes in 2018).
402. Article 106 of Law on Environmental Protection of 2004 (last changes in 2018).
403. Article 2 of LCTI.
404. Articles 17 and 74 of LCTI. The Guarantee Fund was established for the purpose of financial protection of passengers in public transport and third-party claimants in cases where damage has been caused by the use of uninsured or unidentified means of transport, as well as for damages payable by the insurance company in respect of which the bankruptcy proceedings have been initiated.

476. When it comes to insurance against liability to others, direct claim of the injured party against the insurance company shall become time-barred (i.e., unenforceable due to lapse of time) at the same time as the injured party's claim against the tortfeasor.[405]

477. Under LO, the insurance company that compensates the victim becomes 'assignee by operation of law' and subrogates to the victim's claim for compensation against the person liable for damage on whatever ground, up to the amount of compensation the victim was actually paid.[406] Along the same lines, under LCTI, the insurance company that pays compensation to the claimant shall subrogate against any person liable for the damage up to the amount of compensation paid out, interest on such compensation, and the possible costs of the proceedings, unless the insurance company was obliged under the third-party liability insurance contract to bear the costs in question.[407]

478. When deciding on the existence and the scope of the defendant's liability, the courts are not allowed to take into consideration the fact that the defendant is (or is not) insured against liability to others. This argument is never overtly considered by the courts, and may not be found in court decisions, though it is possible that the courts covertly contemplate it.

The development of insurance against liability to others has played an important historical role in the expansion of different types of strict liability. However, at least in Serbian law, this does not mean that the courts may probe into the question of whether the defendant is insured against liability to others when deciding on the merits of the claim in damages against him.

§2. Social Security

479. Comprehensive social insurance is mandatory in Serbia, under the Pension and Disability Insurance Act of 2003 (PDIA, last changes in 2022) and the Health Insurance Act of 2019 (HIA), for nearly every citizen and resident.[408] In cases of personal injury and death, the Health Insurance Fund (HIF) and the Pension and Disability Insurance Fund (PDIF) cover most of the expenses caused by health impairment, injury, disability or death, and may later reclaim these expenses from the tortfeasor.

480. HIF is entitled to compensation from a person who has intentionally or through gross negligence caused illness, health impairment, injury or death of the insured party. If the illness, health impairment, injury or death were caused by an

405. Article 380, para. 5 of LO.
406. Article 939, para. 1 of LO.
407. Article 28 (and Arts 63 and 66) of LCTI.
408. Articles 10–13 of PDIA, Arts 11–23 of HIA. Although the protection is relatively inclusive, the benefits provided are very modest.

employee-tortfeasor, at his work or in relation to work, HIF may claim compensation from the employer. HIF may seek compensation directly from the employee-tortfeasor who has, at his work or in relation to work, intentionally caused health impairment, injury or death of the insured party.[409] HIF has the right to demand compensation from the employer if the illness, health impairment, injury or death of the insured employee occurred as a result of the failure to implement the prescribed safety and health measures at work. In addition, HIF is entitled to compensation from the employer for the paid sum, if the damage occurred from the fact that the insured employee was not submitted to a prescribed prior medical examination, and therefore, it remained unknown that he was not medically fit for the work he was assigned to perform.[410]

481. PDIF is entitled to compensation from a person who has caused disability, bodily impairment or death of the insured party, provided that the disability, bodily impairment or death in question has instigated pension or disability claims. PDIF shall claim compensation from an employer if occupational disease or bodily impairment of the employee was caused by failure to comply with the prescribed workplace safety measures.[411]

The courts have confirmed that PDIF may claim compensation from an employer for the disability benefits paid out to the insured party (the injured employee) if the employee's work-related injury was caused by failure to comply with the prescribed workplace safety measures. The compensation PDIF is entitled to shall be proportionate to the employer's liability for the employee's work-related injury.[412]

409. Article 219 of HIA.
410. Article 220 of HIA.
411. Article 208, paras 4–5 of PDIA.
412. SCS, Prev. 374/2005 of 16 Nov. 2005, *PLex*.

Chapter 7. Other Remedies

§1. Restitution for Unjust Enrichment

482. There is a provision of LO connecting two sets of rules: the rules on tortious liability and the rules on unjust enrichment. As per this provision, after the injured party's claim for damages becomes time-barred (i.e., unenforceable due to lapse of time), the injured party may request from the injurer, under the rules on unjust enrichment,[413] to return what he has acquired from his injurious conduct.[414] The injured party is obviously entitled to restitution for unjust enrichment even prior to the expiry of the claim for damages and, for a time, may opt for either of these remedies.

It is largely understood that the provisions of Articles 210–219 of LO institute a general action of unjust enrichment, covering different types of *condictiones sine causa*, as well as *actio de* in rem *verso*. The general prerequisites include enrichment of one party; impoverishment of another; *sine causa* requirement (something turned to the benefit of another's estate without legal cause); and causality (one was enriched at the expense of another).[415]

483. A claim for damages generally provides for a wider protection, as the injured party may claim damages also for the losses the injurer did not profit from. However, sometimes an action in unjust enrichment may secure protection for the defendant even if he did not suffer any recoverable damage. For instance, where someone has used another's thing, the owner may demand compensation for the benefits gotten, irrespective of claim for damages, and in the absence of any damage.[416]

484. The rebuttable statutory presumption of fault (Article 154, paragraph 1 of LO) eases the position of the injured party opting for the claim for damages. Namely, under the rules of unjust enrichment, an obligation to make restitution arises regardless of liability for wrongdoing, therefore, no proof of fault is required. An action may be brought against the person who has enriched himself at the expense of the plaintiff, even if there is no fault on his side. This is why the plaintiff is normally in an easier position when opting for an unjust enrichment claim. This advantage is less prominent in Serbian law, due to the said statutory presumption.

485. Period of prescription is much longer for the unjust enrichment claims than for the claims for damages: unlike claims under tort law, unjust enrichment claims are not subject to the shortened prescription periods. An action in unjust enrichment may be brought within a period of ten years from the defendant's enrichment at the expense of the plaintiff, that is, the general duration of the prescription period shall

413. Rules on Unjust Enrichment: Arts 210–219 of LO.
414. Article 209 of LO.
415. Comm LO BK, 769.
416. Article 219 of LO.

be pertinent in unjust enrichment cases.[417] In contrast, tort claims are subject to three-year and five-year prescription periods, starting respectively from the injured party's learning of the damage and the tortfeasor's identity, and from the occurrence of damage.[418] Therefore, an action in unjust enrichment may serve as a consolation remedy for the victim of damage, after the expiry of her claim in damages, as the victim may not recover the losses which, at the same time, do not constitute the enrichment for the liable party.

§2. Injunctive Relief

486. As mentioned before, any person may demand from another to eliminate a source of danger, where this source threatens to cause considerable damage to him, or to an unspecified number of persons. Along the same lines, each person may demand from another to refrain from an activity which causes disturbance or generates risk of damage, if disturbance or damage cannot be prevented by appropriate measures. Should the keeper of the said source of danger fail to take the appropriate measures for preventing damage or disturbance, or should he fail to eliminate the source of danger in question, the court shall, at the request of the interested party, order the keeper to do so at his own expense. Damage caused by an activity which was performed in public interest and authorized by the public authorities shall be recoverable only if it exceeds the normal scope of damage under the circumstances. The potentially injured party can, however, demand socially justified measures to be taken, in order to prevent or mitigate the impending damage.[419] As was already stated, some lower courts have taken the position that, once the damage exceeds the normal scope, the injured party is entitled to full compensation.

487. Also, any person may demand from the court, or another competent authority, to order termination of an activity infringing his personal rights, such as human dignity, privacy of personal and family life, etc. The court, or another competent authority, may order the aforesaid termination under the threat of monetary sanction (imposed as a lump sum or per unit of time) to the benefit of the injured party.[420]

§3. Punitive Damages

488. Damages are strictly compensatory under the general rules of Serbian tort law. As was already discussed, under the principle of full or integral compensation (Article 190 of LO), the amount of damages awarded should put the victim in the position he or she would have been in, had the action causing injury not been committed. The victim is entitled to full compensation, and nothing but the full compensation, for the legally recognized (recoverable) losses inflicted on him. The

417. Article 371 of LO.
418. Article 376, paras 1 and 2 of LO.
419. Article 156 of LO.
420. Article 157 of LO.

purpose of compensation is neither to punish the liable party, to better the financial position of the victim, nor to deter the liable party and others from engaging in certain conduct. Therefore, punitive or exemplary damages are generally not available under Serbian law.

489. Where an item of property was destroyed by a criminal offence committed with premeditation, the court may determine the amount of indemnity against the value the item has had for the injured party (Article 189, paragraph 4 of LO). However, this special provision does not change the compensatory nature of damages, it only alters the method of assessment of compensatory damages, in order to better suit the specific type of cases at hand.

490. There was at least one remedy under Serbian copyright law, which seemed like an emergent functional equivalent of exemplary damages. In brief, the victim of a violation of copyright (or a related right/*droit voisin*), was entitled to the threefold amount of what would have been the normal adequate remuneration for lawful exploitation of the copyright (or a related right) in question. The notion of 'victim' was considered to include authors; performers; phonogram, videogram or database producers; broadcasting organizations; holders of exclusive licences for copyright or related rights.[421] This was the so-called triple compensation; it was meant to serve the purpose of deterrence, along with the purpose of compensation; and the victim was entitled to claim it only where the said violation was performed intentionally or by gross negligence. In addition, the triple compensation could have only been claimed *instead of* compensation for patrimonial damage caused by the violation in question, and not together with it.[422] However, these rules were amended in 2019, and the triple compensation has been abolished since.

421. Article 205 of the Law on Copyright and Related Rights of 2009 (LCRR, last changes in 2019). This article was significantly altered in 2019.

422. Article 206 of LCRR. This article was significantly altered in 2019, and triple compensation was abolished.

Selected Bibliography

Tort Law in General

Antić. *Obligaciono pravo* (2008).
Aranđelović. *O odgovornosti za naknadu štete* (1923).
Aranđelović. *Osnovi obligacionog prava (opšti deo)* (1937).
Babić. *Leksikon obligacionog prava* (2022).
Blagojević. *Posebni deo obligacionog prava* (1939).
Blagojević. *Posebni deo obligacionog prava. Ugovori, jednostrani pravni poslovi, građanskopravni delikti* (1939).
Cigoj. *Obligacijska razmerja (Zakon o obligacijskih razmerjih s komentarjem)* (1978).
Cigoj. *Obligacijsko pravo. Poslovne in neposlovne obveznosti* (1962).
Đorđević, A. *Sistem privatnog (građanskog) prava* (1896).
Đorđević & Stanković. *Obligaciono pravo* (1987).
Gams & Đurović. *Uvod u građansko pravo* (1988).
Goldštajn (ed.). *Obvezno pravo* (1978).
Grupa autora. *Građanska odgovornost. Referati i diskusija sa Simpozijuma održanog 11–12. februara 1966. godine u Beogradu* (1966).
Jakšić, A. *Građansko procesno pravo* (2012).
Jakšić, S. *Obligaciono pravo* (1953, 1962).
Jankovec. *Ugovorna odgovornost* (1993).
Konstantinović. *Obligacije i ugovori. Skica za zakonik o obligacijama i ugovorima* (1969, 1996).
Konstantinović. *Obligaciono pravo. Beleške sa predavanja* (1969).
Lazarević. *Osnovi obligacionog prava. Opšti deo* (1956).
Loza. *Obligaciono pravo, opšti deo* (2000).
Marković. *Obligaciono pravo* (1997).
Milošević. *Obligaciono pravo* (1982).
Orlić. *Ogled o odgovornosti za prekid pregovora*, PZ 10/1996.
Orlić. *Ogled o odnosu građanske i krivične odgovornosti*, PZ 10/2011.
Orlić. *Pravna i moralna odgovornost*, PZ 10/2012.
Orlić. *Predugovorna odgovornost u sudskoj praksi*, PZ 10/1995.
Orlić. *Zaključenje ugovora* (1993).
Pajtić, Radovanović, Dudaš. *Obligaciono pravo* (2018).
Perić. *Privatno pravo. Skupljene rasprave iz građanskoga prava* (1912).
Perović & Stojanović (eds.). *Komentar Zakona o obligacionim odnosima* (1980).

Selected Bibliography

Perović (ed.). *Komentar Zakona o obligacionim odnosima* (1995).
Perović (ed.). *Pravni život: Šteta i njena naknada* (1992).
Perović. *Obligaciono pravo* (1990).
Perović. *Predgovor. Zakon o obligacionim odnosima* (2009).
Pop-Georgijev. *Građansko pravo: Obligaciono pravo* (1970).
Poznić & Rakić-Vodinelić. *Građansko procesno pravo* (1999).
Poznić. Komentar Zakona o parničnom postupku (2009).
Prednacrt. Građanski zakonik Republike Srbije (2019).
Radišić, *Predugovorna odgovornost* (1991).
Radišić. *Imovinska odgovornost i njen doseg* (1979).
Radišić. *Obligaciono pravo* (2004).
Salma. *Obligaciono pravo* (2007).
Stanković & Vodinelić, *Uvod u građansko pravo* (1996).
Stanković, Perović & Trajković (eds). *Enciklopedija imovinskog prava i prava udruženog rada* (1978).
Stojanović & Antić, *Uvod u građansko pravo* (2004).
Stojanović. *Istorijski razvoj i ciljevi građansko-pravne odgovornosti za prouzrokovanu štetu*, PZ 9–10/1992.
Vizner. *Građansko pravo* (1969).
Vizner. *Komentar Zakona o obveznim (obligacionim) odnosima* (1978).
Vodinelić. *Građansko pravo. Uvod u građansko pravo i Opšti deo građanskog prava* (2012, 2017).
Vodinelić. *Takozvana zloupotreba prava* (1997).
Vuković. *Obvezno pravo* (1956, 1964).
Vuković. *Opći građanski zakonik, s novelama i ostalim naknadnim propisima* (1955).
Živanović. *Sistem sintetičke filozofije prava* (1959).

Liability for One's Own Acts

Jakšić, A. *Kvalifikacija ugovorne i vanugovorne odgovornosti za štetu*, PZ 9–10/1992.
Jankovec. *Značaj krivice kao pretpostavke za nastupanje ugovorne odgovornosti*, APFB 6/1990.
Klarić. *Pravna osnova odgovornosti za štetu* (1983).
Konstantinović. *Osnov odgovornosti za prouzrokovanu štetu*, Arhiv 3/1952.
Lazarević. *Razlike između građanske i krivične odgovornosti i njen značaj u teoriji i praksi*, APFB 5–6/1969.
Milošević. *Građanskopravna deliktna odgovornost za prouzrokovanu štetu u našem pravu*, APFB 3–4/1970.
Milošević. *Odgovornost maloletnika za štetu – građanskopravna (deliktna) odgovornost maloletnika*, APFB 2–3/1964.
Perović. *Osnov ugovorne i deliktne odgovornosti*, PZ 3–4/2004.
Perović. *Osnov ugovorne i deliktne odgovornosti*, PZ 3–4/2004.
Perović. *Pravičnost i princip naknade ugovorne i deliktne štete*, PZ 5–6/2000.
Pop-Georgiev. *Ugovorna odgovornost prema Zakonu o obligacionim odnosima*, APFB 3–5/1978.

Radišić. *Protivpravnost kao uslov građanske odgovornosti*, APFB 1–4/2001.
Šulejić. *Konkurencija deliktne i ugovorne odgovornosti (problem izbora odštetnog zahteva)*, APFB 1–3/1991.
Vuković. *Pravni osnov odgovornosti za štetu*, APFB 2–3/1967.

Damages

Ivošević. *Naknada štete zbog umanjenja životnih aktivnosti*, APFB 3–5/1978.
Karanikić-Mirić. *Nasledivost prava na naknadu moralne štete*, in: Ignjatović (ed.), *Kaznena reakcija u Srbiji* (2015).
Karanikić-Mirić, *Istorija ideje o moralnoj šteti u modernom srpskom građanskom pravu*, in: Đorđe Ignjatović (ed.), *Kaznena reakcija u Srbiji* (2016).
Karanikić-Mirić, *Non-Pecuniary Loss in Serbian Tort Law: Time for a Change in Paradigm?*, in: *SEE | EU Cluster of Excellence in European and International Law Series of Papers* (2016).
Karanikić-Mirić, *Objektivizovanje moralne štete*, in: Zbornik Matice srpske za društvene nauke 3/2015.
Karanikić-Mirić, Subjektivna koncepcija neimovinske štete, in: Slakoper, Bukovac Puvača, Mihelčić (eds.), *Liber Amicorum Aldo Radolović* (2018).
Petrović, D. *Oblici nematerijalne štete i njena naknada*, PZ 1/1989.
Radišić. *Razgraničenje imovinske i neimovinske štete*, APFB 1–3/1998.
Simonetti. *Naknada troškova sahrane*, PZ 1/1989.
Salma. *Apstraktna šteta (pojam i pravne osobine)*, APFB 1–4/1983.
Stanković. O. *Naknada štete* (Ivošević ed.) (1998).
Stanković. O. *Naknada štete (imovinske i neimovinske) prema Zakonu o obligacionim odnosima*, APFB 3–5/1978.
Trifunović. *Naknada neimovinske štet zbog smrti bliskog lica*, PZ 10/1998.
Trifunović. *Naknada štete zbog izgubljene zarade u obliku rente*, PZ 10/2002.
Vukotić. *Nasledivost prava na naknadu neimovinske štete* (dissertation, 2020).
Vuković. *Odgovornosti za štete* (1971).

Causation

Karamarković, L. *Odgovornost više lica za istu štetu*, PZ 9–10/1992.
Karanikić. *Normativno u poimanju uzročnosti kao osnova građanskopravne odgovornosti*, PZ 10/2005.
Obradović-Begić. *Odgovornost za štetu prouzrokovanu od strane više lica* (1983).
Radišić. *Naknada štete i problem tzv. prestignutog (hipotetičkog) kauzaliteta* (1969).
Salma. *Uzročnost kao determinanta subjekata i obima odgovornosti za štetu*, PZ 10/1997.
Salma. *Uzročnost u deliktnom pravu*, Glasnik 6/1997.

Fault

Ačanski. *Pretpostavljena krivica kao osnov odgovornosti za štetu prema saveznom Zakonu o obligacionim odnosima* (dissertation) (1981).
Karanikić-Mirić. *Krivica kao osnov deliktne odgovornosti u građanskom pravu* (2009).

Selected Bibliography

Karanikić-Mirić. *Odgovornost javnih beležnika u srpskom građanskom pravu*, PZ 10/2014.
Karanikić-Mirić. *Pretpostavka krivice u građanskom pravu*, PZ 11/2009.
Orlić. *Esej o krivici – u građanskom pravu*, PZ 1–2/2009.
Orlić. *Građansko-pravna odgovornost advokata u srpskom pravu*, in: *Odgovornost i osiguranje odgovornosti advokata* (2006).
Orlić. *Subjektivna deliktna odgovornost u srpskom pravu*, PZ 10/2010.

Medical Malpractice

Karanikić-Mirić. *Krivica kao osnov deliktne odgovornosti lekara u građanskom pravu*, PZ 10/2013.
Karanikić-Mirić, *Odgovornost proizvođača vakcine u praksi Evropskog suda pravde*, in: *Srpska politička misao* 4/2017.
Karanikić-Mirić, *Šteta usled neželjenog rođenja i neželjenog života: Osvrt na Zojin zakon*, APFB 1/2016.
Mujović-Zornić. *Medicinska odgovornost za štetu*, PZ 9/2004.
Mujović-Zornić. *Pravna priroda lekarske odgovornosti za štetu*, SPZ 1–2/1999.
Mujović-Zornić. *Ugovor pacijenta sa lekarom*, PZ 9/2003.
Orlić. *Zakon o zdravstvenoj zaštiti i odgovornost lekara za prouzrokovanu štetu*, PZ 7–8/2012.
Radišić. *Lekarske greške u svetlosti pravnih razmatranja*, APFB 3/1995.
Radišić. *Medicinsko pravo* (2008).
Radišić. *Naknada štete u oblasti medicine*, PZ 1–2/1993.
Radišić. *Odgovornosti zbog štete izazvane lekarskom greškom u lečenju i obaveštavanju pacijenta* (2007).
Radišić. *Profesionalna odgovornost medicinskih poslenika* (1996).
Radišić. *Samovoljno lečenje bolesnika i njegova pravna priroda*, APFB 4–6/1998.
Sjeničić. *Pacijent kao oštećeni u građanskom pravu i njegova sukrivica* (2013).

Liability for Acts of Others

Denković. *Osnov odgovornosti za štetu koju građanima prouzrokuju javni službenici*, APFB 1–2/1962.
Draškić. *Odgovornost za drugog*, PZ 1/1989.
Gams. *Odgovornost za radnje trećih lica u privatnom pravu* (1940).
Goldštajn. *Kauzalna deliktna odgovornost privrednih organizacija za službenike i radnike*, Arhiv 4/1952, 4/1953.
Karanikić-Mirić, *Tip odgovornosti pravnog lica po čl. 172 ZOO*, in: Ignjatović (ed.), *Kaznena reakcija u Srbiji* (2014).
Petrović, K. *Odgovornost roditelja za štetu koju prouzrokuju maloletnici* (dissertation) 1974.
Subić. *Odgovornost za štetu koju prouzrokuju maloletnici*, PZ 9–10/1992.

Strict Liability

Andrejević, *Odgovornost za štetu koju pričini životinja* (1969).
Bazala. *Odgovornost za štetu prouzročenu pogonom cestovnih motornih vozila*, NZ 3/1956, 4/1956.

Bazala. *Odgovornost za štetu prouzrokovanu uslijed povećane opasnosti*, NZ 7/1952.

Karanikić-Mirić. General Clause on Strict Liability in Comparative Perspective, in: Jevremovic Petrović, Milisavljević, Živković (eds.), *Law and Transition* (2017).

Karanikić. *Odgovornost za razvojne rizike*, APFB 2/2005.

Karanikić-Mirić. *Objektivna odgovornost* (2013, 2016).

Karanikić-Mirić. *Odgovornost države za štetu usled terorističkih akata, javnih demonstracija ili manifestacija*, in: Ignjatović ed. *Kaznena reakcija u Srbiji* (2012).

Karanikić-Mirić. *Odgovornost za zagađivanje životne sredine*, PZ 9/2007.

Karanikić-Mirić, Građanskopravni tretman životinje u štetnom događaju, in: Vuković, Davinić, Karanikić-Mirić (eds.), *Životinje i pravo* (2016).

Karanikić-Mirić, *Prilog razumevanju pravila o solidarnoj odgovornosti imalaca motornih vozila*, in: Lilić (ed.), *Perspektive implementacije evropskih standarda u pravni sistem Srbije* (2016).

Kostić. *Pojam opasne stvari* (1975).

Mihajlović. *Odgovornost za štetu pričinjenu izvorom povećane opasnosti*, Glasnik 3/1975.

Mihajlović. *Pojam opasne stvari*, Glasnik 3/1971.

Milisavljević. *Naknada štete za neopravdanu osudu i neosnovano lišenje slobode*, PZ 11–12/1992.

Milošević. *Štete od škodljivih materija i pitanje naknade tih šteta* (1972).

Nikolić. *Odgovornost zbog uskraćivanja neophodne pomoći*, PZ 9–10/1992.

Nikolić. *Posebna odgovornost za štetu od terorističkih akata, javnih demonstracija ili manifestacija*, PZ 1/1989.

Nikolić. *Pravičnost kao osnov odgovornosti usled terorističkih akata, javnih demonstracija ili manifestacija*, PZ 10/1995.

Petrović, D. *Odgovornost za štetu od životinja*, PZ 10/1996.

Popović. *Odgovornost za opasnu delatnost u jugoslovenskome pravu*, APFB 5/1986.

Radišić. *Imovinska odgovornost za štetu izazvanu motornim vozilom* (1976).

Stojanović. *Građanskopravna odgovornost za atomske štete prema trećim licima* (1965).

Stojanović. *Odgovornost za naknadu genetičkih, anonimnih i zakasnelih atomskih šteta* (1967).

Tasić. *Odgovornost za rizik*, Arhiv 3/1925, 4/1925, 5-6/1925.

Vilus. *Građanskopravna odgovornost izvođača i projektanta* (1973).

Defences and Exception Clauses

Karanikić-Mirić. *Ograničenja odgovornosti za štetu u srpskom pravu*, APFB 1/2012.

Karanikić-Mirić. *Zastarelost potraživanja naknade štete prouzrokovane krivičnim delom*, APFB 1/2011.

Mijačić. *Krivica oštećenika u domenu vanugovorne odgovornosti* (dissertation) (1978).

Selected Bibliography

Remedies

Danilović. *Neosnovano obogaćenje*, APFB 1–4/2001.

Hiber. *Poreski tretman, naknada štete i reparacija iz osiguranja u svetlu načela integralne naknade*, PZ 9–10/1992.

Karanikić-Mirić. *Odgovornost vlasnika motornog vozila kao preduslov obaveze osiguravača*, PZ 10/2011.

Karanikić-Mirić. *Odmeravanje naknade štete prema vrednosti koju je stvar imala za oštećenika, Crimen* 1/2011.

Konstantinović. *Osiguranje i odgovornost u jugoslovenskom pravu*, APFB 3–4/1982.

Radišić. *Odmeravanje naknade za totalnu štetu upotrebljavane stvari*, APFB 1–2/1970.

Rakić-Vodinelić. *Odmeravanje visine naknade štete slobodnom ocenom*, PZ 9–10/1992.

Petrović-Tomić. *Aktuelnost razlikovanja prava na naknadu štete i prava na osiguranu sumu*, APFB, Special Issue, 2022.

Salma. *Odgovornost za opasnost od štete*, PZ 1/1989.

Spaić. *Pitanje naknade neimovinske štete u našem pravu*, Arhiv 1/1953.

Stanković. *Naknada štete u obliku rente* (1975).

Stanković. O. *Naknada imovinske štete. Iznos naknade kod deliktne odgovornosti* (1968).

Stanković. O. *Novčana naknada neimovinske štete* (dissertation, 1968).

Šulejić. *Osiguranje od građanske odgovornosti* (1967).

Toroman. *Odmeravanje naknade štete u građanskom pravu* (1969).

Vedriš. *Stjecanje bez pravne osnove po Zakonu o obveznim odnosima*, PZ 1/1989.

Vodinelić. *Obligaciono-pravna zaštita ličnosti*, PZ 1/1989.

Index

The numbers here refer to the paragraph numbers.

Index

www.ingramcontent.com/pod-product-compliance
Lightning Source LLC
Chambersburg PA
CBHW061613200626
46927CB00032B/1596
* 9 7 8 9 4 0 3 5 2 8 9 7 7 *